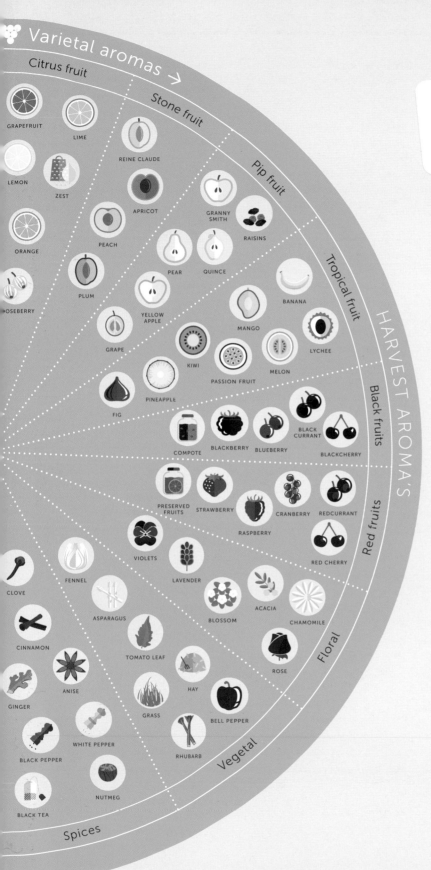

Varietal aromas →

Citrus fruit

Stone fruit

Pip fruit

Tropical fruit

HARVEST AROMA'S

Black fruits

Red fruits

Floral

Vegetal

Spices

GRAPEFRUIT
LIME
LEMON
ZEST
ORANGE
PEACH
REINE CLAUDE
APRICOT
GRANNY SMITH
RAISINS
PLUM
YELLOW APPLE
PEAR
QUINCE
BANANA
OSEBERRY
GRAPE
KIWI
MANGO
MELON
LYCHEE
PASSION FRUIT
FIG
PINEAPPLE
COMPOTE
BLACKBERRY
BLUEBERRY
BLACK CURRANT
BLACKCHERRY
PRESERVED FRUITS
STRAWBERRY
RASPBERRY
CRANBERRY
REDCURRANT
RED CHERRY
VIOLETS
LAVENDER
BLOSSOM
ACACIA
CHAMOMILE
CLOVE
FENNEL
ASPARAGUS
TOMATO LEAF
ROSE
CINNAMON
ANISE
GRASS
HAY
BELL PEPPER
GINGER
WHITE PEPPER
BLACK PEPPER
RHUBARB
NUTMEG
BLACK TEA

D0850121

© 2022 Cees van Casteren MW

Translated by: Heather Willson and Cees van Casteren MW
Edited by. Dr. Jamie Goode and David Ramsay Steele
Illustrated by: Studio Christa Jesse
Designed by: DATBureau.nl
Printed and bound in the United States of America.
Printed on acid-free paper.
Original title: Proeven als een Pro, Treebooks, Netherlands, November 2020.

ISBN 978 1 63770 034 1

All rights reserved. No part of this publication may be copied or reproduced or utilized in any form or by any means, electronic or mechanical, including photocopying, recording or by any information storage and retrieval system, without the prior written permission of the publisher, Carus Books, 315 Fifth Street, Peru, Illinois, 61354.

Library of Congress Control Number 2022943987

Picture Credits
Front and back cover: Carlo ter Ellen
11 Cees van Casteren MW
20 Kosmos
22 www.dreamstime.com/gyuszko
24 Cees van Casteren MW
26 © Riedel Crystal
65 © DrLoosen photo Chris Marmann
75a © Reichsrat Von Buhl
75b © Consejo Regulador de Jerez-Xérès-Sherry
78a www.dreamstime.com/hel080808
78b © MoëtHennessy
78c © DrLoosen photo Chris Marmann
79a www.dreamstime.com/phbcz Richard Semik
79b www.dreamstime.com/freeprod
79c www.dreamstime.com/sergejsbelovs
93 © Joseph Drouhin
All bottle shots: the respective producers
328 © Coravin
329 © Riedel Crystal
330 © Eurocave

Anyone Can Taste Wine

OPEN UNIVERSE
Chicago

Contents

Part III   100

Anyone Can Taste Wine, You Just Need to **Combine Method with Knowledge**

Part IV   128

Anyone Can Taste Wine, You Just Need **Practice**

For Wine Lovers, Not Wine Snobs

Richard Pratt is a well-known wine connoisseur and gourmet. Every now and then he is invited to the Schofield family where his host Mike Schofield makes small bets with Pratt to see if he can guess what wine is being served.

On one particular evening, Mike Schofield is serving a Bordeaux and throws out an especially stern challenge to Pratt. Schofield claims that Pratt could not possibly guess where the wine came from. Pratt not only accepts this challenge, but also raises the stakes. Tough talk follows, ending in an absurd wager. Pratt says that he wishes to bet for the hand of Schofield's daughter in marriage; he promises in turn, that if he loses, he will give Schofield both of his London houses. Schofield, convinced that Pratt will be unable to guess the wine, accepts the outrageous bet - much to the horror of his wife and daughter.

Mother and daughter watch anxiously as Pratt tastes the wine. They observe how he studies the color, how he puts his nose in the glass and breathes in the aromas, how he sucks the wine into his mouth and how, by rolling and chewing, he absorbs the layers of taste - all the while describing the wine in as feminine, demure, tender, gentle, bashful, and even, a little naughty. Pratt goes on to name the region, the commune, the vineyard, the year... and finally, he names the chateau. He comes to the uncannily concise and correct conclusion that the wine must be 'a fourth cru from the municipality of Saint-Julien, namely the small Château Branaire-Ducru, from 1934'.

Pratt has succeeded. The Schofields are in shock. At this moment, however, the maid walks in and returns Pratt's reading glasses, revealing to all that Pratt had left the glasses on the cabinet where the bottle had been placed in order to reach room temperature. Pratt's deception is exposed. He cheated.

This short story 'Taste' by Roald Dahl from 1945 satirises the world of wine tasting as a pompous display of ego between a bunch of upper-class twits with seemingly nothing better to do than to engage in ludicrous guessing games involving specialized snobbery such as discerning the differences between Bordeaux Grands Crus Classés from especially good years. The story illustrates the folly of believing that one could accurately 'guess' a wine, in all its layers of detail, including the year and the producer, in a blind tasting. Indeed, the plot reveals that the only way this could be done is by cheating.

Needless to say: 'guessing' and 'cheating' are not the central tenets of this book. This book is intended for wine lovers who are genuinely interested in developing their knowledge about wine, and in particular, in developing their skills in describing the taste of the wines they experience, using their own words and objective descriptors that - similar to a scientific experiment - might be understood by another person and replicated if another person were to try the same wine. This book aims to give enthusiasts more self-confidence, not only to taste wines blindly but also to talk about wine in company and to offer objective and meaningful observations about grape variety, origin, winemaking and quality. No need to cheat or bluff or fake it. And all of this without the help of the label telling you what you are tasting! This book will train you, so you know for yourself what you are tasting and how to describe your own taste in your own words.

I wish you much reading pleasure.

Cees van Casteren MW
Amsterdam, July 14, 2022

*A bottle of wine contains more philosophy
than all the books in the world.*

– Louis Pasteur

Part I

Anyone Can Taste Wine, You Just Need a Method

This part of the book will focus on two aspects of wine tasting. First, what you need to know and notice when you taste wine. And second, how to describe what you taste in an objective manner. There are surprisingly few books that help you with these concurrent and complex demands.

I first experienced the frustration of not knowing how to organize and describe my growing knowledge about wine tasting when I was studying for the Master of Wine qualification. I was quick enough to master the techniques of wine tasting (observing, smelling and tasting), but to then translate that knowledge into words, continued to be a struggle. I needed a method. So I developed one.

1
The Holy Grail of Wine Tasting

(Well, it worked for me!)

Honest and objective wine tasting
demands a combination of knowledge
and experience. That is precisely why
the constructive method introduced in
this chapter, designed to assist you in
framing your expansion of knowledge,
might well be hailed as the Holy Grail
of Wine Tasting.
Well, it worked for me.

Many people typically believe that the ability to taste comes from some kind of inborn, innate aptitude – as though 'taste' were a genetic hand-me-down – something that you either have, or you don't have. But that's not true. Wine tasting is a skill. *Anyone can taste wine*, as long as they have normally functioning senses of smell and taste. Anyone (that is) who is motivated to learn and practice – a lot – can become a good wine taster. Genes or no genes. Much of this skill will involve awareness of how to train your senses.

While there are genetic differences between humans in terms of smelling and tasting, these innate differences do not make one taster better than another. Research by taste professor Linda Bartoshuk, previously at the University of Yale, has shown that a wine taster's ability to taste is mainly due to the amount of training that the taster has experienced. Specifically, exercises dedicated to recognizing wine scents and developing an attendant wine language are the main contributing factors in developing wine tasting abilities. The difficulty that most besets inexperienced tasters is a lack of suitable vocabulary that would

enable them to name and describe the flavors and scents that they taste and smell. This vital skill, being able to describe flavors and aromas in words, remains a common problem, even for the most experienced of wine tasters. According to Professor Tim Jacob of Cardiff University, a method that will enable you to associate smells and flavors with a suitable repertoire of words will contribute greatly to the enhancement of tasting skills... that is... *you just need a method*. The more user-friendly, the easier it will be to learn and remember.

And that's exactly what I realized at the start of my Master of Wine studies. The method had to be user-friendly in order to help me to remember all relevant aspects for tasting, describing and analyzing the wine.

Relevant Aspects

In search of these aspects, I started with... the wine itself. At this fascinating blend of water (colorless, odorless, tasteless), alcohol (colorless, odorless, slightly sweet), acids, sugars, pigments, aromas and tannins which together give wine its color, smell and taste.

.

< 1.1%   OTHER

< 14.0% ALCOHOL

< 0.01% OTHER
          INCLUDING
          AROMA PRECURSORS,
          TANNINS, PIGMENTS
< 0.1% SUGARS
< 0.5% GLYCEROL
< 0.6% ACIDS

< 84.9 % WATER

In addition to water and alcohol, a wine mainly consists of sugars, acids, some glycerol and miniscule concentrations of aroma precursors, tannins and pigments.

And I was quite quick to learn that this very curious and complex combination of color, aromas, alcohol, acids, sugars and tannins actually were the 'relevant aspects' I was looking for, and therefore the targets of my attention while developing a method. The answer to my quest was indeed in the wine itself!

Introducing the CHARACTER Method

For reasons of user-friendliness, I developed an acronym, using the first letters of each of the relevant aspects: color, aromas, alcohol, acids, sugars and tannins. The acronym I developed, is: 'CHARACTER', as in to 'characterizing' wines, describing them, typifying, labelling and profiling them. Not only did this acronym – let's start to call it the 'CHARACTER Method' – help me to pass the

Master of Wine exam, but also I still use it every day when tasting wines professionally. The method uses the letters in the word 'CHARACTER' to introduce a systematic approach to tasting wine and writing effective notes. If you take the time to learn the procedures behind each letter, they will guide you, step by step, through the complex process of wine tasting (from color to smell to taste) as well as through the process of winemaking (from harvesting the grapes to winemaking).

C Color

H Harvest Aromas

A Aromas of Winemaking

R Ripening Aromas

A Acidity

C Candy

T Tannins

E Ethanol

R Relative Fruit Intensity

In Chapter 2: *Anyone Can Taste Wine, You Just Need a Method* – I will demonstrate the CHARACTER Method which is the core technique of this book. I will do this by using a couple of benchmark wines – a Marlborough Sauvignon Blanc and a Barossa Shiraz – to show first how to taste, and then how to describe these wines in an objective way.

Then, in PART II: *Anyone Can Taste Wine, You Just Need (a Lot of) Knowledge* – the book will really begin to build up a detailed system of knowledge pertaining to the three main factors which determine the taste of wine – namely, the influence of the harvest (chapter 3); the influence of the winemaker (chapter 4); and the ripening or evolution of some wines in the bottle (chapter 5).

What follows here is an outline of how we will continue to systematically build the knowledge needed to apply the CHARACTER Method that will enable us to pursue the ultimate goal of this book: to be able to taste wine and draw conclusions about the grape variety, the origin of the grapes, the winemaking and the age of the wine.

Man versus Machine

I could hardly believe David Bird MW when he argued in his book *Understanding Wine Technology* that most chemical analyses would not be able to distinguish between Château Latour and a basic Bordeaux table wine. According to Bird, machines can't measure the differences, despite the vastly different qualities and consumer prices. I was convinced humans could do better. But could they?

In the first year of my MW studies I decided to put Bird's claim to the test. At the laboratory DSM, I compared a Château Lafite Rothschild 1996 with an ordinary AOC Bordeaux (Réserve Spéciale) from the same vintage. I analyzed each wine using gas chromatography. Think of a long, heated tube filled with absorbent substances through which an inert gas flows. Wine concentrate is injected into the device so that the volatile wine components become even more volatile and pass through the tube at different speeds. This ensures a separation of substances at the end of the tube where a detector is located to transmit the concentrations to the computer, which records the outcomes graphically in a gas chromatogram.

My findings matched those of David Bird. Even with the most accurate detector – a mass spectrometer with an estimated detection limit of 10 ppb (parts per billion), the machine concluded that the measured substances found in both samples were at a similar level. At the same time, I had both samples organoleptically assessed by a panel of Masters of Wine. And guess what? The MWs had no problems in finding the differences between the two samples.

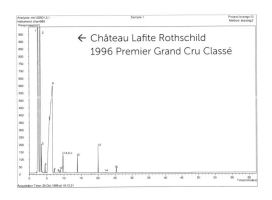

← Château Lafite Rothschild 1996 Premier Grand Cru Classé

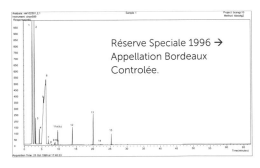

Réserve Speciale 1996 → Appellation Bordeaux Controlée.

[1] 'It is the concentration of all these components that creates fine wines. The complexity of these components makes it almost impossible to define quality of a wine in terms of chemical analysis. The simple analysis of Château Latour of a good vintage, for example, would be identical to that of a basic vin de table.' *Understanding Wine Technology*, DBQA Publishing, 2000, page 23.

Benchmark Wines

A benchmark wine is a reference against which other wines can be compared. It is a benchmark in the sense that it often is a great example of a grape variety or regional style, and recognized as such by both consumers and winemakers.

Sancerre, for example, is a benchmark Sauvignon Blanc with its unique restrained and mineral character. Just as Marlborough is also a benchmark wine for Sauvignon Blanc with its outspoken aromatic intensity, racy acidity, and harvest aromas..

In PART III: *Anyone can taste wine, you just need to combine method and knowledge* – (chapter 6 and 7) I will expand the CHARACTER Method by drawing conclusions from as many of our observations of the wine as possible, combining these with the freshly acquired knowledge from previous chapters.

Last but not least, in PART IV: *Anyone can taste wine, you just need practice* – (chapters 8 and 9) I will go crazy with the CHARACTER Method by applying it to no fewer than 175 benchmark wines. The idea behind this broad application of the method is that most wines you will taste, from anywhere, will typically display the characteristics of one of these benchmark wines. If you learn to recognize the typicity of each wine you taste – 'in what way a Chablis tastes like a Chardonnay' – you will be equipped to use the method to improve your tasting skills and draw more replicable and objective conclusions.

Practice the method and you'll see that wine tasting and making good tasting notes become second nature. The more often you apply the CHARACTER Method and the more knowledge you gain, the better you will finally be able to say after tasting a wine which grape it is made of, where it comes from, how it was made and how old it is.

Just like Richard Pratt, but without being a 'prat'; that is, without cheating.

2
Test of a Wine's Character

Demonstration of the Method

The test of a wine's character entails understanding of its origin, production and evolution, as well as being able to observe its characteristics in the context of the grape variety. This chapter will demonstrate how to use the CHARACTER Method and how to apply it to two benchmark wines.

The CHARACTER Method is powerful and intuitive because it demands that we engage our senses, starting with sight, then smell, then taste and mouthfeel, to collect 'data' about the wine. Parallel to our senses, we follow the letters in the acronym, and for each letter we try to (1) rate the intensity and (2) describe our observations.

I acknowledge that the sophistication and accuracy of your observations will depend on how much knowledge and experience you begin with. That is also why this chapter, with the exception of the first letter of the acronym, offers a different approach for novices versus advanced tasters.

After the letter C, when you then continue to activate your sense of smell, novice tasters will skip the letters H and R and focus solely on the letter A which stands for Aroma. Advanced tasters want their noses to discern between three types of aromas: (i) Harvest aromas (primary aromas originating from the harvested fruit), (ii) Aromas of winemaking (secondary aromas originating from the actions of the winemaker in the cellar) and (iii) Ripening aromas (tertiary aromas which develop from aging in the bottle). It may be helpful to pretend you have three nostrils each a separate specialist in – harvest, winemaking and ripening aromas. For example the Barossa Shiraz:

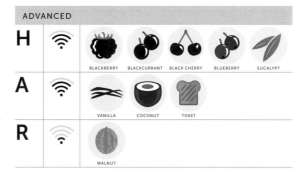

For the A of Aromas, novice tasters try to score the aromatic intensity in the wifi pictogram and the most appropriate *aroma group(s)* from the Aroma Wheel on the flyleaf as observations. Such as black fruit, spices and oak.

Advanced tasters answer the same two questions as the novice tasters but now for each of the three types of aromas: Harvest aromas, Aromas of winemaking and Ripening aromas. In addition, advanced tasters try to identify aromas as precisely as possible – that is, within the individual aroma groups of the aroma wheel.

On the next two pages, I will take you letter by letter through the acronym explaining the techniques that can be used to make appropriate observations at each stage.

Follow the LETTERS		Rate the INTENSITY
C	COLOR	Always pour the same amount of wine into your glass and hold it against a white background. Observe red wines from above and note the opacity (how clearly can you see the stem through the wine?) With whites, the hue helps to determine the intensity.
H	HARVEST AROMAS	Swirl the wine in the glass. Put your nose into the glass and sniff in short bursts (like a dog). Determine how weak or strong are the aromas derived from the harvest, such as fruity, floral, herbal, and spicy aromas.
A	AROMAS OF WINEMAKING	Now swirl and sniff once more and try to focus on the aromas derived from winemaking, such as from yeast, malolactic fermentation, and oak. Try to rate the intensity from dominant (highest score) to not detectable (lowest).
R	RIPENING AROMAS	A final round of swirling and sniffing, now to determine the age of the wine. Ripening in bottle causes oxidative aromas and specific bottle age aromas to develop. Do you smell them (a lot) or not at all?
A	ACIDITY	Acidity in wine causes your mouth to water. The sudden creation of saliva prepares the body to neutralize and dilute the acids by lining the mouth with a protective layer. The more salivation you experience, the higher the acidity in the wine.
C	CANDY	A level of 5 grams of residual sugars will be noticeable for most tasters. More than this and the wine will begin to taste a little sweet. The perception of sweetness depends not only on the sugars but also on sugars versus acidity (they mask each other).
T	TANNINS	Tannins have the opposite effect from acidity; they react with the proteins in the saliva, including the mucins that lubricate the mouth, causing a feeling of roughness. The more tannins, the drier this sensation (called astringency).
E	ETHANOL	You can perceive alcohol by observing the weight, or so-called body of the wine, in your mouth. Also pay attention to the sensations in your throat: if the alcohol level is high it activates the pain receptors in the throat causing a burning sensation.
R	RELATIVE FRUIT INTENSITY	Swirl the glass one more time and re-assess the intensity of the harvest aromas and flavors versus wines of the same grape variety. Compared to other wines of the same grape variety, is the relative fruit intensity high or low?

Describe your OBSERVATIONS

Follow the SENSES

SIGHT

By shining light sideways through the wine you can observe the suspended particles (clarity). The hue of red wine is best perceived by inspecting the rim, while the hue of white wine is best observed by looking into the core.

SMELL

Use the Aroma Wheel on the flyleaf to help you to determine the individual harvest aromas which you detect in your glass, such as citrus, stone fruit, tropical fruit, red and black fruit, floral aromas, herbal and spicy aromas.

After rating the intensity of Aromas of winemaking, then we now try to describe them. Looking at the Aroma Wheel, which of the aromas of yeast, malo, or oak can be distinguished in this wine?

If, and only if, you have detected any ripening aromas, it's time to consult the Aroma Wheel and check out whether you can recognize any of the oxidative and/or bottle age aromas in your wine.

PALATE

Although tartaric acid is dominant in all wines, white wines may be styled to contain a deliberate ratio between malic and lactic acids. Malic acids are tart; lactic acids are softer and so it is helpful to pay attention to the type of acids we experience.

Dry white wines with high acidity might be balanced by residual sugars or aging on the lees which gives an oily texture. Pay attention to flavors in sweet wines such as honey or raisins because these can give you clues about the type of sweet wine.

Tannins from grapes tend to dry out your whole mouth; while the tannins from (new) oak are especially noticeable on the front teeth; they are also more drying and offer wood flavors, even though they diminish more rapidly when matured in the bottle.

Alcohol is the basic indicator of the body of a wine, although factors as acids, residual sugars, concentration, and tannins also contribute. Does the wine feel 'heavy' in your mouth? Or 'light'? This might mean making a personal judgment.

Even if the grape variety may not be determined, please assume a certain grape variety and assess the relative fruit intensity versus the extremes for that imaginary grape variety.

We always begin wine tasting with vision. That's not because it is the most important aspect of tasting but because humans are visual beings, and what we see unconsciously influences our ability to taste.

We Taste What We See

In fact, our sight plays such an important role in forming our perceptions that it can overrule all of our other impressions. There is a famous experiment from 2001 in which prospective winemakers were asked to taste a white wine that had been colored with red dye. The winemakers placed so much trust in what they saw that they chose aromas such as strawberry, cherry, and cedarwood that are typically designated for red wines to describe what they 'tasted'. In reality, they were tasting the same white wine in which they had previously recognized flowers, peach, citrus, and honey. We taste what we see!

In addition to tasting what we see, we tend to taste what we read and what we perceive. A glimpse at the label of a bottle of wine will inevitably plant powerful preconceptions about the taste even before we taste it. The reputation of the producer, the region of origin and the vintage can all contribute to our personal enjoyment when drinking wine, but do be aware, these factors also influence our perception of the taste. For these reasons, I encourage all those motivated, inquisitive people to taste 'blind' as much as possible; that is, without seeing the bottle or label.

The first step in wine-tasting is to activate our sense of sight and evaluate the intensity of the color, and to also check the clarity of the wine, which happens to be represented by the first letter C in the CHARACTER acronym.

The color intensity of white wines coincides with the hue or color itself. The table below shows the color intensity for white wines alongside the color descriptors and for each of them representative wine examples.

COLOR INTENSITY		COLOR	EXAMPLE
🛜	deep	amber/brown	Oloroso
🛜	intense	orange	Tokaj Aszú
🛜	medium	gold	Alto Adige Gewürztraminer
🛜	pale	lemon	Marlborough Sauvignon Blanc
🛜	colorless	watery	Very young Muscadet

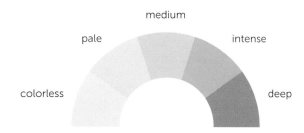

Your observations about intensity and color will reveal preliminary information about the amount of oxygen the wine has been exposed to, the color of the grape skin (e.g. Gewürztraminer), the type of wine and the age.

To be Clear, about Clarity
In addition to observing the color we also use our visual sense to observe the clarity of the wine. To check this, hold the glass by the stem and observe it against a fairly dark background allowing some light (day or artificial) to shine through it sideways. If the wine contains a large number of suspended particles these will scatter the light making the wine less transparent. This might simply be caused by winemaking techniques (e.g. without fining and/or filtering) but it might also indicate a fault in the wine. The only way to find out is to taste the wine.

If you are unlucky enough to find a faulty wine, you will need knowledge of wine faults to understand what the problem might be. See pages 28 and 29.

Bubbles

Bubbles are, of course, the essence of sparkling wines, but still wines also contain some residual CO_2 from the fermentation process. Usually this carbon dioxide is invisible to the eye and largely imperceptible on the palate. However, as our sense of touch is more sensitive to carbon dioxide than our vision, visibly imperceptible amounts of CO_2 may be still experienced as a familiar tingling on the palate. Noticeable presence of bubbles in still wines may be caused by a second fermentation in the bottle (which would be a wine fault) or deliberately added during bottling for more freshness. Think of certain wines from the Vinho Verde in Portugal and Alsace in France.

Wine Crystals

Wine crystals are tartrate crystals (salts of tartaric acid) that are sometimes discovered on the bottom of the bottle or on the cork. They look like sugar crystals, or more alarmingly, pieces of glass, but are completely harmless by-products of wine. The crystals are composed of potassium hydrogen tartrate formed when tartaric acid binds with potassium to form potassium bitartrate (cream of tartar used in cooking).

Let's put the CHARACTER Method to work. We start with a very characteristic and distinct white wine. Please meet the Young Marlborough Sauvignon Blanc!

Benchmark Wine
Young Marlborough Sauvignon Blanc

It was Sauvignon Blanc that put the Marlborough region of New Zealand on the map. The sunny, cool, windy north of the South Island in combination with the Sauvignon Blanc grape variety created a unique style that could not be ignored or imitated. What makes Marlborough special is its unusual combination of long days, cool nights, intense sunlight and – in most years – its dry autumn months, which give the grapes plenty of time to fully ripen without losing their signature grapefruit – like acidity. The longer the season, the fuller-bodied Marlborough Sauvignon Blanc can be. The differences with Sancerre (also Sauvignon Blanc, but then from the Loire Valley in France) are significant, both in terms of intensity of the Harvest aromas and the Harvest aromas themselves. In the case of Marlborough, the harvest aromas are pronounced, as in gooseberry and grapefruit.

This outspoken New Zealand style gave the pioneering winery, Cloudy Bay Vineyards, situated in Marlborough, a cult status from the late 1980s. The success of Cloudy Bay was further instrumental in establishing an international reputation for Marlborough and New Zealand in the decades that followed. Marlborough is now a household name in the world and a true benchmark wine for Sauvignon Blanc.

STEP 1 SIGHT

We now activate our sense of sight to evaluate the color intensity and the color itself.

C COLOR

Looking at the young Marlborough Sauvignon Blanc, I note the low color intensity and the lemon color.

NOVICE

C 🛜 lemon

ADVANCED

C 🛜 lemon

Marangoni's Tears

When using your visual senses you may observe so-called 'tears' (also known as 'wine legs' or 'fingers' or 'curtains') in your wine glass, often mythologized as a sign of quality. Here we need to separate fact from fiction.

In fact, any mixture of water and alcohol will leave tears on the glass. If you swirl your wine around the glass it will not simply slide back. Rather, some of the wine forms a ring on the inside of the glass because the alcohol percentage of the wine liquid here becomes lower than the level of alcohol in the wine itself. The stronger forces of the water molecules suck up the wine and create a liquid-ring around the inside of your swirl. Then gravity turns it into droplets that slide back down into the wine. The effect is named after the Italian physicist Carlo Marangoni who wrote his doctoral thesis on the subject of wine tears in 1865.

Tears, or legs, are a sign that you have washed the wine glasses correctly – that is, just with water, and without dishwashing detergent. If any residual detergent remains in a wine glass, no tears will form. And that would be sad, so please just use hot water.

We Taste What We Smell

While our taste-buds can only perceive a handful of primary tastes (sweetness, acidity, saltiness, bitterness, and umami), we can discern an overwhelming number of scents. In fact no one knows exactly how many smells the human nose can detect; even the scientists are divided on this number and the estimates range from thousands to millions. In any case, this infinity of scent impressions is precisely what makes wine tasting so fascinating.

How does the sense of smell work? The human body has some 20,000 genes and 400 of those genes are dedicated scent genes whose job it is to control the production of olfactory receptors. These scent receptors have their headquarters in the olfactory epithelium, at the top of the nasal cavity amongst six million specialized nerve cells all operating within a 10 cm2 patch of tissue that detects smell molecules. What we perceive as one scent is always an interplay of tens – if not hundreds – of scent molecules. An espresso contains about eight hundred scent molecules and a Chateau Margaux would probably match that number. When those scent molecules reach the olfactory epithelium, the olfactory receptors send signals to brain areas that process all this information, after which we recognize the scent as espresso or Chateau Margaux.

The next step in our method would be to parse out the separate aromas in the espresso and in the Chateau Margaux. This is one of the challenges addressed in this book because both of these beverages are composed of hundreds and thousands of odor molecules in a composite mixture, from which the human nose can only hope to distinguish a mere handful.

The Laing Limit

It will probably be gratifying to note that although, in theory, we can distinguish perhaps thousands of scents, research by an Australian psychologist called David Laing showed that when multiple scents are combined in a mixture, then the human nose on average cannot distinguish more than four scents. This limitation is known as the 'Laing limit' and that is why, when discussing the benchmark wines in this book, you will never encounter more than five aromas in the CHARACTER Method. That doesn't mean that these are the only aromas detectable in a particular wine, but these are the most obvious ones. Due to the 'Laing limit' you might not be able to distinguish all aromas at the same time, so please give yourself a break, and understand that sometimes your knowledge of the aromas (that are typically found in certain wines) might exceed your ability to actually detect all those aromas with your nose. Let's be honest about that.

Before we activate our sense of smell, we first swirl the wine in the glass. If you have never done this before, pour a little bit of wine in the glass (about two fingers) and place the glass on a smooth surface such as a table. Take the stem with thumb and index finger and gently slide the glass on the surface in a circular manner. This will cause the wine to swirl along the glass wall. You thus increase the wine surface that gives off aromas. Tilt the glass, bring your nose just above the rim of the glass and take a short sniff.

First impressions are usually the most telling and that is because our sense of smell gets used – adapts – to what it is smelling and as a result becomes less sensitive to it. This is called adaptation. Adaptation is also the reason why you do not smell yourself and why you no longer perceive the canteen smells within 10 to 20 seconds after you entered the canteen. As a result of adaptation it's better to smell the wine for a few seconds, then leave the glass alone for a while, and then go back to it. Our sense of smell tires rapidly, but it recovers rapidly too.

On that first sniff, try to focus on 'cleanliness' first. If the wine does not smell clean there may be something wrong. Please read the possible causes on the next pages.

Next we try – as advanced tasters – to focus on the so-called 'Harvest Aromas' (or Primary Aromas). These are the aromas in the wine which originate from the harvest (grape variety and vineyard). We will try to compare the intensity of the harvest aromas of this wine with the harvest aromas of all other white wines you have previously smelled. This is scoring the *absolute* intensity of the harvest aromas, which, in a way, means comparing apples with pears.

To assist you in scoring this absolute intensity of the harvest aromas, in the table below, for each aromatic intensity, I have listed some white benchmark wines as references. The abbreviations OW and NW stand for Old World (this is Europe) and New World (all wine countries outside of Europe).

HARVEST AROMAS OF WHITE WINES		
	very high	Riesling, Sauvignon Blanc, Gewürztraminer, Muscat, Torrontés,
	high	Viognier, Kerner, Roussanne, Marsanne
	medium	Albariño, Chenin Blanc (NW), Chardonnay (NW), Grüner Veltliner
	low	Garganega, Chenin Blanc (OW), Chardonnay (OW), Pinot Grigio
	very low	Melon de Bourgogne, Pinot Blanc, Trebbiano, Macabeo

Metaphors

In addition to estimating the intensity of the harvest aromas, advanced tasters also try to determine the harvest aromas themselves. Harvest aromas are divided into grape and vineyard aromas which in turn are divided into subgroups such as 'citrus' and 'floral'. Do you smell something 'floral' or 'citrusy'? Then try to specify it further (for example, 'lime' or 'blossom').

The words we choose for these aromas are metaphors: we give each scent the name of the product in which it occurs most often. Such as 'grapefruit' (as in a grapefruit), 'Granny Smith' (as in a Granny Smith apple) and 'gooseberry' (as in gooseberries). If aromas are less recognizable than those in the young Sauvignon Blanc, please use the Aroma Wheel on the flyleaf for inspiration.

Five Wine Faults

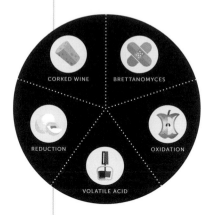

Although the number of flaws in wine has fallen sharply in the last fifty years, they still do occur. The most common are outlined.

CORKED WINE

Just to clear up a common misconception: a corked wine is not a wine that has bits of cork floating around in it. In fact, a wine that is described as 'corked' is one in which a contaminant called TCA (trichloroanisole) from the cork has found its way into the bottle giving the wine an off smell. The extent to which TCA or cork taint occurs in the wine varies. At a low level of contamination, the taste can hardly be perceived. In its most extreme form it gives out a musty smell like moldy cardboard, wet dog, or old church books. Once infected, there is no way back and the only solution is to return the wine.

BRETTANOMYCES

Brettanomyces (or Brett for short) is a type of yeast that can cause smells of sweaty horse, band aids, or cardamom in a wine. Although some enthusiasts actually like this, strictly speaking Brett is a winemaking flaw. Brett often turns up in cellars with poor hygiene. The difference between reduction and Brett – both cause a wine to be stinky - is not always immediately clear. In both cases you would be advised to decant the wine. Over time, Brett will only get worse after opening the bottle, while reduction will decrease.

OXIDATION

Oxidation is a contamination of the wine caused by exposure to too much oxygen. This can happen if mistakes have been made in winemaking or if the wine has not been properly sealed. Fresh fruit scents turn into candied or dried fruit, or disappear completely. Oxidation that is brought about by evolution in the bottle is not (necessarily) a wine fault. Neither is oxidative character in wines such as Madeira, which are made by intentional oxidiation. However, if a young wine has the aromatic impressions of an old one, then something is wrong.

VOLATILE ACID

Volatile acids are released as soon as a wine comes into contact with oxygen. As such, all wines contain volatile acids to some extent. However, if the wine starts smelling like acetic acid, acetone, and/or nail polish remover, then the acids are a bit too volatile and you can begin to speak of a wine fault.

REDUCTION

A wine is called 'reductive' if we can smell volatile sulfur compounds (like boiled eggs). These sulfur compounds are produced by yeasts when they are stressed. Much confusion arises from the fact that reduction often occurs when too little oxygen is added to the must or wine. And that is called 'reductive' wine making. However, it is wrong to see oxidation and reduction as opposite wine errors. Volatile sulfur compounds can be made by yeasts even with enough oxygen (although they are more common without). It is even possible to have a wine that is both oxidized and reductive. And because not all sulfur compounds are volatile, you cannot always correct the reduction by decanting the wine.

STEP 2 SMELL

I now take a profound second sniff and try to focus on what I am smelling. More precisely, I try to focus on the harvest aromas.

H HARVEST AROMAS

In this wine, all aromas I detect seem fruit-driven, that is, aromas which I would associate with the harvest. They are pronounced. I indicate this with a maximum rating of the wifi pictogram. I then go on to identify the aromas as gooseberry, grapefruit, Granny Smith, lime, and passion fruit, and duly note those aromas in the second row of my CHARACTER Chart.

NOVICE		
H		
A	📶	citrus, stone fruit, tropical fruit
R		

ADVANCED						
H	📶	🫐 GOOSEBERRY	🍊 GRAPEFRUIT	🍏 GRANNY SMITH	🍋 LIME	🟣 PASSIONFRUIT
A						
R						

After detecting these harvest aromas then advanced tasters are encouraged to look for Aromas of winemaking (or Secondary Aromas). These don't occur in every wine because many wines are made to uniquely express the harvested fruit. Aromas of winemaking are created by the winemaker in the cellar, for instance through extended contact with yeast, the use of bacteria, and/or use of oak. See the aroma wheel for inspiration.

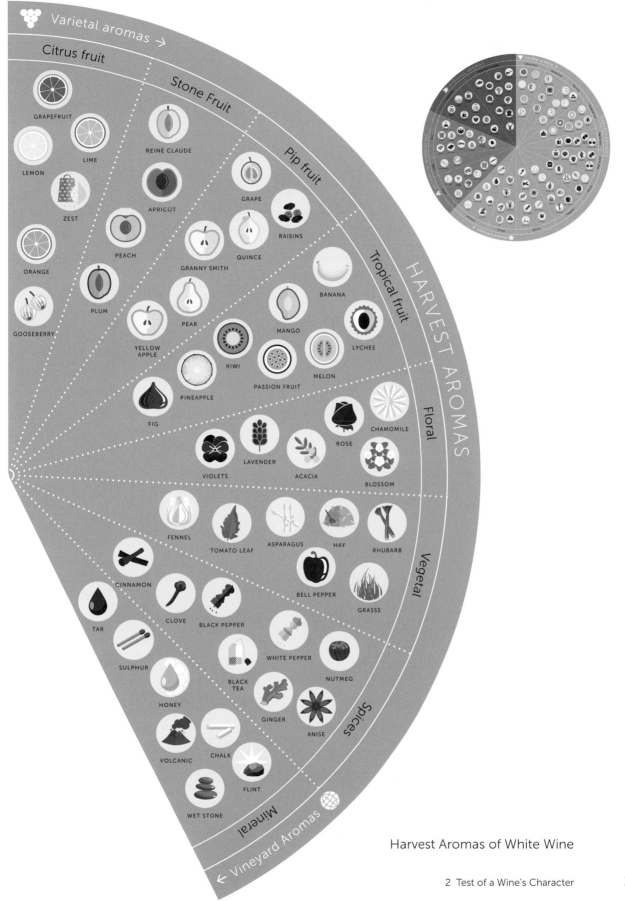

Citrus fruit

GRAPEFRUIT

LEMON

LIME

ZEST

ORANGE

PEACH

GOOSEBERRY

PLUM

Stone Fruit

REINE CLAUDE

APRICOT

YELLOW APPLE

GRANNY SMITH

PEAR

Pip fruit

GRAPE

QUINCE

RAISINS

KIWI

PINEAPPLE

FIG

PASSION FRUIT

Tropical fruit

BANANA

MANGO

MELON

LYCHEE

Floral

ROSE

CHAMOMILE

VIOLETS

LAVENDER

ACACIA

BLOSSOM

FENNEL

TOMATO LEAF

ASPARAGUS

HAY

RHUBARB

Vegetal

CINNAMON

BELL PEPPER

GRASSS

TAR

CLOVE

BLACK PEPPER

WHITE PEPPER

NUTMEG

SULPHUR

BLACK TEA

HONEY

GINGER

ANISE

Spices

VOLCANIC

CHALK

FLINT

WET STONE

Mineral

HARVEST AROMAS

← Vineyard Aromas

Harvest Aromas of White Wine

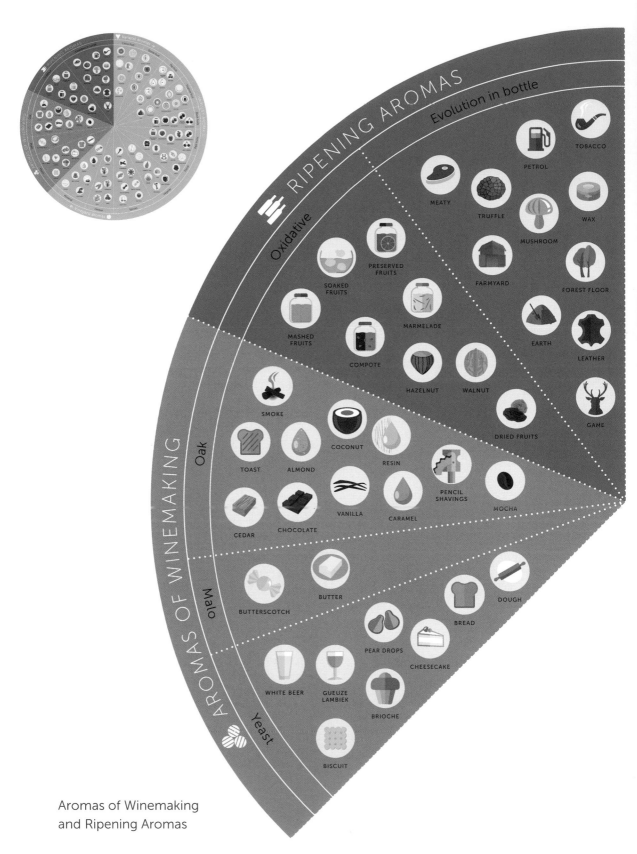

Aromas of Winemaking
and Ripening Aromas

A AROMAS OF WINEMAKING

So, I take another sniff of the benchmark wine. Unsurprisingly I do not detect any aromas of winemaking and I record this in the CHARACTER Chart as nil.

NOVICE			ADVANCED						
H			H	📶	GOOSEBERRY	GRAPEFRUIT	GRANNY SMITH	LIME	PASSIONFRUIT
A	📶	citrus, stone fruit, tropical fruit	A	📶					
R			R						

R RIPENING AROMAS

Finally, with my sense of smell still activated, I take a third sniff to ascertain whether the wine contains Ripening Aromas (or Tertiary Aromas). Refer to the aroma wheel on the previous page for an overview. Any evidence of oxidation in the smell is mostly likely also signalled in the development of the color of the wine (STEP 1). That said, in this young Marlborough Sauvignon Blanc, I detect no ripening aromas and express this with a minimum rating of the pictogram.

NOVICE			ADVANCED						
H			H	📶	GOOSEBERRY	GRAPEFRUIT	GRANNY SMITH	LIME	PASSIONFRUIT
A	📶	citrus, stone fruit, tropical fruit	A	📶					
R			R	📶					

We Taste What We Savor and Feel

Strictly speaking, our sense of taste is limited to the taste buds on our tongue. They can distinguish the five primary tastes: sweet, sour, salty, bitter and a fifth taste called 'umami'. This is a Japanese word for 'savory' and refers to the taste of amino acids (the building blocks for proteins) such as glutamate. The receptors for all five flavors are evenly distributed on the tongue. This may come as a surprise to you, as many books on the subject show a 'tongue map' where each taste would have its own area on the tongue. However, recent studies, such as those conducted by Professor Linda Bartoshuk of Yale, relegate this teaching to the land of fables. So don't bother trying to locate the flavors of wine in separate parts of your tongue because that's not how it works.

In a broader sense, most of what we call taste, is in fact smell. The brain uses the sense of touch to locate flavors perceptually. When you put a piece of salmon in your mouth, the input from both the taste buds and the olfactory epithelium, is combined in the brain in such a way that you perceive that the information is coming from where you 'feel' the salmon in your mouth. Take a sip of wine and similarly, the taste sensation (flavors) seems to come from your mouth – even though technically the flavors are determined by the aromas.

Retronasal versus Orthonasal

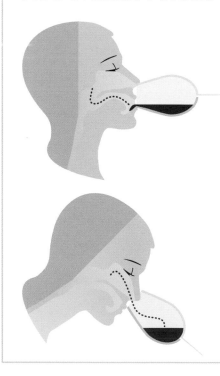

When you use the term 'smell' you probably mean 'orthonasal smell', or the smell that enters directly through your nose. But when the same odor molecules travel through the mouth to the nasal passages, the 'retronasal smell' will be affected by the warmth of the mouth, contact with saliva and/or food. According to Professor Linda Bartoshuk these different neural pathways can even produce different sensations. To fully experience the retronasal smell, I encourage you to gently suck in some air while you have the wine in your mouth – just like you slurp spaghetti. And do not worry: in wine tasting that is not considered bad manners. However, if you have never done this slurping before, I advise you to try it out with water in the shower, as it requires some technique (and sifting/salivating, especially red wine, can be embarrassing in public).

STEP 3 PALATE

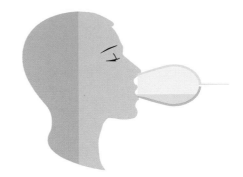

Since the taste sensations of salt and umami do not typically occur in wine, we will focus on the remaining tastes contained in the letters A for acidity, C for candy (residual sugars), A for Alcohol and T for tannins.

The letter A in the acronym stands for acidity in the wine. The most important acids in wine are tartaric, citric, malic, and lactic. The presence of these acids in the wine will cause your mouth to water; the more acidity, the more saliva is produced. Malic acid is the sharpest acid, lactic acid the softest. In some wines, such as the Sauvignon Blanc from Marlborough, malic acid is part and parcel of the wine's character. But with some other white wines, such as white Burgundies, it is precisely the softer lactic acids that fit the style. Wines with low levels of acidity feel rounder and softer in your mouth; whereas wines with high levels of acidity feel fresher and tighter.

Tricky Sensations
This all seems simple enough. But some focus is needed when evaluating acidity levels because there are a couple of tricky circumstances that you need to pay attention to. The first thing is that acidity and residual sweetness can mask each other. Secondly, alcohol can sometimes cause a burning sensation that is easily confused for acidity. If in doubt, check again - does the wine make your mouth water? That's how the presence of acidity can be differentiated from the burning sensation of alcohol.

How do We Measure Acidity?
In most places in the world acidity is typically measured using the amount of 'tartaric acid' as the unit of measurement. Another way of measuring acidity is via the pH, which is the concentration of free hydrogen ions. Even though it does not technically measure the acids themselves, pH is effectively a measure of how acidic the wine is. The higher the pH; the lower the acidity. Moreover, the pH is measured on a logarithmic scale with each value ten times higher than the previous one. So, a wine with a pH of 3 is ten times more acidic than a wine with a pH of 4.

To illustrate the pH in the table, I have added some examples of fruits or vegetables.

ACIDITY		PH	
🛜	very high	< 3.1	Rhubarb, gooseberry
🛜	high	3.2-3.3	Quince, British strawberries
🛜	medium	3.4-3.7	Golden Delicious, canned pineapple
🛜	low	3.8-3.9	Nectarine, raisins
🛜	very low	> 4.0	Canned pears, vegetable juice

So, how acidic is wine compared to other common beverages? The next table might help.

How Acidic Is My Beverage?

	Drink	pH	Benchmark wine
high	Coca Cola	2.4	
		2.5	
		2.6	
	Red bull / Bitter Lemon	2.7	
	Diet Coke / 7-Up	2.8	Riesling Eiswein
	Dr. Pepper	2.9	Assyrtiko Santorini
	Fanta	3.0	Champagne
		3.1	Chablis
	Ice Tea lemon (still)	3.2	Marlborough Sauvignon Blanc
	7-Up light	3.3	Prosecco
	Spa fruit orange	3.4	Chardonnay Napa Valley
		3.5	Chianti Classico
acidity	Apple Juice	3.6	Haut-Médoc
	Liptonice	3.7	Mendoza Malbec
	Bottled Water (sparkling)	3.8	Barossa Shiraz
		3.9	Chateauneuf-du-Pape
		4.0	
	Heineken	4.1	
	Buttermilk	4.7	
	Bottled Water (still)	6.3	
	Tap water	7.0	
low	Milk	7.3	

A ACIDITY

I take the first sip of the young Marlborough Sauvignon Blanc and note that this wine scores very high in terms of its acidity. This wine not only makes my mouth water but it also has a pronounced malic acid feel which contributes largely to the style of the wine. I note this observation in the CHARACTER Chart – malic in character. And continue.

NOVICE		
A	📶	
C		
T		
E		

ADVANCED		
A	📶	malic
C		
T		
E		

The letter C for 'candy' is used in the acronym as a word to denote sweetness, which in wine tasting refers to residual sugars from unfermented grape sugars or refers to sugars which were added.

Just as acidity is measured by pH, candy (or residual sweetness) is measured in grams of sugar per liter.

The notion of 'grams per liter' is rather difficult to imagine when tasting the wine so it is helpful to illustrate residual sugar scores alongside more familiar beverages and the appropriate German wines.

SWEETNESS		GR/L	
📶	luscious	> 130	Yakult, Trockenbeerenauslese, and Eiswein wines
📶	sweet	70-129	Fruit Juice, most soft drinks, and Beerenauslese wines
📶	medium sweet	40-79	Milk, and both Spätlese and Auslese wines
📶	medium dry	10-49	Vegetable juice, and Kabinett wines
📶	dry	0-9	Water, and most Trocken wines

C CANDY

Now, as I taste and feel the Marlborough Sauvignon Blanc in my mouth, I need to think about the presence of sweetness of any kind. I feel a certain texture, richness and roundness on the palate which seems to balance some of the very high acidity. We will discuss the origin of that texture, that roundness in Chapter 4, but for now it is relevant to note the texture in the CHARACTER Chart. As for the sensation of sweetness, I realize more compellingly, that the wine is completely dry.

NOVICE		
A	📶	
C	📶	
T		
E		

ADVANCED		
A	📶	malic
C	📶	rich texture
T		
E		

Tannins are substances present in the bark of many trees, in kernels, leaves, stems and in the skins of many fruits. The sense of touch is important in the assessment of tannins. Unlike acids (which will make your mouth water), tannins bind with the proteins in saliva as black tea can do. As a result, your mouth will not water but dry out for a moment. In that respect, tannins give the opposite effect compared to acids in your mouth. This effect will be more relevant when tasting red wines such as the Barossa Shiraz in the following demonstration of the method.

T TANNINS

No tannin sensation can be detected in the taste of the young Marlborough Sauvignon Blanc so it scores nil in the CHARACTER Chart.

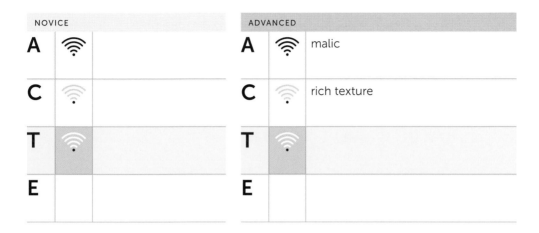

We now move on to an important part of assessing the wine: ethanol, also called 'ethyl alcohol', or simply alcohol. Ethanol is naturally produced during the fermentation of sugars by yeast. However, ethanol itself has no odor and just a slight sweet taste which normally is not noticeable. As such, you cannot taste it properly. But you can still perceive it.

First of all, because of the weight of the wine in the mouth: does it feel like a heavy or a light wine? A lot of ethanol makes the wine heavy, little ethanol makes the wine light. Ethanol is therefore the most important factor in what we call the 'body' of the wine.

We thus feel the presence of ethanol, rather than taste it. This sensation is part of the impression we call 'body' or 'weight' in a wine. A wine with a very high ethanol percentage is often described as 'full bodied', while a wine with a low ethanol percentage is often referred to as 'light'. Ethanol is also a carrier of the flavors of the wine in the mouth.

In addition to the 'body' or 'weight' of the wine, a high or very high ethanol percentage in the wine can be perceived in your throat as it will activate the pain receptors causing a burning sensation in your throat.

ALCOHOL		ABV	
📶	very high	> 15%	Usually fortified wines
📶	high	14 to 15%	Very ripe wines or fortifieds
📶	medium	12 to 13.5%	Most wines from moderate climates
📶	low	5.5 to 11.5%	Early harvest wines, sweet wines or wines which have been corrected for alcohol
📶	no	< 0.5%	Wines which have been corrected for alcohol

The letter E of ethyl alcohol or ethanol is the same as alcohol. They are synonyms.

E ETHANOL (ALCOHOL)

The young Marlborough Sauvignon Blanc scores 'medium' in terms of ethanol content, and also medium in body, so I note this in the CHARACTER Chart.

NOVICE				ADVANCED		
A	📶			A	📶	malic
C	📶			C	📶	rich texture
T	📶			T	📶	
E	📶			E	📶	12.5 to 13.5%, medium body

R RELATIVE FRUIT INTENSITY

The final letter of the CHARACTER Chart stands for Relative fruit intensity. The *relative* fruit intensity — or *relative* intensity of the Harvest aromas — is a variation of the *absolute* intensity of the Harvest aromas (H). Whereas for scoring the absolute intensity of the Harvest aromas we compare the fruit intensity of wines made from all grape varieties with each other — like apples and pears, remember? — in the case of the relative fruit intensity, we just compare the fruit intensity of all wines made from the same grape variety with each other — like apples and apples.

NOVICE		
C	📶	lemon
H		
A	📶	citrus, stone fruit, tropical fruit
R		
A	📶	
C	📶	
T	📶	
E	📶	
R	📶	

ADVANCED		
C	📶	lemon
H	📶	GOOSEBERRY GRAPEFRUIT GRANNY SMITH LIME PASSIONFRUIT
A	📶	
R	📶	
A	📶	malic
C	📶	rich texture
T	📶	
E	📶	12.5 to 13.5%, medium body
R	📶	

In this case we want to compare the fruit intensity of the Marlborough Sauvignon Blanc to the fruit intensity of all other Sauvignon Blancs in the world, including benchmarks like Sancerre and Pouilly Fumé. And in doing so, we would score the relative fruit intensity of the Marlborough Sauvignon Blanc as very high. Probably higher than any other Sauvignon Blanc in the world.

In case we are not sure about the grape variety the wine is made of, we have to make an assumption for an imaginary variety and decide whether the relative fruit intensity of the wine is high or low. This may sound a bit abstract for now, but we will come back to Relative fruit intensity in more detail later in the book. For now, it will suffice to score the Relative fruit intensity very high in the chart.

With rating the Relative Fruit Intensity we have completed all letters of the acronym. Following the intensity scores and observations will automatically give a tasting note of this wine.

Tasting Note
Marlborough Sauvignon Blanc

Novice tasters
This pale, lemon colored white wine has intense aromas of citrus, apple and tropical fruit. In the mouth the wine is dry, with a lot of acidity and medium alcohol.

Advanced tasters
This pale, lemon colored white wine has pronounced aromas of gooseberry, grapefruit, Granny Smith, lime, lemon and passion fruit. On the palate, the wine is dry, has intense acids (malic in style), and a rich texture, medium alcohol content of 13%, medium body, and a very high relative fruit intensity.

This is not only an accurate description of this wine, but it is also expressed in simple, clear words. No subjective pretensions, no distracting embellishments. Everyone will understand what has been tasted.

Let's do it again.

Now I will repeat the journey, this time with a red benchmark wine with harvest aromas, aromas of winemaking, and ripening aromas and which, like the Marlborough Sauvignon Blanc, is very outspoken. Meet the mature Barossa Shiraz!

Benchmark Wine
Mature Barossa Shiraz

If you could choose one wine region to illustrate the history and development of Australian wine, it would be the Barossa Valley. Here you will find sixth-generation wine families who are stewards of the largest collection of ancient vines in the world, with vineyards dating back to 1840. Anno 2020, the Barossa Valley is still the beating heart of Australia's viticulture and best known for its muscular, oaked Shiraz. Barossa is located inland from Adelaide in South Australia and has a very warm, sunny and dry Mediterranean climate. In the summer it can be particularly hot. But Shiraz (which is the same grape variety as Syrah) has adapted well to those conditions. In the Barossa Valley it gives wine a full body, moderate acidity, high alcohol, and firm (but silky) tannins. The local vegetation of eucalyptus trees usually lends a minty, eucalypt note to the deep purple Shiraz fruit. In terms of winemaking, the wine is usually aged in (at least partly) American oak, which contributes characteristic notes of vanilla and coconut. 'Mature' in this Shiraz means that it is ready to drink, or approximately three to five years old.

STEP 1 SIGHT

We activate our sense of sight to evaluate both the intensity and hue of the wine.

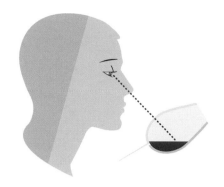

Intensity and Hue
They are two different things.

SIGHT		EXAMPLE
	deep	Cabernet Sauvignon, Sagrantino, Saperavi, Touriga Nacional
	dense	Blaufränkisch, Carignan, Malbec, Syrah
	medium	Barbera, Marselan, Merlot, Tempranillo
	light	Dolcetto, Grenache, Mencía, Zinfandel
	pale	Cinsault, Frappato, Nebbiolo, Pinot Noir

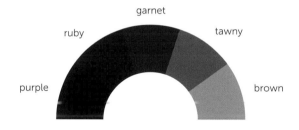

C COLOR

I look into the dark depths of this exemplary red, and it scores the maximum 5 stripes on the wifi bar for color intensity: I can't even see the stem of the glass when I look into the center of the glass from above. After 3 to 5 years of bottle aging, the hue has evolved from purple to ruby. This color, a visible sign of the maturation process, needs to be noted in the chart.

About Clarity

Sediment

Some red wines accumulate sediment as a result of winemaking (vintage port for example) or as a result of ripening in the bottle (usually after 10 years). This sediment, or 'fine lees' can be a mixture of precipitated tannins, pigments, dead yeast, tartrate crystals, and proteins leftover from the winemaking. Most winemakers fine or filter these solids before bottling while others leave them in. As such fining and filtration are a trade-off between a desire for full stability while accepting some flavor loss versus risking biological problems without compromising aromas or flavors.

Cloudiness

Sediment can cause cloudiness. Put the bottle at least half an hour before opening upright to allow the sediment to settle.

Now, there is decanting and decanting

Decanting to aerate
Aeration is the process of purposefully invigorating wine with air to bring about changes in aroma, flavor and tannins. This is usually done by decanting the wine into a decanter (glass carafe) and sometimes even by decanting it back into the original bottle (so-called double decanting).

Decanting to separate
Decanting for the purpose of clarification is the process of separating the sediment from the clear wine. Although decanting will do some aerating by default, it is much gentler in doing so.

STEP 2 SMELL

Next we activate our sense of smell to assess the aromas and their intensity.

Swirl the wine in the glass. Insert your nose into the glass and sniff in short bursts (like a dog sniffs). Is the wine clean? Good news! If not, investigate possible problems (see page 28 and 29 Wine Faults).

Just like the way we assessed the Marlborough Sauvignon Blanc, novice tasters will try to determine the intensity of the smell and focus on the applicable aromas in the aroma wheel. Advanced tasters will do the same but separately for the harvest aromas (H), the aromas of winemaking (A) and the ripening aromas (R).

H HARVEST AROMAS

I take a long whiff to detect the first scent of harvest aromas. I can smell pronounced purple fruit: blackberries, black cherry, and blueberry. These intense aromas score high in the chart. In addition, I clearly smell a scent of mint or eucalypt. I note all of this in my chart.

NOVICE		
H		
A	📶	purple fruit, spice, vanilla
R		

ADVANCED						
H	📶	🫐 BLACKBERRY	🫐 BLACKCURRANT	🍒 BLACK CHERRY	🫐 BLUEBERRY	🌿 EUCALYPT
A						
R						

The white wine had no aromas of winemaking but we can expect something quite different here.

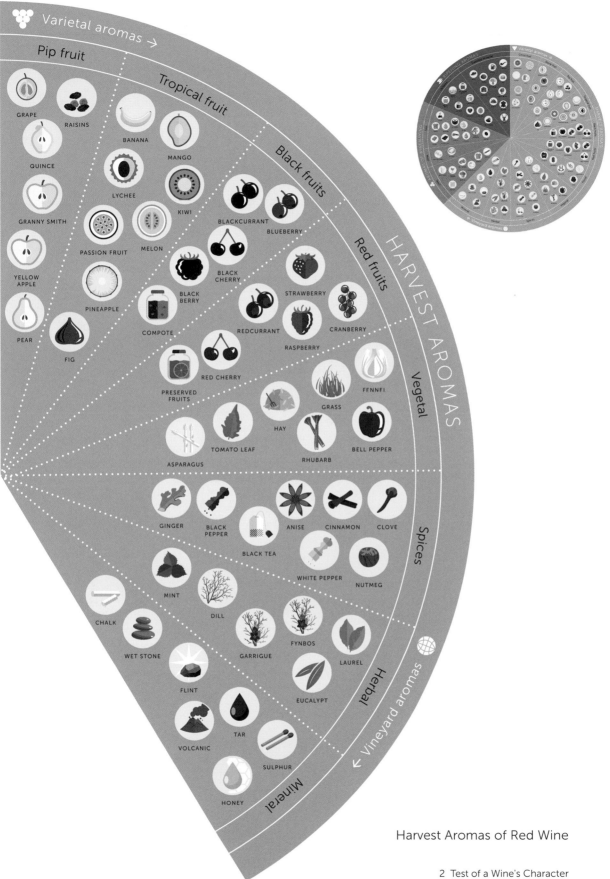

Pip fruit

GRAPE

RAISINS

Tropical fruit

QUINCE

BANANA

MANGO

GRANNY SMITH

LYCHEE

KIWI

Black fruits

YELLOW APPLE

PASSION FRUIT

MELON

BLACKCURRANT

BLUEBERRY

PEAR

PINEAPPLE

BLACK CHERRY

Red fruits

FIG

COMPOTE

BLACK BERRY

REDCURRANT

STRAWBERRY

HARVEST AROMAS

RED CHERRY

RASPBERRY

CRANBERRY

PRESERVED FRUITS

Vegetal

FENNEL

HAY

GRASS

ASPARAGUS

TOMATO LEAF

RHUBARB

BELL PEPPER

GINGER

BLACK PEPPER

ANISE

CINNAMON

CLOVE

Spices

BLACK TEA

WHITE PEPPER

NUTMEG

MINT

DILL

CHALK

GARRIGUE

FYNBOS

WET STONE

LAUREL

FLINT

EUCALYPT

Herbal

VOLCANIC

TAR

Vineyard aromas

SULPHUR

Mineral

HONEY

Harvest Aromas of Red Wine

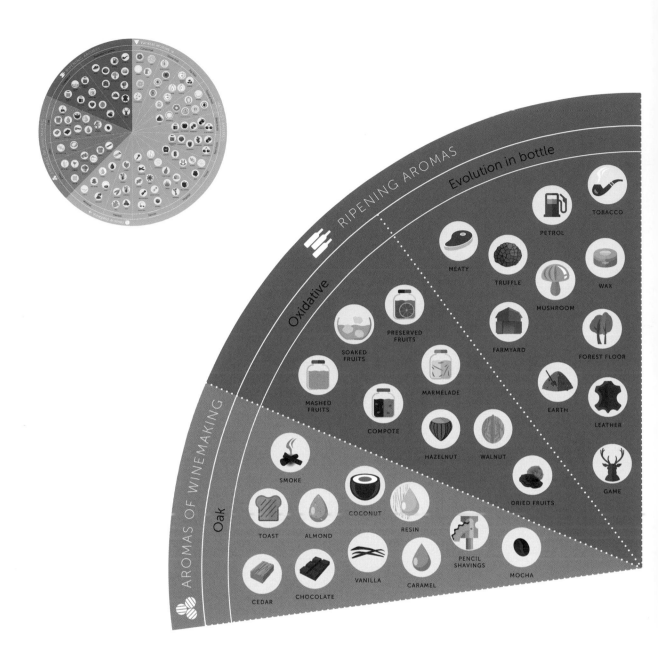

Aromas of Winemaking and Ripening Aromas of Red Wine

A AROMAS OF WINEMAKING

Second sniff. Now I smell clear impressions of vanilla, coconut, and toast. They are almost as defined as the harvest aromas and again, score high and require some brief comments in the chart: vanilla, coconut, toast.

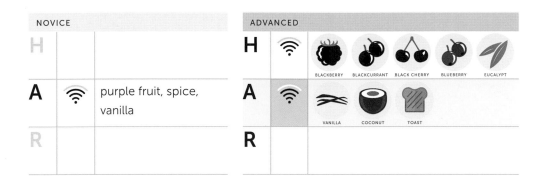

R RIPENING AROMAS

Smell again, third time lucky? Hmmm, the Shiraz reveals again the harvest and cellar aromas, even after five years of bottle age. But there also seem to be certain nutty aromas which are indicative of ripening in the bottle, even though these ripening aromas are not as intense as the harvest and cellar aromas. I note these ripening aromas in the comments for as well: walnut.

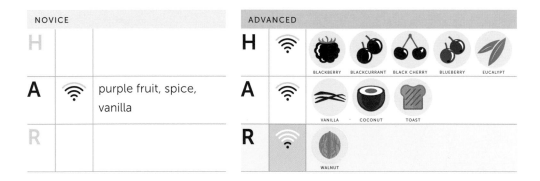

Now we have assessed the appearance and smell of the Shiraz, i's time to take a first mouthful – and here we go again.

STEP 3 PALATE

Just like with white wines, we will focus on the letters A for acidity, C for candy (residual sugars), E for ethanol and T for tannins.

A ACIDITY

The acidity of this Shiraz, scores below average; I don't experience much salivation.

NOVICE		ADVANCED	
A	🛜	A	🛜
C		C	
T		T	
E		E	

C CANDY

This Shiraz is dry and scores nil for the C of candy.

NOVICE		ADVANCED	
A	🛜	A	🛜
C	🛜	C	🛜
T		T	
E		E	

Tannins are substances that bind with proteins in a solution and then precipitate. The term *tannin* (from *tannum*, oak bark) refers to the use of oak and other bark in tanning animal hides into leather. Tannins in grapes are based on gallic acid and are sometimes also referred to as tannic acid. But don't let that name fool you, because tannins have the exact opposite effect from acids in wine tasting. Whereas acidity in wine makes your mouth water and thus causes more saliva, tannins have the opposite effect. Tannins are substances which bind with proteins in a solution and then precipitate. And that is what happens in your mouth when tasting red wines. The tannins combine with and coagulate the tannins in your saliva which then loses its normal lubricant properties and this causes a drying and puckering sensation in your mouth.

Astringent Versus Bitter
If you try several astringent wines in succession, the protein in your saliva runs out and your mouth becomes as dry as leather, causing a temporary loss of taste until the protein level recovers. Astringency is not assessed by your sense of taste, but sense of touch. It is a mouthfeel. Bitterness, however, is assessed by the sense of taste and something you can get used to – that is, you can develop a taste for it. Just drink a popular IPA beer. The first sip is bitter because of the high hop content, but soon your mouth gets used to the taste and it becomes pleasant for most people.

When assessing tannins, we tend to focus on the drying, furring, and puckering sensation in your mouth. The drier the sensation, the more astringent the tannins. In chapters 3 and 6 we will learn that tannins in red wine have two sources: the skin and pips of grapes, and new wooden barrels. We will also learn that the degree of astringency is determined by both the thickness of the skins and the degree of ripeness of the harvested fruit. For now, we will use the table on the next page as guide.

When tasting wine, we try to estimate tannin levels by organizing them relative to each other from low to high. In our notes we try to deduce something about the maturity and the origin of the tannins. The table below organizes the degrees of astringency to certain benchmark wines.

TANNINS		
📶 astringent		Wines made from very thick-skinned grapes like Tannat (Madiran), Sagrantino (di Montefalco) and Nebbiolo (Barolo)
📶 high		Wines made from thick-skinned grapes like Cabernet Sauvignon (Médoc), Malbec (Cahors) and Sangiovese (Chianti)
📶 medium		Most red wines
📶 low		Wines made from thin-skinned grapes such as Pinot Noir or made by short, cold or carbonic maceration such as Beaujolais
📶 very low		Most white wines, sparkling wines, and rosés

In the same way that tannins bind with proteins in saliva, they also bind with proteins in meat (and cheese). This is the main reason that tannic wines are less drying if you drink them with food. Tannins and acids can mask and compensate each other to a certain extent – because the extra saliva (generated by acidity) is partly bound by the tannins. This is a phenomenon that often occurs with Italian wines.

Back to the Barossa Shiraz.

T TANNINS

This big wine has lots of tannin content derived from both the grapes and the oak. They are ripe, smooth, yet firm. These observations about the tannins seem to correlate with my other observations about the ripeness of the wine. I briefly note my observations about the sensation of the tannins in this wine: firm yet smooth and ripe tannins.

NOVICE		
A	📶	
C	📶	
T	📶	
E		

ADVANCED		
A	📶	
C	📶	
T	📶	ripe and smooth
E		

The Tannin Tower

astringent

Nebbiolo	Tannat
Sagrantino	Vranac
Saperavi	Xinomavro

high

Aglianico	Negroamaro
Alicante Bouschet	Nerello Mascalese
Baga	Nero d'avola
Blaufränkisch	Pinotage
Bobal	Primitivo
Cabernet Sauvignon	Petit Verdot
Carignan	Sangiovese
Durif	Syrah
Feteasca Neagra	Touriga Franca
Malbec	Touriga Nacional
Monastrell	Trincadeira

medium

Agiorgitiko	Marselan
Barbera	Mencía
Bonarda	Merlot
Cabernet Franc	Montepulciano
Carmenere	Tempranillo
Dolcetto	Tinta barocca
Dornfelder	Zinfandel
Grenache	Zweigelt

low

Cinsault	Lambrusco
Corvina	Pinot Noir
Frappato	Regent
Gamay	Sankt Laurent

E ETHANOL

The Shiraz from Barossa gives a slightly burning sensation in your throat, even if it is not unbalanced in this wine. We estimate the alcohol percentage at 14.5%.

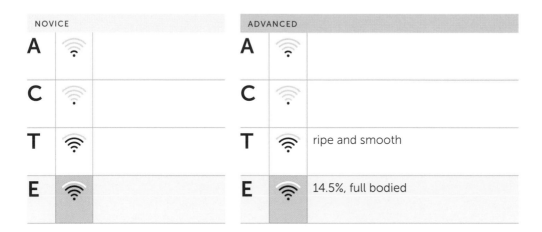

NOVICE				ADVANCED		
A	📶			A	📶	
C	📶			C	📶	
T	📶			T	📶	ripe and smooth
E	📶			E	📶	14.5%, full bodied

We describe the Shiraz as full bodied while we assessed the body of the Marlborough Sauvignon Blanc as medium.

Just like astringency, the body of a wine is also more about tactile sensations than taste. Nevertheless, they are part of the overall flavor of the wine. With 'body', or mouthfeel we assess the 'weight' of the wine in the mouth. Would it be easy to 'knock back' (half) a bottle of this wine on a summer afternoon? Or would it be a task to get through even one glass on such a day? In the first case we would probably refer to the wine as 'light bodied' while in the latter case we most likely would call the wine 'full bodied'.

We might make a further comparison with skimmed and whole milk. Although the difference in weight between them is caused by only one factor – the fat content, in wine, the body is determined by an array of factors of which alcohol is the dominant one. Other influences are extract (concentration), sweetness, acidity and tannins. This is further complicated by the fact that oftentimes these forces work in opposition to each other – some increasing the body, others decreasing it. It is the total of all these influences which ultimately gives the wine its body, or weight.

For example, an Amarone della Vapolicella, is a wine made from dried grapes which leads to a red wine with high to very high alcohol (15% is no exception), moderate acidity, (often) some residual sweetness, high extract and ripe, smooth tannins. While they all add to the full body, the maturation in oak barrels give extra complexity further increasing the body.

By contrast, an Aged Hunter Semillon, is produced from barely ripe grapes and higher yields resulting in a white wine with low alcohol (11% is no exception), high to very high acidity, no residual sweetness and no oak complexity at all. The only factor which increases the body to a degree is the added complexity of several years of bottle age.

The table below organizes the degrees of body associated with certain benchmark wines, both whites and reds, and offers some cool vocabulary for describing the body of your wine.

BODY			
full bodied	rich, heavy, full, robust, big	Amarone della Valpolicella Smaragd Grüner Veltliner
	firm, solid, muscular, intense	Pauillac (Grand Cru Classé) Meursault (Premier Cru)
medium bodied	moderate, average, decent	Barbera d'Alba Pinot Gris Alsace
	athletic, elegant, delicate,	Pinot Nero (Alto Adige) Vinho Verde
light bodied	light, slender, thin, slim, frail	Frühburgunder Ahr Aged Hunter Semillon

Going back to the Barossa Shiraz: not only do I feel a burning sensation in my throat, the wine also produces a heavy mouthfeel, indeed the alcohol content is 14.5%. Body is sometimes the best way to estimate the alcohol level, especially in the case of Amarone style wines. Alcohol might seem balanced in these big wines, and estimating body might be the best technique to determine the alcohol level.

R RELATIVE FRUIT INTENSITY

The final letter of the CHARACTER Chart of the Barossa Shiraz also stands for Relative fruit intensity, or the *relative* intensity of the Harvest aromas.
In this case we would compare the fruit intensity of the Barossa Shiraz to the fruit intensity of all other Syrah/Shiraz in the world, including benchmarks like Hermitage or Côte-Rôtie in the northern Rhône in France. And in doing so, we would score the relative fruit intensity of the Barossa Shiraz as very high.

In case we are not sure about the grape variety the red wine is made of, we have to make an assumption for an imaginary variety and decide whether the relative fruit intensity of the wine is high or low. This may sound a bit abstract for now, but we will come back to Relative fruit intensity in more detail later in the book. For now, it will suffice to score the Relative fruit intensity high in the chart.

NOVICE		
C	📶	ruby
H		
A	📶	purple fruit, spice, vanilla
R		
A	📶	
C	📶	
T	📶	
E	📶	
R	📶	

ADVANCED		
C	📶	ruby
H	📶	BLACKBERRY, BLACKCURRANT, BLACK CHERRY, BLUEBERRY, EUCALYPT
A	📶	VANILLA, COCONUT, TOAST
R	📶	WALNUT
A	📶	
C	📶	
T	📶	ripe and smooth
E	📶	14.5%, full bodied
R	📶	

Tasting Note
Barossa Shiraz

Novice tasters
This deeply colored, ruby red wine has a distinct nose of purple fruit and herbs. The wine is dry with low acidity, a lot of tannins and also a lot of alcohol.

Advanced tasters
This deeply colored, ruby red wine has a pronounced nose with harvest aromas such as blackberry, black currant and black cherry, mint, and eucalyptus, as well as aromas of winemaking such as vanilla and coconut and a ripening note of walnut. The wine is dry with pronounced fruit ripeness, low acidity, many but ripe, round tannins, and high alcohol (14.5%), full body and a high relative fruit intensity.

And with this tasting note we close chapter 2. It was all about the CHARACTER Method in action. That is to say, the first part of the method. With this first part, the systematic approach to wine tasting, it proved to be a piece of cake to write a tasting note.

However, the goal is not just being able to write tasting notes, but also, to draw conclusions from them. Conclusions about the grape variety, the origin, the method of winemaking, and the age of the wine. This, we can only do with a big reservoir of wine-knowledge and repeated practice, and only then will this method develop its potential into the promised 'holy grail of wine tasting'.

So, we'd best get on with the job of building the reservoir of wine knowledge.

Part II

Anyone Can Taste Wine. You Just Need (a Lot of) Knowledge

Wine is fascinating. More and more people are falling under the spell of fermented grape juice. As you become beguiled by wine you will not only develop a thirst for new wine experiences but also welcome a thirst for wine knowledge.

3
Is Wine Made in the Vineyard?

Reap the Harvest

'Wine is made in the vineyard' is a cliché which should not be taken too literally. It simply implies that you can't make great wine from a poor harvest. It also means that you can't make a Marlborough Sauvignon Blanc in Sancerre. Or a Vosne-Romanée in Sonoma (sorry). In this chapter we'll find out why.

Grape Expectations

Our investigation into the taste of wine will start with how the harvest — a combination of grape variety and vineyard — leaves its own signature on the identity of the wine, in terms of its color, aromas, and taste.

Consider the grape as the only raw material of wine. The DNA of the grape is in the skin but the DNA of the vineyard is in the pulp. Although the grape and vineyard are destined, therefore, to influence each other in a natural and symbiotic relationship, it will be helpful to temporarily set these partners apart and first study their effects in isolation. In this chapter, we will start with a close up study of the grape as the basis of every wine.

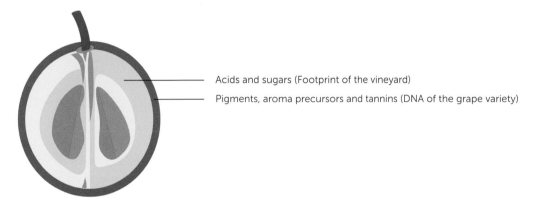

Acids and sugars (Footprint of the vineyard)

Pigments, aroma precursors and tannins (DNA of the grape variety)

Every grape variety has unique qualities which impact the color, smell, and taste of the wine. This comes about via the skin of the grape. Indeed, you might even say that the importance of the grape is skin-deep because it is the skin that contains the variety's typical:

- **Pigments**
- **Aroma precursors**
- **Tannins**

These three are collectively known as 'phenolics'. Notwithstanding their influence being (only) skin-deep, the unique aroma precursors and tannins in the skin directly influence the taste of the wine, while the pigments are directly responsible for the color of the wine. It is, therefore, crucial to learn more about these influencers — Pigments, Aromas, and Tannins - and discover how the variety impacts the wine. So, let's establish some 'grape expectations'.
In fact, I will start with the pigments, since the sense of sight coincides with STEP 1 of the CHARACTER Method.

The Impact of Pigments

Red and Rosé

The color intensity of red (and rosé) wine depends on (1) the grape variety and (2) the technique and length of the maceration. Some grapes, just like some people, are thicker-skinned than others. And it is the thick-skinned types who are potentially the champions when it comes to contributing color to the wine. In a nutshell: the thicker the skin, the deeper the potential color. Note the term 'potential'. This little caveat is needed because – no matter how thick the skin – if the winemaker decides for a short maceration, the wine will nevertheless be light in color. This is how rosé is made. Some red grape varieties are famed for their fabulously thick skins (the thickies?) such as Tannat, Cabernet Sauvignon and Petit Verdot. Other red grape varieties are, by nature, thin-skinned. Pinot Noir is the most famous of the thin-skinned types. Its wines are usually light in color; if however a deeper colored wine is desired the only thing the winemaker can do is to blend with a deeper colored wine.

The thicker the skin, the more color goes in (potentially).

CHARACTER		
thick-skinned	C	📶
thin-skinned	C	📶

White and Orange

But let's not ignore the whites just because their color pales in comparison to the reds. White wines are yellow because they are fermented without their skins. However, this yellowness can still vary in intensity, mainly depending on exposure to oxygen (either during winemaking and/or aging in the bottle). Also, the grapes of some varieties, such as Gewürztraminer and Pinot Gris, tend to develop a light red color towards the maturation in the vineyard which thus impacts their yellowness.
And if, a winemaker uses red winemaking with white grapes, which means maceration on the skins, then you end up with a so-called 'orange wine'. In one sense, orange wines hark back to a historical winemaking past when macerating the grapes on the skins and thus extracting tannins from the wine was the only way to keep white wines fresh for a little longer. But now it seems that orange wines are also 'back to the future' because they are especially fashionable among hipster sommeliers.

Orange wines are orange because the white grapes are macerated on their skins.

CHARACTER		
orange	C	📶
white	C	📶

The Impact of the Aromas

Aromatic Intensity

Just as the pigments determine the potential color intensity, it is the aroma precursors in the skin which determine the aromatic intensity of the wine. However, unlike the pigments, which directly transfer their color to the must, most aromas are still 'bound' when they enter the must and are only released during alcoholic fermentation. When that finally happens, there are big differences between grape varieties, especially whites.

Some white grape varieties contribute such an intensity of aromas to their wines, that we call them 'the aromatics'. Wines made from these grape varieties are often easy for us to identify because they are so pronounced in their aromatic intensity. Among them are Gewürztraminer, Muscat, Riesling, Sauvignon Blanc, Torrontès, and Viognier.

Other white grape varieties are much less outspoken in their display of aromas and we would describe these simply as 'neutral'. 'The neutrals' include Melon de Bourgogne, Pinot Blanc, and Trebbiano among others.

In terms of aromatic intensity there is huge varietal difference.

CHARACTER

| aromatics | H 🛜 |
| neutrals | H 🛜 |

Aromatic Identity

Whatever the color of your skin and whether you are an 'aromatic' or a 'neutral' grape variety, all varieties contribute unique aromas – signature smells – to your glass of wine, no matter where in the world they are grown. It is not that origin doesn't matter (because it does) but each wine made from Cabernet Sauvignon in the world will show to some extent blackberries and blackcurrant. Just like wine made from Viognier from anywhere will smell more or less of peach and apricot. It is their aromatic identity.

It's therefore useful to know the unique aromas of the most common grape varieties as it makes it easier to recognize them in wine tasting. To assist you, we listed the typical harvest aromas (and other characteristics) of some 175 benchmark wines in Chapters 7 and 8.

In terms of aromatic identity each variety contributes unique aromas.

CHARACTER

H   HARVEST AROMAS

The Impact of Tannins

Thick- versus thin- skinned types

Tannins are the astringent little bitey-bits found in the skin of the grapes and therefore they have a direct influence on the taste and style of wine. To understand how this works, we just need to return to our knowledge of the thick-skinned and thin-skinned types and promptly add a new generalization to our list of grape expectations. The thicker the skin, then potentially, the more intense will be the tannins of the wine. The same caveat about the word 'potentially' is needed here because again the winemaker may choose to dose the tannins in the winemaking throughout the maceration process. Also, the degree to which tannins have a drying effect in your mouth depends on the ripeness of the skin.

This is because tannins in plants play a protective role against predators; if the fruit is not completely ripe, the tannins can be still quite astringent, making it less attractive for predators to eat them. If however, the fruit is fully ripe and ready to be eaten and spread by predators, the tannins turn sweet and smooth.

This explains why a Madiran (made from Tannat, a grape with a very thick skin) from the moderate climate of the French Sud-Ouest is so much more astringent than the same Tannat from Tarija in Bolivia. The higher UV at 2,000 meter altitude takes care of a significant higher degree of ripeness of the tannins.

The riper the grape, the less drying the tannin. So, it is not only the grape but also the vineyard, including its climate, location, and soil, which plays an important role.

The thicker the skin, the more tannins go in. The riper the grape, the softer the tannin.

CHARACTER		
thick-skinned	T	📶
thin-skinned	T	📶
orange	T	📶

Summary

It is vital to remember that the skin of the humble grape influences the wine in our glass in important ways because it contains:

- **Pigments** - influence the color
- **Aromas** – unique for each grape variety; vary in intensity and identity
- **Tannins** - influence style

In order to broaden our knowledge, we can now zoom out to see the grape in the bigger picture: the vineyard. As it is the location of the vineyard which also leaves its metaphorical footprint in our glass of wine.

Footprint of the Vineyard

The Impact of Terroir

By the term 'vineyard' we mean the natural environment of the vine, also known as Terroir. This quintessential French term has no English equivalent, but the theory behind it is simple: that even small differences in climate, topography and the soil type of a given vineyard can have a marked impact on the style (and quality) of the wine produced there. And thus give a wine a 'sense of place'.

The footprint of the vineyard is determined by the three factors of terroir:
- Climate
- Topography
- Soil

Before we dig deeper, I will need to draw some boundaries around the scope of this discussion and limit myself to those vineyard factors that have a direct impact on the color, smell or taste of wine. There is much more to write about climate, soil and topography, but not all these aspects can be tasted in a wine.

The Impact of Climate

Climate is defined here as the average weather measured over a longer period of time; while weather can be defined as the short-term temperature, sunlight, rain, and wind. Of all the climates in the world, only certain combinations of temperature, humidity and precipitation are suitable for viticulture. According to Dr. Gregory Jones, a climatologist specializing in viticulture, within all ranges of suitable climates, each grape variety has its own 'optimum zone' in terms of temperature, sunlight, precipitation, humidity, and drought. In this zone, the grape ripens optimally, with good sugar levels and ripe flavors, in a balanced way.

Some grape varieties, for example, Riesling, will only thrive in cool climates. In warmer climates, Riesling not only loses its hallmark acidity but also its aromatic intensity and even the aromas themselves. Mourvèdre, similarly, will only thrive in warm to hot climates. Place Mourvèdre in a cool climate and it will not ripen — leaving it to suffer from unripe flavors, astringent tannins, and unbalanced acids. These grape varieties are indeed fussy about where in the world they survive or thrive. As a result of their quite narrow optimum zone, stylistically Riesling and Mourvèdre tend to be homogeneous.

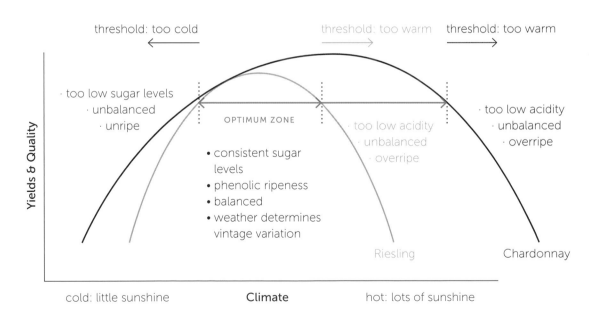

Source: Dr. Gregory V. Jones

Temperature

Chardonnay and Syrah, on the other hand, tend to adapt and feel at home in a much wider variety of climates as illustrated in the graph. As a result of their much wider optimum zone, Chardonnay and Syrah display a much wider spectrum of styles than Riesling or Mourvèdre. That's why we call them heterogeneous.

It took viticulturists like Gregory Jones many decades to work out the optimal zones for particular grape varieties – then along came climate change. The impact of climate change on the practice of grape growing has been so profound that climates in certain regions of the world have moved out of the optimum zones for the grape varieties which have thrived there for centuries. This phenomenon is presenting new dilemmas, especially to winemakers of the least adaptive grape varieties.

Of the five aspects of climate (temperature, sunlight, precipitation, wind and humidity), we will first take a look at temperature, and in particular at the relationship between temperature and the acidity in grapes and wines.

The rate of acid loss in the grapes as they ripen (thus the acidity level of the resulting wines) is determined by the climate. The cooler the climate, the higher the acidity in the wine. And the warmer, the lower the acidity.
To illustrate this, it's fun to compare what happens to the acidity levels in a wine made from the same grape variety but from different climates. For this experiment, we need to turn to adaptive varieties like Chardonnay and Syrah. A Chardonnay from the cool climate Chablis region indeed has much higher acids than a Chardonnay from the hot climate Riverland in Australia. And compare a Chilean Syrah from San Antonio (cool climate) with one from the heart of Maipo (warm climate). These regions are not even fifty kilometers apart, but exhibit a world of difference in acidity!

The cooler the climate; the higher the acidity.
The warmer the climate; the lower the acidity.

 # Water

Water is important when it comes to the growth and ripening of the grapes. Every plant needs water from time to time. Some water stress is okay, but stress for a prolonged period is definitely not good, neither for us nor for the vine. This is because water stressed vines become dehydrated which affects the growth and ripening of the grapes. In large parts of Europe, we are used to dryland vineyards (not irrigated), because for hundreds of years we had enough rainfall in combination with soils with good water-holding capacity. But dryland vineyards do not necessarily lead to better quality, as growers who are allowed to irrigate can more or less 'manage' the water stress of the plant. This gives them a unique advantage over the winemakers who depend on Nature. Obviously, precipitation can mean more than just rain. Precipitation can also be snow, or worse, hail, which can destroy the harvest in a matter of minutes.

 # Wind

Wind can be friend or foe to the vines. In the role of a friend, wind can help to prevent the effects of mold and rot in the vines. Moreover, the alternating land and sea winds in the Mediterranean climate, for example, can have very favorable effects on the health of the vines in these regions. The friendly, dry winds that visit in the evenings reduce the risk of fungal diseases, while the humid sea breezes that sweep in during the day can reduce the water stress. Too much wind, however, is seen as the enemy of the vines. Strong winds can cause dehydration, water stress and even physical damage to the vine itself.

In some climates, the wind plays a formidable role in the environment of the vineyard. The Cape Doctor, for example, is said to have got its name from its function of cleansing the air of germs and mildew. Then there's the Mistral, which sweeps across the vineyards in the South of France. The wind can even determine the style of the wine; the Levante and the Poniente in Andalusia determine whether it will be a Fino or a Manzanilla! The answer my friend is blowin' in the wind, and quite plausibly, the answer can also be detected in your glass of wine.

 # Sunlight

In addition to temperature, rain, and wind, sunlight contributes to ripening in terms of a build up of sugars, phenolic compounds such as anthocyanins (pigments for color) and flavor pre-cursors and softer, less drying tannins.

Sunlight and Alcohol
The amount of sunlight that a vineyard receives directly influences the amount of sugar in the grapes via the process of photosynthesis. This in turn determines the potential amount of alcohol in the wine. The more sunlight, the more sugar in the grape, and the more alcohol in the wine. Again, such logic is helpful.

The more sunlight; more sugar in grapes; more alcohol in wine.

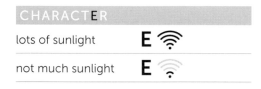

CHARACTER		
lots of sunlight	E	📶
not much sunlight	E	📶

Sunlight and the Old versus New World Theory
After more than 25 years of non-stop travel to wine regions all over the world, I have noticed a few stylistic differences in wines from the Old World (Europe) versus the New World. These stylistic differences manifest themselves in the glass in fruit intensity and astringency of tannins. Over time, I used this experience to develop my own totally non-scientific 'Old versus New World Theory'.

The *Old versus New World Theory* starts with the fact that most wine regions in the New World have a warmer and sunnier climate than those in Europe at comparable latitudes. Most New World wine regions benefit from cold currents (or high altitudes) to moderate their temperatures. At the same time, the opposite is happening in Europe where a colder and less sunny climate is compensated – heated this time – by the warm North Atlantic Drift. Currents play a special role in this Old and New World Theory.

Current Affairs: Oceans in Motion
'The movement of warm or cold waters off the coasts of continents can profoundly affect the local climates and growing conditions', writes Wayne Belding on Wine Review Online. Take the Humboldt Current which brings cold water near the Chilean coast.

In the westerly wind belt, moisture laden air is pushed towards the Chilean coast. As the moisture laden westerly wind passes over the Humboldt Current it is cooled. Since cold air cannot hold as much water vapor as warm air, it drops its moisture load over the Pacific. The then already-dried air dries out even more as it is pushed over the Chilean coastal range and by the time it reaches the wine regions it is so dry it creates a diurnal shift benefiting flavor develop-ment in the grapes and inhibits the development of fungal diseases, leading to healthier fruit.

This phenomenon is repeated in other New World regions, such as California (the California Current), South Africa (the Benguela Current), Australia (the West Australian Current) and New Zealand (the Antarctic Circumpolar Current).

In contrast, most of Europe's wine-growing regions are moderated by the warm North Atlantic Drift which arguably raises the latitude of viti-cultural viability in France and Germany by three degrees. While, as a result, average temperatures in wine regions in the Old World might not be that different from many wine regions in the New World, the intensity of the sunlight is quite different. The intensity of the sunlight (UV) is not affected by the currents which means that – at similar latitudes – New World wine regions have more sunlight than Old World wine regions. This has an effect on the fruit intensity and tannins.

Sunlight and Tannins

Remember the role of tannins in plants to protect against predators? More sunlight hours and stronger UV in New World wine regions cause wines to have overall riper fruit and smoother, less drying tannins.

CHARACTER		
New World	T	smooth
Old World	T	astringent

Sunlight and Relative Fruit Intensity

The fruit intensity of wines is determined by the intensity of the harvest aromas and flavors. The aromatics (remember the whites?) have a high fruit intensity and the neutrals a low fruit intensity. This is an 'absolute fruit intensity' as we are comparing all grape varieties. However, if we're only comparing wines from the same grape variety, we are talking about the 'relative fruit intensity'.

The sunnier the New World climate and the higher the UV radiation, then the higher this 'Relative Fruit Intensity'.

CHARACTER		
New World	R	〰
Old World	R	〰

Take for example Marlborough Sauvignon Blanc (influenced by the cold Antarctic Circumpolar Current) and compare it to Sancerre in the Loire Valley in France (influenced by the warm North Atlantic Drift). Made from the same grape variety, with similar varietal aromas, but hugely different in terms of fruit intensity.

Give that a thought when you next sip your glass of wine. The pull of the ocean may have helped shape the climatic conditions that enabled the relative fruit intensity and tannins of these wines.

The Impact of Topography

When we talk about the topography of a vineyard we need to consider its latitude, aspect, direction, altitude, and proximity to bodies of water (rivers, seas, lakes), and hills and mountains.

Proximity to Mountains

Alsace is a northerly wine region in France and as a result should receive more rain than the south of France. But the opposite is true. Alsace owes this to its location behind the Vosges mountains. This ridge blocks the clouds brought in by westerly winds which are forced to dump all their rain and snow on the mountains. As a result, the vineyards behind the Vosges remain relatively protected from moisture from the west.

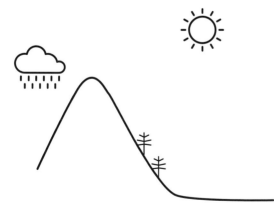

A similar phenomenon occurs in the Pfalz (protected by the Haardt mountains) the Hawke's Bay (protected by the Ruahine and Kaweka Ranges) and many other wine regions globally.

Thermal Zone

A thermal zone is a phenomenon in which warm valley air is replaced by descending (heavier) cool mountain air. It happens each afternoon in the Chilean summer but only at close proximity of the foothills of the Andes. When it happens just as if someone comes in and turns on the air conditioner. Thermal zones enable the grapes to maintain their acidity, whereas wine made from a vineyard a few kilometers into the valley will not benefit from this air conditioning effect. Thermal zones can happen in any vineyard with significant air temperature difference at proximal altitudes.

Direction and Slope

Let's recognize the importance of direction. In a cool climate, a south-facing vineyard (in the Northern Hemisphere) can mean the difference between ripe and unripe grapes. And since we prefer ripe grapes, south-facing vineyards matter. The same applies to an ideal slope on a hill. It's all about sun exposure. A steep north-facing slope (this time in the Southern Hemisphere) will equally provide the best sun exposure and the best chance of ripening. Especially in marginal climates.

Altitude and Latitude

Another aspect of location is the altitude of the vineyard. Each 150 meter increase in altitude correlates with an average temperature decrease of approximately 1°C. At the same time, the UV increases, as does the diurnal temperature variation. Usually this leads to riper tannins and more acidity. That said, the most favorable altitude for a vineyard depends on the latitude of the vineyard (its location in relation to the equator). Think about it: as you travel closer to the equator, latitudes get lower, and the lands get warmer, more tropical.
If you want to grow vineyards in these conditions, you will need to find higher altitudes.

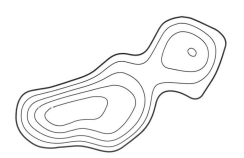

Proximity to Water

The vineyard's proximity to water masses such as a sea, a lake, or a river is also significant. Such water masses can have a tempering effect on the temperature in an area which is mainly due to the circulation of the air: cool air from above the water masses is drawn across the land (think of sea breezes) to replace the warm air rising above the vineyards as the land heats up. These breezes cool the vines throughout the afternoon. At night, the opposite happens, and the cool air above the land surface flows back towards the relatively warm water surface. In addition, the confrontation of warm air above land with cool air above sea can cause condensation and thus fog (as in large parts of the California coast) or cloud cover (such as in the Hunter Valley).

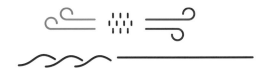

Lakes and rivers can also cause noble rot to develop due to condensation and morning mist. Think of the Neusiedlersee and Sauternes. In the latter, fog is caused by the temperature difference between two rivers: the warmer Garonne and the cooler Ciron whose water comes from an underground river that rises above the ground here.

Proximity to Vegetation

The singularity of provincial aromas can hardly be understated. Think of the eucalyptus trees that grow close to the Chilean and Australian vineyards. Take an imaginary whiff of the natural minty fragrances given out by the foliage. The substance that causes these aromas and flavors is called eucalyptol. The oil from the eucalyptus tree evaporates and then precipitates on the grapes (and is also transmitted through eucalyptus leaves that find their way into the picking bin). Its aromas and flavors are only evident in red wines, since, as we well know, only these are made with prolonged maceration.

Eucalypt trees near the vineyard can cause harvest aromas of eucalypt and mint.

CHARACTER

H
EUCALYPT   MINT

In the South of France there are few if any eucalyptus trees, but there is a myriad of game vegetation such as juniper, thyme, rosemary and lavender, that grow together like weeds. These plants impart gamely delicious smells like a 'Provencal spice mix' and when that smell finds its way into your glass of wine you will recognize it by the term 'garrigues'.

Vegetation of juniper, thyme, rosemary and lavender near the vineyard can lead to harvest aromas of garrigue.

CHARACTER

H
GARRIGUE

And then there is the aromatic influence of the wily shrubland plants in parts of South Africa known as 'fynbos'. The wine regions in the Western Cape are located in the middle of the so-called Cape Floral Kingdom which is the smallest but richest plant kingdom in the world. More plant species are grown in the thousand-kilometer stretch between Port Elizabeth and Cape Town, than in the entire Northern Hemisphere! Fynbos has a characteristic rooibos and buchu-like spiciness that you can taste in many Cape reds. It is often erroneously dismissed as 'burnt rubber', but it is my theory that the aroma comes from that native vegetation. It is the whiff of the vineyard, right there in your wine.

Indigenous vegetation from the Cape Floral Kingdom can cause harvest aromas of fynbos.

CHARACTER

H
FYNBOS

The Impact of **Soil**

Sense of Place?

We often imagine, or even romanticize about how a wine is reminiscent of its particular place of origin. Tasting notes in wine magazines (including those I've contributed myself) routinely use the word 'minerality' to describe the taste. A typical example would be tasting notes describing wines from the Chablis region as imparting aromas and flavors that are 'mineral' or 'flinty' or 'steely'. But is that really so? Can we taste the soil?

Soil and the Scientists

Scientists cannot actually prove that the soil in Chablis directly influences the aromas in the wine. The minerals in the soil, or so the 'lab-report' reads, do not affect the taste or aromas of the grape and therefore the wine, because (the evidence goes on) mineral concentrations in the grape are below the human tasting threshold. According to these reports, the soil is just a nutritional source (of minerals), a heat regulator, and makes no other contribution to the vine.

First Taste, then Believe

Nonetheless, I consistently recognize Chablis in blind tastings as a style that cannot be reproduced anywhere else in the world. And while we're at it,

I also usually recognize Assyrtiko from the Greek island of Santorini, and Nerello Mascalese from the Etna for their unmistakably 'volcanic' style. Just as I tend to recognize Pfalz Rieslings from basalt soils, Grüners from loess soils and Hermitage from granite surfaces.

I'm not in the habit of rejecting scientific evidence. But I maintain that there is some mysterious influence, from the soil, on the aromas of the grape and the taste of the wine – because I can taste it myself. First taste; then believe. It is difficult to explain the mechanism through which I am able to detect these aromas and flavors but perhaps the answer lies in the capacity for human tasters to outperform machines in tasting ability.

Reason enough to take a closer look at the ground beneath our feet.

Black is for Warmth

Think about the black basalt from the German Pfalz. We don't need to imagine that we can smell the basalt or that our wine will contain a 'touch of darkness'; no, in this case, the science shows us how the black soil contributes by being warmed by the sunlight during the day and then generously releasing this warmth at night, enabling the grapes from such soils to become riper than those from

other soils in the same region. Even the scientists would agree that, in this way, the soil here can have a measurable influence on the style and quality of the wine. And there are many more examples.

Shield of White

Now consider the albariza soils in Jerez, Spain (albarizo means whiteish). These whiteish soils, like those in Chablis, are rich in limestone. This extends all the way up to the surface of the vineyard giving an intense, white color to the soils (don't forget your sunglasses when visiting Jerez!). Like a shield, this bright, light-colored soil reflects the searing Spanish sunlight back into the sky and provides relief from the heat.

Summary

We have now followed the footprint of the vineyard all the way into our glass. Hopefully, we're beginning to appreciate the impact of climate, soil, and topography, on the style and quality of the grapes. Within their complex interplay, they determine alcohol, acidity, tannins and relative fruit intensity. Finally, the presence of vegetation in the proximity of the vineyard can add specific flavors such as eucalyptus, garrigues and fynbos to the wine.

In Chapter 4 we will go into the cellar and come to understand the influence that the winemakers themselves can have on the color, smell, and taste of the wines they create.

4
Winemakers Make Wine

Right?

Yes, they do. You can't make great wine
from a poor site. But a great site is no
guarantee for a great wine, either.
Without expert intervention by skillful
winemakers, there is no timely harvest,
no diligent selection of grapes, no
skilled conversion in the cellar and
therefore, no great wine.

Styles differ

It's true that even small differences in the climate, topography and soil type of a given vineyard can have a marked impact on the style and quality of the wine produced there. Hence terroir is the basis of famous geographic indication systems such as in Burgundy and the Mosel. However, the idea that terroir – or some form of divine intervention – is solely responsible for the wine in your glass is nonsense. "I've had more than enough disappointing bottles from great vineyards to recognize a more important truth: that the best wines are produced by people who have refined and mastered their craft", says Tim Atkin MW and I couldn't agree more.

For entry level wines, that craft includes masterful blending, adjustment of acidity, alcohol, residual sugar, and usually reductive winemaking; all focused on achieving a certain quality and style at a given price point.

For fine wine, winemakers are usually more focused on optimum picking times, the health of the harvest, and keeping the fruit of these exceptional blocks and vineyards separate during vinification. Usually, they do not aim their winemaking toolbox to achieve a specific price point but to maintain the integrity and authenticity of the unique terroir. That's why they usually interfere much less than in the case of entry level wines. This is also the reason why you will hear winemakers of many top wines in the world say their job is easy because they do as little as possible.

However, no matter how much or little the winemakers interfere in the process, they will have their impact on the final wine. This begins with the decision when to harvest and continues when the fruit arrives at the winery, setting in motion a series of decisions and activities in the cellar that will have a direct impact on the color, aromas, and flavors of the wine. In much the same way as the previous chapter, we will only investigate the most impactful cellar activities. We will do this in separate columns linking specific cellar activities to specific letters in the golden bar of the acronym CHARACTER.

All of the cellar activities are put into context on page 80 for white winemaking and page 86 for red winemaking. The cellar activities with a blue caption are optional (such as malolactic fermentation for whites), while those with a black caption are mandatory (such as malolactic fermentation for reds).

Harvest

People often imagine that the only consideration for deciding when to harvest is the ripeness of the fruit. However, in real life, several other factors also play a role, such as availability of tank space, personnel, harvesters, or pickers; whether the weather or the weather forecast allows or demands it; and last but not least decisions required in order to get the desired wine style (such as Aged Hunter Semillon which is deliberately picked early to obtain this light style).

SPARKLING

Early Harvest

The time of harvest is also critical for the production of sparkling wines. For most bubblies you need grapes with high acidity and relatively low sugars. And that means an early harvest! Acidic grapes with low sugars produce base wines with high acidity and low alcohol. The low alcohol subsequently enables a second fermentation without exceeding 12 or 12.5% in the final wine; the high acidity absorbs the dosage (addition of sugars) and gives the wine its freshness.

CHARACTER

C

E

SWEET

Late Picked

The decision to harvest late is often associated with sweet wines. As a rule of thumb: the later you harvest, the more sugars the grapes develop, and the more opportunity to leave residual sugars in the wine, without the alcohol content becoming too low. Most late harvest wines such as Spätlese or Vendange Tardive come from cool climates, as the grapes – even harvested late – retain enough acidity to balance the sweetness.

CHARACTER

A

Dried

Another way to concentrate the sugars (and acidity) in the grape is to allow the grapes to dry. This can be done on the vine, but also on mats in well-ventilated areas. The drying process can take from several weeks to several months. Vin Santo, Recioto, Strohwein, Vin de Paille and Liqueur Muscat are typical benchmark wines made from 'dried' or 'raisined' grapes. Hence drying usually lends the wine aromas and flavors of raisins.

Late Picked: Noble Rot

A third vineyard technique is the so-called 'noble rot' or Botrytis Cinerea. Fully ripe grapes are subjected to moisture from morning mists. Fungus attacks the grapes, perforating their skins and causing them to lose water, which concentrates the sugars and acids. Botrytis gives these wines recognizable honey flavors. Thin-skinned varieties such as Riesling, Semillon, Chenin, and Furmint are most susceptible to noble rot.

Last Picked: Ice Wine

A fourth vineyard technique is to wait until winter and watch the grapes freeze to minus 8 Celsius (18 Fahrenheit). This concentrates the flavors, acids, and sugars because the water in the grape is transformed into ice crystals. Ice wine is perhaps the ultimate 'late harvest' wine. The challenge is to protect the grapes from mold, birds, and vermin until it freezes. In Europe, Eiswein (Icewine) is commonly made without oak, occasionally (in Canada) with oak.

CHARACTER

H
RAISINS

A

C

CHARACTER

H
HONEY

A

C

CHARACTER

A

C

Winemaking WHITES

blue captions: optional steps in the process
black captions: mandatory steps in the process

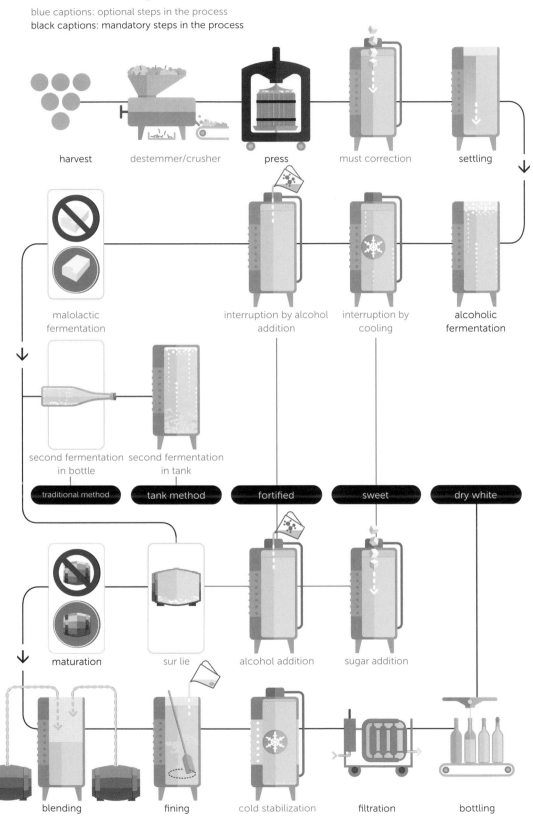

harvest

destemmer/crusher

press

must correction

settling

malolactic
fermentation

interruption by alcohol
addition

interruption by
cooling

alcoholic
fermentation

second fermentation
in bottle

second fermentation
in tank

traditional method

tank method

fortified

sweet

dry white

maturation

sur lie

alcohol addition

sugar addition

blending

fining

cold stabilization

filtration

bottling

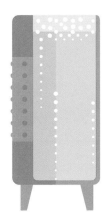

Orange wine
Back to the Future

If you make wine from white grapes in the way of red wine (with maceration of the skins) then you get a so-called 'orange wine'. In addition to color, the maceration also gives the wine some tannins, a different mouthfeel and a different aromatic intensity and identity than conventional white wines. Orange wine is 'back to the future' as all white wine was made that way centuries ago, before temperature control and stainless steel tanks, yet it is enjoying growing popularity under hipster sommeliers.

Alcoholic Fermentation

The process of alcoholic fermentation turns grape must into wine. During fermentation yeasts convert sugars into alcohol and carbon dioxide and free the aroma precursors which were bound to sugars, releasing the aromas in the wine. The lower the temperature of fermentation the less oxygen, the more fruit forward the wines will be. This is called reductive winemaking and it requires inert materials such as stainless-steel tanks and gases such as nitrogen and carbon dioxide, all designed to keep out the oxygen.

Interruption fermentation

Refrigeration or addition of alcohol will stop the yeasts from fermenting and unfermented sugars will remain. Addition of alcohol will also create a fortified wine (varying from 15 to 20%). Think of Vin Doux Naturel for whites, white port and madeira. The timing of the fortification determines the residual sweetness, the earlier, the sweeter (Malmsey); the later, the drier (Sercial). For wines whose fermentation has been interrupted by cooling, addition of sulfur dioxide and sterile filtration is necessary before bottling. Think of Kabinett, Spätlese, and Auslese.

CHARACTER
C

T

CHARACTER
H
HARVEST AROMA'S

CHARACTER
C   cooling

CHARACTER
C   fortifying

E   fortifying

Malolactic Fermentation
Go Malo!

The most important reason that malolactic fermentation (malo) is carried out in white wines is to reduce acidity and sometimes also to add a buttery aroma. As such, malo results in a fuller body, rounder mouthfeel, and usually a buttery aroma with a bit more complexity. Some grape varieties (remember the neutrals? – Chardonnay and Chenin Blanc for instance - wines which are less outspoken in their harvest aromas) have an affinity with malo, just as they have with oak. Especially the more premium styles from Burgundy, the Western Cape, and Rioja.

CHARACTER

BUTTER

A 📶

Malolactic Fermentation
No Malo?

For some whites, such as Sauvignon Blanc and Riesling (remember the aromatics?) or wines which are already low in acidity, the winemaker may not wish to lower acidity and/or add a buttery aroma. Malo can be inhibited by cooling the new wine (the bacteria will get too cold to start converting) and measuring appropriate additions of sulfur dioxide (stunning the bacteria into submission), followed by sterile filtration as well, before bottling. This will preserve the malic acids which can be an integral part of the style of the wine. Think of Sauvignon Blanc and Riesling.

CHARACTER

Second fermentation in bottle
The Remains Remain

Base wine is bottled with some addition of sugar and yeast which triggers a second fermentation after which the dead yeast remains in the bottle, varying from nine months to nine years. The longer the remains remain, the more of the deceased yeast cells will be broken down, and the more the wine will taste of the cadaver – although we prefer to use words such as brioche, biscuit, and toast, to describe the yeast feast in our wine. This is called 'autolysis' and it is common practice for champagne and other traditional method sparklings (Franciacorta, Cava, English, and New World sparklings, and Crémants). After autolysis, the yeast is removed from the wine (disgorgement), sugars may be added (dosage) and the bottle will be closed.

CHARACTER

A^2

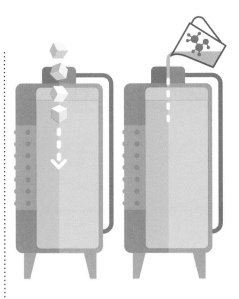

Second fermentation in tank
The Remains Removed

With the Charmat or Tank Method, you add yeast and sugars to a pressure tank with base wine, resulting in a second fermentation in the tank. As the resulting carbon dioxide cannot escape, the wine becomes sparkling. In order to preserve the harvest aromas and limit the impact of the dead yeast, the sparkling wine is, immediately after the second fermentation filtered and bottled under pressure. Typical examples of Tank method sparklings are Prosecco and most Sekt. For the Asti Method, the must becomes a sparkling sweet wine as the fermentation is arrested by cooling at approximately 100 grams per liter of residual sugars.

Sur lie
Deceased Yeast Adds to the Body - Sure-ly Not?

Sur lie is the first stage (3 to 9 months) of autolysis. If you leave the dead yeast after alcoholic fermentation in the wine, the enzymes of the yeast cells break down the yeast (the same as what happens to us when we die). The decay starts with the cell walls: let's say the tummy of the yeast, which gives fattiness and adds body, complexity, and palate weight to the wine. It is an alternative to residual sugar and common practice for high-acid wines outside of Germany such as Muscadet de Sèvre et Maine (sur Lie) and white Burgundies, and Chenin and Chardonnay elsewhere. Stirring the dead yeast through the wine is known as bâtonnage.

Addition of sugars or alcohol

By adding sugars, must, or grape juice concentrate (dosage for sparkling wines and mistela – a mixture of must and pure brandy – for sherry) to a dry base wine, the winemaker can make certain still, sparkling, and fortified wines more or less sweet. The addition of alcohol to a dry base wine is another method of fortification. This often results in a high alcohol content of 15 to 20%. Think of sherry. All base sherry wines are dry. To make a sweet sherry, such as a Medium or Cream, the dry base sherry must be sweetened before bottling.

CHARACTER
C
E 📶

CHARACTER
H 📶

CHARACTER
C creamy mouthfeel

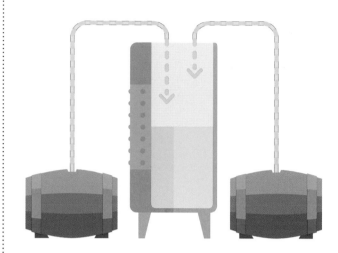

To Oak
That's the question

Remember our earlier analogy of the winemaker as a magician-alchemist able to magically add flavors of vanilla, coconut, mocha, chocolate, cedar, toast, spice, to the wine? Well, the real magic lies in the properties of oak which works behind the scenes, in the sense that it helps to naturally clarify and stabilize wines. Some of the most famous white wines in the world owe their style and greatness to their maturation in oak barrels. And I'm not just talking about Burgundy and Bordeaux but most premium whites in the world. And for all these reasons, it's hard to imagine not wanting to use oak.

or Not to Oak

But there are good reasons for leaving it out too. If winemakers wish to preserve the purity of the harvest aromas, then the use of (new) oak is generally not recommended. Think again of those aromatic grape varieties – like the benchmark Sauvignon Blanc from Marlborough – whose fruit-intense perfume is an integral part of their appeal. Naturally, winemakers prefer not to cloud that perfume with a woody sauce. And some of the neutral varieties are so fragile that even a touch of oak can be too much.

CHARACTER

A 📶

AROMAS OF WINEMAKING

T 📶

Blending

Blending wines from different white grape varieties, vineyards and / or vintages (such as in champagne) is a proven method for synergy. Both in obtaining more complexity and quality, as well as masking minor shortcomings and obtaining a consistent style. Famous white blends are Sauvignon Blanc with Semillon (Bordeaux) or with Chardonnay (Australia), Garganega with Trebbiano for Soave and Macabeo, Perralada with Xarello for Cava.

CHARACTER

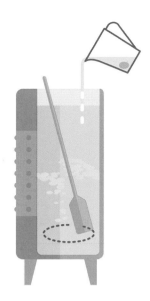

Clarification
to be clear

The purpose of clarification obviously is to keep the wine clear. This is done by putting a medium through the wine (fining) and putting the wine through a medium (filtration). Fining agents can be egg whites, albumin, pvpp, casein, isinglass, gelatin, or bentonite. They remove all invisible negatively or positively charged substances – depending on the charge of the fining agent – and thus protect the wine from future cloudiness. If you don't fine, the wine can still become cloudy and/or spoil later in the bottle.

Cold Stabilization

Cold stabilization is cooling a tank to freezing temperature for a few days to a week to allow the unstable tartaric acids to crystallize. If the winemaker does not do that, the wine can develop those tartrate crystals later in the bottle (remember?). Tartrate crystals are innocent and no problem for the connoisseur, but the inexperienced consumer can mistake them for sugar or, worse, 'broken glass', file a complaint and return the wine.

Filtration

Filtration finally, doesn't put a medium through the wine, but puts the wine through a medium – a filter in this case, which may remove any residues of fining, crystals and, if necessary, even yeasts and bacteria (sterile filtration).

All clear.

CHARACTER

C clear

CHARACTER

C clear

CHARACTER

C clear

Winemaking REDS

blue captions: optional steps in the process
black captions: mandatory steps in the process

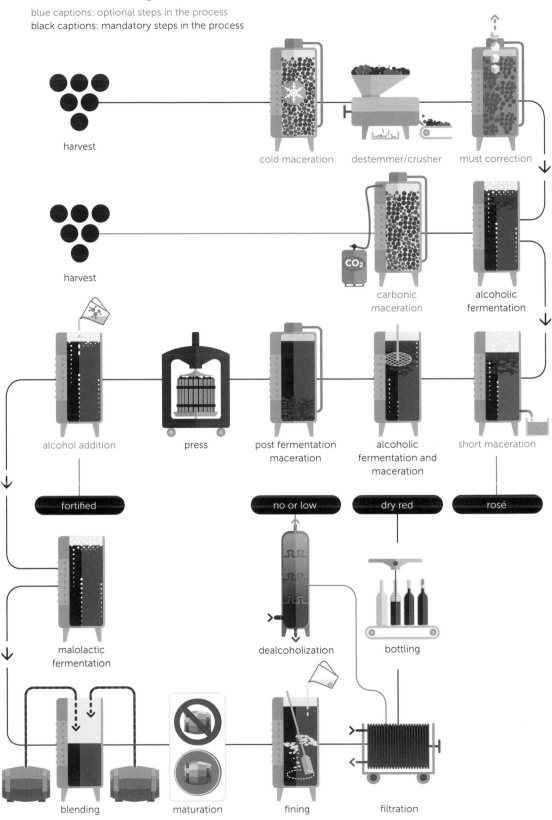

harvest · cold maceration · destemmer/crusher · must correction

harvest · carbonic maceration · alcoholic fermentation

alcohol addition · press · post fermentation maceration · alcoholic fermentation and maceration · short maceration

fortified · no or low · dry red · rosé

malolactic fermentation · dealcoholization · bottling

blending · maturation · fining · filtration

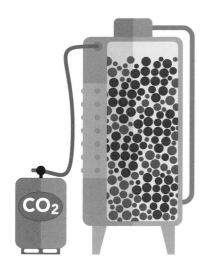

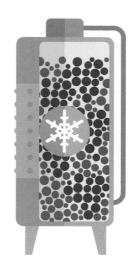

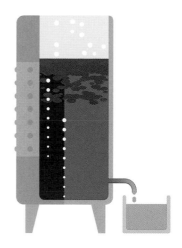

Carbonic Maceration

Maceration means soaking grapes on the skins to extract color, aromas, and tannins. Carbonic maceration is when whole bunches go into a closed pressure tank, and carbon dioxide is either injected or created by the fermentation of the crushed grapes at the bottom of the tank. After a week, this maceration is followed by a short alcoholic fermentation, producing a fruit-intense wine, low in tannins and ready to drink. As with Gamay in Beaujolais and Carignan in the South of France.

Cold Maceration

Freshly crushed grapes are parked in a large refrigerator, where it is too cold for the yeasts to become active. A maceration takes place but without any fermentation yet. Because tannins are not soluble in an aqueous solution, but pigments and aroma precursors are, the must absorbs color and aroma precursors but no tannins. Cold maceration, macération préfermentaire or cold soak is more popular worldwide then macération carbonique because you only need a cooling compartment for it.

Short Maceration
Bleeding

In making rosé, first of all, the winemaker seeks the right color, while preserving aromas and flavors. This can be accomplished by a short maceration, or by 'bleeding' which involves draining up to 20% of the must after a few hours of maceration. Bleeding serves two purposes: it concentrates the red wine because the remaining 80% of the must macerates in 100% of the skins, and it enables the winemaker to make a rosé as a by-product of the drained pink must.

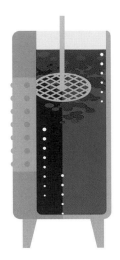

Alcoholic Fermentation

Compared to alcoholic fermentation in whites, fermentation temperatures in reds are usually higher and oxygen plays a more prominent role. As a result, harvest aromas may be less 'fresh' compared to reductive winemaking, a bit more confit, jammy or dried and usually aromas of winemaking are added such as vanilla, toast, or cedar. What sets fermentation further apart from white winemaking is that fermentation is combined with maceration on the skins and pips. Two techniques dominate the cellars, although it would be difficult to decide by taste which technique has been used.

Pigeage

The alcoholic fermentation creates a strong stream of bubbles which pushes the skins and pips to the top of the red must until a thick layer (the 'cap') is formed. In order to keep it in contact with the must, the winemaker punches down the cap either manually or with a hydraulic punch down machine. Sometimes it is even done by foot. This technique is called 'pigeage' (punching down) and is traditionally popular in Burgundy, and elsewhere with Pinot Noir. Pigeage, like other maceration techniques such as remontage and délestage, extracts color and tannins from the grape skins.

Remontage

Instead of putting the cap back into the must, the must can be put back into the cap. 'Remontage' (pumping over) is in vogue in Bordeaux. Red must is pumped from the bottom of the tank and sprayed over the cap like a shower, after which it finds its way back to the fermentation as a percolator. 'Délestage' (rack and return) is a variant of remontage. Now the tank is pumped over to another tank in one go, causing the cap to collapse, after which the tank is refilled. This is common practice in the Languedoc. You have to be an expert (more than I, because I can't) to be able to taste which maceration method has been used.

CHARACTER

H   HARVEST AROMA'S

CHARACTER

C

T

CHARACTER

C

T

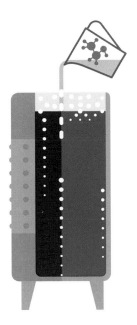

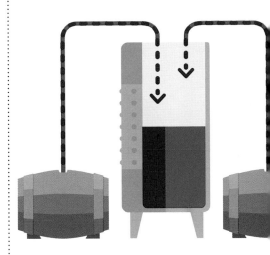

Adding Alcohol

With red Vin Doux Naturel and Port, not only the alcoholic fermentation but also the maceration is interrupted by the addition of alcohol. This results in 16 to 17% alcohol for most Vin Doux Naturel and 20% alcohol for Port (and about 100 grams of residual sugars per liter). Ruby, LBV and Vintage Port are reductive in style and therefore dominated by harvest aromas while tawny, colheita and 10 to 40 year old tawny are oxidative in nature and thus dominated by ripening aromas.

Maceration Post Fermentation

For some wines, aging potential is such an important part of the wine style – such as for Grands Crus Classés – that extended maceration is required after alcoholic fermentation. The cap will disintegrate and fall to the bottom of the tank after fermentation, but as tannins are soluble in alcoholic liquids, maceration will continue, even without techniques such as pumping over or punching down.

Blending

When must has become red wine, the winemaker can still leave their mark on the style, via both reductive or oxidative maturation and by blending: blending of grape varieties (as in Bordeaux, Chianti, Rioja, and the Southern Rhône) and blending of vineyards (as in South East Australia). Blending can provide synergy (in terms of color, smell, and taste), as well as mask a defect. Winemakers may blend immediately after alcoholic fermentation or just before clarification and bottling.

CHARACTER

R

CHARACTER

T

CHARACTER

5
Evolution Theory

Drink it, or Save it?

So far, we have built up some systematic knowledge about the evolution of our wine: from grape variety to vineyard to cellar and into the bottle. But the evolution of the wine does not end when the cork is squeezed into the bottle, or with the last twist of the screw top. Wines are not forever young. They live on in a new world inside the bottle. Well, some wines do...

One of the most persistent misconceptions about wines is that they all get better with age. But this is really not the case. In fact, 99% of all wines are at their best upon release and possess neither the concentration nor structure needed to improve. And even if the quality of the wine does allow for evolution in the bottle, success will still depend on the way the wine is stored, the type and quality of the closure, the protective effect of sulfites, the cellar conditions, and other factors such as the size of the bottle.

When wines of suitable quality are skillfully stored and allowed to age in the bottle, their original harvest aromas and cellar characteristics fade. These aromas do not die, they change. They evolve. Parallel, fascinating, new 'ripening' aromas and flavors develop. Time and chemistry are the magicians at work in the bottle and when they perform their magic, they can dramatically transform the taste of your wine over the span of say, ten years... or more.

So, bottle evolution can make us feel that wines are getting better. But that's also a Holy Grail of wine tasting: that wines get better with age. But how?

The key question of this chapter is: what actually happens to the wine inside the bottle while the bottle, on the outside, is gathering dust? Which aspects of the CHARACTER Method Chart are impacted? And how do we predict when a wine is peaking?

Impact of Hydrolysis

Hydrolysis is, in a sense, the opposite of polymerization: it breaks down molecules into smaller molecules (monomers). The release (hydrolysis) of harvest aromas by fermentation enzymes such as glucosidases does not stop with the alcoholic fermentation but continues during bottle maturation. Compounds like trimethyldihydronapthalene (TDN) in Riesling are basically carotenoids produced by the plant to protect it against intense sunlight. They cannot be smelled until they are liberated aromatically by enzymatic hydrolysis, either during alcoholic fermentation or later in the bottle (goût de pétrol). The same occurs with aromas like wax, mushroom, and earth.

CHARACTER

R

RIPENING AROMAS

Candy

Sweet wines seem to lose their sweetness over time. They *seem* to become notably drier and sometimes even develop surprising savory ripening aromas. I always used to assume that sweet wines actually lose some of their residual sugars with the passing of time, that sugars get more integrated in the wine with age or break down over time (or form a compound) and create sediment. However, several experiments have proved that the measurable sugar level does not change during bottle maturation. It is the same after 20 years as it was at the bottling. Nonetheless the wine tastes less sweet.

Perception of Residual Sugar dimishes

CHARACTER

C

Without scientific explanation, I was going to contribute this to the alchemy, or magic, of what happens in the bottle. However, the English wine writer Jamie Goode suggests it is not the wine that has changed, but our perception.

Based on Linda Bartoshuk's research on strawberries and tomatoes, Goode assumes that the aromas (and flavors) we detect when we smell a wine (both orthonasal and retronasal, remember?) affect our perception of sweetness. We cannot smell sweetness, but some fruity aromas (in young wines) give us a sweet perception because we have learned to associate them with sweetness. As an example, Goode takes a young Sauternes with many fresh harvest aromas like apricot, passion fruit and peach. In the bottle, over time, the Sauternes loses these fresh harvest aromas and instead develops other, sometimes even savory, ripening aromas. As these ripening aromas are not associated with sweetness, it is therefore not surprising, according to Goode, that the bottle matured wine is perceived as less 'sweet'.

There's food for thought.

The Optimum Zone

Finally, some thoughts about how to predict when a wine will be peaking. After all, the processes of micro-oxidation, polymerization and hydrolysis do not stop when we think the wine is at its best. Tragically, you only realize when a wine has reached its peak after it's too late. Wait too long and you will experience the smell and taste of decay in your glass. Think mold and mushrooms, bad breath, soil, rotting fruit. Yes, it is proverbially better to drink the wine a year early than a day late.

Just as a grape variety and climate have their optimum zone, so do wine and age. The optimum zone is different for every wine. For most wines – white, rosé, and red – that optimum zone starts on the day the wine hits the shelf.

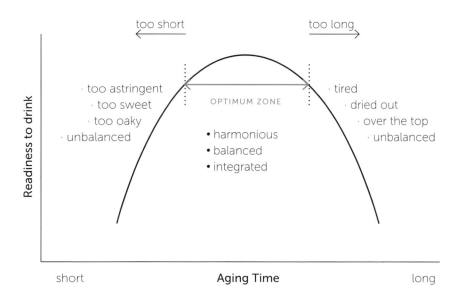

Because the best time to drink a wine is when all relevant aspects of the wine (in the CHARACTER Method) are in harmony. And that does not only depend on the acids, residual sugars, alcohol, tannins and aromas, but also on the cellar conditions. And it's also a matter of taste, often culturally determined. In Bordeaux they prefer their Margaux when it's five to seven years old, but in England this is seen as infanticide.

Whatever your taste preference, the 'moment suprême' when the wine reaches its proverbial climax is hard to predict. Fortunately, some wines can maintain their peak for some time, some even for years. Clive Coates has a theory about it. According to him, a wine can be matured for as long as it took the wine to get ready to drink. For example, if a wine took five years to get ready to drink, then according to Coates the wine will stay fit for another five years, with the climax sometime in that period.

Cellar Conditions

Optimal cellar conditions include a low temperature, as constant as possible (with only gradual fluctuations), a dark and humid environment with as little vibration as possible. Especially, the ultraviolet radiation from sunlight can cause free radicals and oxidation. In extreme cases, this can lead to odors of boiled cabbage, wet wool, soy, or corn. Protection from ultraviolet radiation is the main reason wine is bottled in colored glass. Sunlight contains thousands of times more ultraviolet light than fluorescent tubes and is – for wines – thus much more harmful.

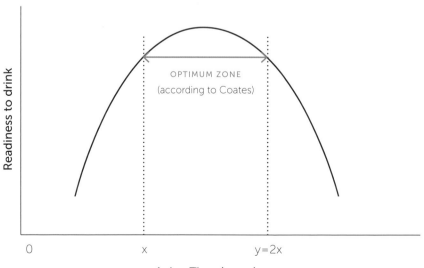

OPTIMUM ZONE
(according to Coates)

Readiness to drink

0   x   y=2x

Aging Time (years)

The question is to what extent humidity really is important for optimal cellar conditions? As well as to the related question of whether bottles need to be stored horizontally.

Natural corks are elastic because they consist of 85% of air. Due to constant compression of the cork inside the bottle neck that air is slowly lost. This way, even the best corks will lose their elasticity after 20 to 25 five years of cellaring, causing the wine to slowly evaporate and oxidize. High humidity of the cellar will just slow down this process of evaporation. But it won't prevent it. If you wish to safely cellar wines for longer than 25 years or so, it is best to recork them.

So, what about the premise of having to store bottles horizontally? Well, I couldn't find any scientific proof that without cellar conditions of 70% humidity corks will dry out. Natural corks have a moisture content of 5 to 8% which they manage to maintain at cool temperature. It is not the lack of moisture on the outside but the abundance of moisture on the inside. Here, not only is the humidity 100%, but the liquid is acidic with a high alcohol content which will cause the cork at some stage to corrode. Maybe, storing the wine horizontally is not necessary at all.

Conclusion

The evolution theory for wine can be explained in scientific terms such as micro-oxidation, polymerization and hydrolysis. Yet, these chemical processes manage to produce a magical mix of colors, aromas, and flavors.

Wine is a living thing, even in the bottle. Please recall, or look it up if you haven't seen the movie 'Sideways', the scene in which the character Maya delivers a personal monologue about her reasons for loving wine and closes with a final, better than scientific, tasting note:
'I like how wine continues to evolve, like if I opened a bottle of wine today it would taste different than if I'd opened it on any other day, because a bottle of wine is actually alive. And it's constantly evolving and gaining complexity. That is, until it peaks, like your '61. And then it begins its steady, inevitable decline... And it tastes so f*****g good.'

Part III

Anyone Can Taste Wine You Just Need

to Combine Method with Knowledge

The time has come to put our systematically constructed knowledge - about how wine gets its color, aromas and taste - into practice. In other words we are going to put our knowledge where our mouth is... Therefore, the next step is to learn to apply our knowledge thus far, to the CHARACTER Method.

A second acronym will be introduced as well as method for assessing quality: CACHET!

6
True to Taste

To Determine Wine's Distinction

In this chapter we are going to put the
acquired knowledge of the previous
chapters to the tasting test.
If we do this well, we will be able to
draw conclusions about the wine: about
the wine's grape variety, its origin, the
winemaking and its age.

Like Pratt, but without cheating.

We Taste What We See

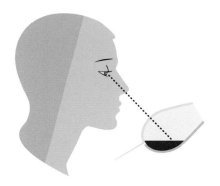

It is time to put method and knowledge together, starting with the letter C of the CHARACTER Chart, but now with more demands on your critical thinking skills.

To that end, I have mapped and collected everything we have learned in the past three chapters and organized it by each letter of the acronym CHARACTER, starting with the letter for Color. I then reversed the relations we learned from the previous chapters. For instance, if in Chapter 3 we concluded that a grape variety with a thick skin (potentially) gives a wine with a deep color, we can now conclude that a wine with a deep color has been made from a grape variety with a thick skin.This has resulted in a checklist of all possible aspects which you should include when you want to draw conclusions from your tasting note.

The table below brings together our observations about color and clarity and organizes them alongside possible conclusions we might make about the wine.

C COLOR

COLOR INTENSITY	CONCLUSIONS
deep	Therefore, thick-skinned grape
pale	Therefore, thin-skinned grape, short maceration, or very old wine

COLOR OBSERVATIONS	CONCLUSION
purple to brown	Therefore, spectrum - young to old (red)
lemon yellow to brown	Therefore, spectrum - young to old (white)
pink to tuile	Therefore, spectrum - young to old (rosé)
orange	Therefore, orange (white grapes with short maceration)

OTHER OBSERVATIONS	CONCLUSION
crystals	Therefore, wine - crystals of tartaric acid (harmless by-product)
sediment	Therefore, not filtered or fined? or an aged wine?
cloudiness	Therefore, not filtered or fined?... possible wine fault?

We Taste What We Smell

We now turn to our nose. The following tables bring together our observations about the aromas and organize them alongside possible conclusions we might make about the wine, starting with the harvest aromas.

H HARVEST AROMAS

Assessment of the intensity and freshness of the harvest aromas may lead to conclusions about the aromatic nature of the grape varieties present and about the type of winemaking applied. Observations about specific varietal aromas may lead to conclusions about the individual grape varieties present in the wine.

INTENSITY OF HARVEST AROMAS	CONCLUSIONS
🛜 to 🛜	Therefore, aromatic grape variety
🛜 to 🛜	Therefore, neutral grape variety
OBSERVATIONS OF HARVEST AROMAS	**CONCLUSION**
fresh fruit	Therefore, reductive winemaking
developed fruit	Therefore, oxidative winemaking
specific varietal aromas	Therefore, specific grape variety
EUCALYPT FYNBOS GARRIGUE	Therefore, Australia/Chile (eucalypt); Southern France (garrigue); Cape (fynbos)

A AROMAS OF WINEMAKING

These aromas are likely to be dominated either by aromas relating to oak, or due to white wine making techniques such as malo and autolysis.

INTENSITY OF AROMAS OF WINEMAKING	CONCLUSIONS
🛜 to 🛜	Therefore, malo, oak, or autolysis
🛜 to 🛜	Therefore, no malo, oak or autolysis
OBSERVATIONS AROMAS OF WINEMAKING	
BUTTER	Therefore, malo
BRIOCHE BISCUIT DOUGH BREAD	Therefore, autolysis
TOAST CEDAR VANILLA NUTMEG CLOVE	Therefore, French oak
VANILLA COCONUT	Therefore, American oak
MOCHA CHOCOLATE	Therefore, high toast, oak chips

R RIPENING AROMAS

A complex and mysterious combination of micro-oxidation, polymerization and hydrolysis turn fresh harvest aromas into more mature expressions.

INTENSITY RIPENING AROMAS	CONCLUSIONS
🛜 to 🛜	Therefore, mature, old or very old wine
🛜 to 🛜	Therefore, young or youthful wine
OBSERVATIONS OF RIPENING AROMAS	
preserved, candied, dried fruit, nutty aromas	Therefore, oxidative development in bottle
TOBACCO SOIL WAX KEROSINE MUSHROOM	Therefore, extended ripening in bottle

We Taste What We Savor and Feel

Next we turn to our palate. The following tables link the findings of our senses of taste and touch to the relevant aspects of vineyard, climate and topography. Starting with acidity.

A ACIDITY

The table below brings together our observations about acidity and organizes them alongside possible conclusions we might make about the wine.

ACIDITY	CONCLUSIONS
	Therefore, very cool climate
	Therefore, cool climate
	Therefore, mild climate
	Therefore, warm climate
	Therefore, hot climate
OBSERVATIONS ACIDITY	
creamy	Therefore, malic acids (through malolactic fermentation)
green, apple, citrus	Therefore, lactic acids (malolactic fermentation blocked)

C CANDY (RESIDUAL SUGARS)

Residual sugars are inevitable if harvested grapes contain so much sugar that the yeasts cannot possibly convert it all into alcohol.

CANDY	GRAM PER LITRE	CONCLUSIONS
	> 130 gr/l	Therefore, very sweet
	80 to 129 gr/l	Therefore, sweet
	40 to 79 gr/l	Therefore, medium sweet
	10 to 39 gr/l	Therefore, medium dry
	< 9 gr/l	Therefore, dry
OBSERVATIONS CANDY		
HONEY RAISINS		Therefore, botrytis/dried grapes

Residual Sugar Scatter

This Residual Sugar Scatter Graph shows the sweetness of the most common sweet wines relative to their alcohol contents. Sweet wines can owe their sweetness to:
– noble rot (Botrytis Cinerea) > quadrant 1 (yellow)
– drying grapes > quadrant 2 (orange)
– fortified (addition of alcohol) > quadrant 3 (blue)
– a late harvest or added sugars > quadrant 4 (green)

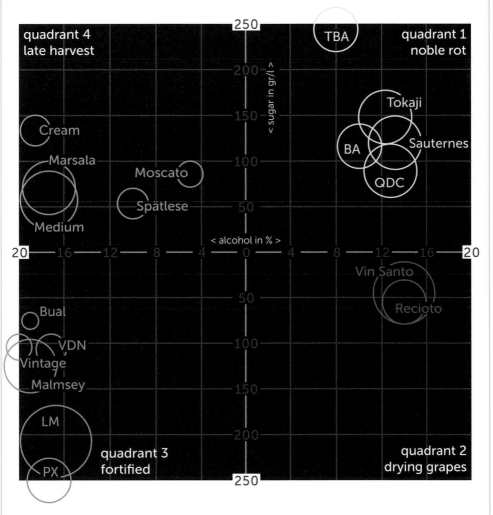

● BA = Beerenauslese, TBA = Trockenbeerenauslese, QDC = Quarts de Chaume, Tokaji = Tokaji Aszú 5 puttonyos ● VDN = Vin Doux Naturel, Vintage = Vintage port, Bual = Madeira Bual, Malmsey = Madeira Malmsey, LM = Liqueur Muscat ● Medium = Medium sherry, Marsala = Marsala Semisecco, Cream = Cream sherry, Moscato = Moscato d'Asti

WINE	ALCOHOL IN % ABV	SUGAR IN GRAM/LITRE
Kabinett (67 to 85 Oechsele)	10	18 to 50
Spätlese (76 to 95 Oechsele)	10	34 to 70
Auslese (83 to 105 Oechsele)	10	34 to 90
Beerenauslese (110 to 128 Oechsele)	10	90 to 140
Eiswein (icewine) (110 to 130 Oechsele)	8	110 to 160
Trockenbeerenauslese (more than 150 Oechsele)	8	more than 220
Vouvray demi-sec	12 to 14	15 to 30
Vouvray moelleux	12 to 14	30 to 80
Layon/Quarts de Chaume/Bonnezeaux	12 to 14	60 to 120
Sauternes	13 to 14	90 to 150
Tokaji Aszú 5 puttonyos	12 to 13	more than 120
Tokaji Aszú Essencia	12 to 13	more than 150
Ausbruch	10	110 to 160
Vin Santo	11 to 17	10 to 80
Recioto	13 to 15	30 to 80
Moscato d'Asti	5 to 5.5	70 to 100
Asti	7 to 9.5	70 to 90
Champagne Extra Dry	12	10 to 20
Champagne Sec	12	15 to 35
Champagne Demi-Sec	12	35 to 50
Champagne Doux	12	more than 50
Vin Doux Naturel	15 to 20	90 to 125
Vintage port/old Tawny	20	90 to 120
White port	16.5 to 20	15 to 50
Madeira Sercial	18 to 20	less than 50
Madeira Verdelho	18 to 20	50 to 75
Madeira Bual	18 to 20	75 to 100
Madeira Malmsey	18 to 20	more than 100
Liqueur Muscat	17 to 19	170 to 250
Dry	15 to 20	5 to 45
Medium	15 to 20	25 to 90
Marsala Secco	15 to 20	less than 40
Marsala Semisecco	15 to 20	40 to 100
Marsala Dulce	15 to 20	more than 100
PX	15 to 20	more than 250
Pale Cream	16 to 20	45 to 115
Cream sherry	17 to 20	115 to 150

T TANNINS

Tannins are a matter of texture, mouthfeel rather than taste. Recall how we observed: the thicker the skin of the grape variety, the more (potential) tannins can be in the wine, analogous to the assessment of color. However, other than color, the assessment of tannins is not just defined by the concentration of the tannins but also by the ripeness of the tannins. And the ripeness of the tannins is determined by sun exposure (especially UV radiation).

In addition, hydrolysable tannins from contact with oak tend to have a different 'feel' than condensed tannins from skins and pips. These tannins tend to stick to your front teeth (usually with a distinct oaky taste – what else?) while grape tannins tend to affect the whole oral cavity.

TANNIN INTENSITY		CONCLUSIONS
📶	very high	Therefore, very thick-skinned grape variety
📶	high	Therefore, thick-skinned grape variety
📶	medium	
📶	low	Therefore, thin-skinned grape variety or short, cold or carbonic maceration
📶	none	Therefore, white, sparkling or rosé wine
TANNIN + COLOR		CONCLUSIONS
T 📶 + **C** 📶		Therefore, particular grape varieties such as Nebbiolo, Aglianico, Nerello
T 📶 + **C** 📶		Therefore, cold or carbonic maceration
OBSERVATIONS TANNIN		
bitter, astringent (drying)		Therefore, Old World
ripe, sweet tannins		Therefore, New World

E ETHANOL

Apart from having an effect on the mouthfeel, acidity, residual sugar and tannins also are flavors in their own right. Alcohol, however, is not a flavor, but a flavor carrier; you can feel it from the weight (mouthfeel, body) of the wine in your mouth and – in case the alcohol is high – from a burning sensation in the back of the throat.

ALCOHOL	%	CONCLUSIONS
🛜	> 15%	Therefore, most likely fortified
🛜	14 to 15%	Therefore, warm, sunny climate, or fortified
🛜	12 to 13.5%	Therefore, moderate climate
🛜	5.5 to 11.5%	Therefore, cool climate, or corrected in the cellar
🛜	< 0.5%	Therefore, corrected in the cellar

We finally have come to the last letter of the CHARACTER acronym: the R of Relative Fruit Intensity. This letter however, only comes into play if and after we have been able to draw conclusions about the possible grape variety.

R RELATIVE FRUIT INTENSITY

After assessment of the wine has led to the conclusion of an international grape variety (mainly the ones of Chapter 7), we assess the fruit intensity (both for harvest aromas and flavors) relative for the chosen grape variety.

RELATIVE FRUIT INTENSITY	CONCLUSIONS
🛜 to 🛜	Therefore, New World
🛜 to 🛜	Therefore, Old World

Summary, So Far...

Whether a wine seems quite familiar to us or really completely unexplored territory, armed with the above deductions we will now be able to add to our observations and mere descriptions logical interpretation and conclusions.

Adding Higher Order Thinking to Our Drinking

To train our interpretive, deductive reasoning skills, we will repeat the demonstration of the CHARACTER Method using the same Sauvignon Blanc and Barossa Shiraz from Chapter 2 and add some higher order thinking to our drinking.

We already know the drill, so we can practice further, putting method and knowledge together.

Analysis of the Marlborough Sauvignon
I Taste; Therefore, I Conclude...

C COLOR

The pale intensity leads to the conclusion of reductive winemaking and the lemon color leads to the conclusion of a young wine.

CLOUDY BAY, MARLBOROUGH SAUVIGNON BLANC, NEW ZEALAND				
C	📶	Therefore, reductive winemaking	lemon	Therefore, young

H HARVEST AROMAS

The high intensity of the Harvest Aromas leads to the conclusion of an aromatic grape variety.

The specific aromas of gooseberry, grapefruit, granny smith, lime and passion fruit are all very helpful indicators that this is a Sauvignon Blanc. This conclusion is added immediately next to the observations column in the diagram.

CLOUDY BAY, MARLBOROUGH SAUVIGNON BLANC, NEW ZEALAND				
H	📶	Therefore, an aromatic grape variety	GOOSEBERRY GRAPEFRUIT GRANNY SMITH LIME PASSIONFRUIT	Therefore, Sauvignon Blanc
A				
R				

A AROMAS OF WINEMAKING

We did not observe any aromas of winemaking – no butter, no vanilla, toast or brioche. From the absence of these aromas and in combination with the freshness of the harvest aromas, we can confirm that this wine has been made reductively, without any use of oak, malolactic fermentation or autolysis.

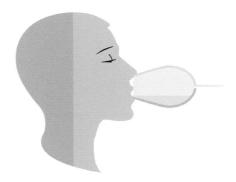

CLOUDY BAY, MARLBOROUGH SAUVIGNON BLANC, NEW ZEALAND									
H	📶	Therefore, an aromatic grape variety	GOOSEBERRY	GRAPEFRUIT	GRANNY SMITH	LIME	PASSIONFRUIT		Therefore, Sauvignon Blanc
A	📶	Therefore, reductive winemaking							
R									

R RIPENING AROMAS

Again, we did not observe any ripening aromas and this helps to confirm our previous conclusion, derived from the color, that this is a young wine.
Again, we will add this conclusion next to the intensity column in the diagram.

CLOUDY BAY, MARLBOROUGH SAUVIGNON BLANC, NEW ZEALAND									
H	📶	Therefore, an aromatic grape variety	GOOSEBERRY	GRAPEFRUIT	GRANNY SMITH	LIME	PASSIONFRUIT		Therefore, Sauvignon Blanc
A	📶	Therefore, reductive winemaking							
R	📶	Therefore, young							

A ACIDITY

We experienced a lot of salivation and duly noted that this was an acidic wine. From this we can conclude that the wine hailed from a cool climate. More specifically we noted that the acidity had a distinct malic character (citrus rather than cream) thus leading to the conclusion that this wine did not undergo malolactic fermentation.

CLOUDY BAY, MARLBOROUGH SAUVIGNON BLANC, NEW ZEALAND				
A	📶	Therefore, cool climate	malic acids	Therefore, no malo
C				
T				
E				

C CANDY

We did not detect any residual sugars, so we conclude that this is a dry wine. The oily, fatty mouthfeel suggests that this wine might have undergone a few months of 'sur lie' (aging on the lees). Again, we will add these conclusions next to the intensity and observations columns in the diagram.

CLOUDY BAY, MARLBOROUGH SAUVIGNON BLANC, NEW ZEALAND				
A	📶	Therefore, cool climate	malic acids	Therefore, no malo
C	📶	Therefore, dry	rich texture	Therefore, sur lie
T				
E				

T TANNINS

We did not feel any tannins which is logical for a white wine. This also confirms that the wine was not aged in oak.

CLOUDY BAY, MARLBOROUGH SAUVIGNON BLANC, NEW ZEALAND				
A	📶	Therefore, cool climate	malic acids	Therefore, no malo
C	📶	Therefore, dry	rich texture	Therefore, sur lie
T	📶	Therefore, no maturation in new oak		
E				

E ETHANOL

We observed that the alcohol content was medium and therefore estimated it to be between 12.5% and 13.5%, suggesting it has a medium body.

CLOUDY BAY, MARLBOROUGH SAUVIGNON BLANC, NEW ZEALAND				
A	📶	Therefore, cool climate	malic acids	Therefore, no malo
C	📶	Therefore, dry	rich texture	Therefore, sur lie
T	📶	Therefore, no maturation in new oak		
E	📶		12.5 to 13.5%, medium body	

R RELATIVE FRUIT INTENSITY

For the final deductions we really need to engage our knowledge (or build it!) about how this Sauvignon Blanc compares – in relative fruit intensity – with other Sauvignon Blancs around the world.

The high Fruit Intensity leads to the New World. But not only that... the style is so pronounced that only Sauvignon Blancs from Chile, South Africa, and New Zealand would be eligible contenders in our conclusive analysis of this wine. Thinking it through – Sauvignon Blancs from the Cape are grassier in style. And Sauvignon Blanc from coastal Chile are more tropical with dominant passion fruit notes. The pronounced gooseberry and grapefruit aromas clinch the deal and lead us to New Zealand. Most likely, to Marlborough.

CLOUDY BAY, MARLBOROUGH SAUVIGNON BLANC, NEW ZEALAND				
C		Therefore, reductive winemaking	lemon	Therefore, young
H		Therefore, an aromatic grape variety	GOOSEBERRY GRAPEFRUIT GRANNY SMITH LIME PASSIONFRUIT	Therefore, Sauvignon Blanc
A		Therefore, reductive winemaking		
R		Therefore, young		
A		Therefore, cool climate	malic acids	Therefore, no malo
C		Therefore, dry	rich texture	Therefore, sur lie
T		Therefore, no maturation in new oak		
E			12.5 to 13.5%, medium body	
R		Therefore, New World		

This completes the circle. Richard Pratt couldn't have done it better.

Analysis of the Barossa Valley Shiraz
I Taste; Therefore, I Conclude...

C COLOR

The deep color intensity leads to the conclusion that this wine is made from a thick-skinned grape variety. And the ruby color suggests a youthful wine of 3 to 5 years.

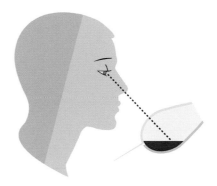

We add this conclusion to the observations column in the diagram.

		YALUMBA, BAROSSA VALLEY SHIRAZ, AUSTRALIA		
C	📶	Therefore, a grape with a thick skin	ruby	Therefore, 3 to 5 years of age

H HARVEST AROMAS

The aromas of eucalyptus are so distinct, the wine has to originate from either Australia or Chile. And the harvest aromas of blackberry, blackcurrant and black pepper suggest Shiraz rather than Cabernet.

		YALUMBA, BAROSSA VALLEY SHIRAZ, AUSTRALIA		
H	📶		BLACKBERRY BLACKCURRANT BLACK CHERRY BLUEBERRY EUCALYPT	Therefore, Chili or Australia / Shiraz (or Cabernet)
A				
R				

A AROMAS OF WINEMAKING

Vanilla, coconut and toast suggest the wine was matured in (partly) new American oak.

YALUMBA, BAROSSA VALLEY SHIRAZ, AUSTRALIA								
H	📶		BLACKBERRY	BLACKCURRANT	BLACK CHERRY	BLUEBERRY	EUCALYPT	Therefore, Chile or Australia / Shiraz (or Cabernet)
A	📶	Therefore, maturation in oak	VANILLA	COCONUT	TOAST			Therefore, maturation in (partly new American) oak
R								

R RIPENING AROMAS

We did, to some extent at least, identify ripening aromas in this wine which confirms that the wine is no longer young. The combination of the relatively fresh harvest aromas and the slightly nutty sensation leads us to the more specific conclusion that the wine probably had a few years of bottle age.

YALUMBA, BAROSSA VALLEY SHIRAZ, AUSTRALIA								
H	📶		BLACKBERRY	BLACKCURRANT	BLACK CHERRY	BLUEBERRY	EUCALYPT	Therefore, Chile or Australia / Shiraz (or Cabernet)
A	📶	Therefore, maturation in oak	VANILLA	COCONUT	TOAST			Therefore, maturation in (partly new American) oak
R	📶	Therefore, 3 to 5 years	WALNUT					

A ACIDITY

The low acidity leads us once again to the conclusion that the grapes must have come from a warm climate.

YALUMBA, BAROSSA VALLEY SHIRAZ, AUSTRALIA				
A	📶	Therefore, warm climate		
C				
T				
E				

C CANDY

We did not observe any residual sugars in the wine so we can conclude that this is a dry wine.

YALUMBA, BAROSSA VALLEY SHIRAZ, AUSTRALIA				
A	📶	Therefore, warm climate		
C	📶	Therefore, dry wine		
T				
E				

T TANNINS

We have already noted the intense color of this wine; similarly we recognized the high intensity of the tannins. Both of these observations contribute to the conclusion that this wine is from a thick-skinned grape variety. Then there is the softness and velvety feel of the tannins which means these are very ripe tannins from a sunny climate. This confirms the conclusions from the harvest aromas of eucalypt that this is a Shiraz from either Australia, Chile or maybe South Africa.

YALUMBA, BAROSSA VALLEY SHIRAZ, AUSTRALIA				
A		Therefore, warm climate		
C		Therefore, dry wine		
T		Therefore, grape variety with a thick skin	ripe and smooth	Therefore, New World
E				

E ETHANOL

The high alcohol confirms a warm and sunny climate. At this stage of our analysis we can come to an overall conclusion that this wine is a Shiraz from a vineyard with eucalyptus vegetation and a warm climate, probably Australia or Chile.

YALUMBA, BAROSSA VALLEY SHIRAZ, AUSTRALIA				
A		Therefore, warm climate		
C		Therefore, dry wine		
T		Therefore, grape variety with a thick skin	ripe and smooth	Therefore, New World
E		Therefore, a sunny climate	14 to 14.5%, full bodied	

R RELATIVE FRUIT INTENSITY

The high Relative Fruit Intensity confirms the New World. However, the aromas of winemaking including coconut impressions of American oak makes us veering in the direction of Australia, rather than Chile.

YALUMBA, BAROSSA VALLEY SHIRAZ, AUSTRALIA

C	Therefore, grape with thick skin	ruby		Therefore, 3 to 5 years of age
H		BLACKBERRY BLACKCURRANT BLACK CHERRY BLUEBERRY EUCALYPT		Therefore, Chile or Australia / Shiraz (or Cabernet)
A	Therefore, maturation in oak	VANILLA COCONUT TOAST		Therefore, maturation in (partly new American) oak
R	Therefore, 3 to 5 years	WALNUT		
A	Therefore, warm climate			
C	Therefore, dry wine			
T	Therefore, grape variety with a thick skin	ripe and smooth		Therefore, New World
E	Therefore, a sunny climate	14 to 14.5%, full bodied		
R	Therefore, New World			

Told You it Was the Holy Grail!

This CHARACTER Method has been my own 'Holy Grail' of wine tasting since the days of study for the MW. In the same way that it has supported my own journey of knowledge and experience, I hope that it can serve you too: to organize your observations and knowledge, draw objective conclusions about the grape variety, the wine-making methods, the evolution in the bottle, and the location of the vineyard.

7
Cachet

for Quality

As the CHARACTER Method does not help you with assessing quality, a separate acronym has been designed for quality. Cachet is synonym to 'distinction' and refers to quality being subjective.

Cachet
is easier to detect than to define

Wine quality, as Maynard Amerine once said, is easier to detect than to define. This is, according to Ronald Jackson in *Winetasting*, partially due to "quality being primarily subjective, and strongly influenced by extrinsic factors" such as bottle, label, host and venue. He thus concludes that defining wine quality in terms of its chemistry will never be more than partially successful. "Nonetheless, most serious wine professionals tend to agree on what constitutes wine quality, that is, what they subjectively have come to like through extensive tasting."

Balance seems to be one of those characteristics. Length, concentration and complexity too. Some include typicity or aging potential, even though many of these characteristics mean different things to different people – even among wine critics. That's why consensus about wine quality is rare and ratings tend to differ even between leading critics. Illustrative is the disagreement between Jancis Robinson MW and Robert Parker about the quality of the 2003 Château Pavie; Robinson gave 12/20 (unacceptable), Parker 95/100 (exceptional).

So, what constitutes wine quality?
ISO 9000 defines quality as the degree to which a set of inherent characteristics fulfils requirements. Applied to wine, the question is what are these 'inherent characteristics', and which 'requirements' have to be fulfilled?

As for the 'inherent characteristics', I would like to limit these to those attributes which can be assessed organoleptically such as concentration, complexity, length, and balance precluding as much as possible extrinsic factors such as bottle (shape, weight, price), label (producer, reputation, vintage, origin, grape variety, et cetera), occasion, host, and venue.

As for the second part of the ISO definition, I would like to link the 'requirements' to hedonistic characteristics such as satisfaction, pleasure, enjoyment, delight, maybe even happiness. These hedonistic criteria are not only subjective but also dynamic; they tend to evolve over time, just like hedonistic quality criteria for food, music, movies, and books.

Parallel to the CHARACTER acronym, I am now introducing another acronym for assessing quality: CACHET. Cachet is synonymous with class and distinction. It is a word which refers to quality and is easy to remember. The six letters of CACHET include the more-or-less established criteria for quality plus a hedonistic one: enjoyment.

Part IV

Practice

To facilitate practice, I have added chapters 8 and 9. Chapter 8 includes the G-20 of grape varieties – those internationally considered the most important grape varieties in the world. For each variety there is a selection of benchmark wines. Chapter 9 follows with over 100 national, regional, or local grape varieties with their benchmark wine. For all of these wines, I have applied the CHARACTER Method and drawn the appropriate conclusion regarding grape variety, origin, and winemaking techniques used.

8

The G-20

Wine's Internationals

The G-20 are the 'internationals' among the grape varieties, from Cabernet Franc to Tempranillo. Together they make up about half of the vineyard plantings worldwide. They are planted in both the Old and the New World. The more heterogeneous a grape variety, the more signature wines will follow.

This is an overview of the G-20 grapes in terms of area planted. The bunches of grapes (in the legend at the bottom) indicate the importance of the plantings. You will also find them on the header of each dashboard page of Chapter 7 and each benchmark wine in Chapter 8, followed by the percentage they make up of global plantings.

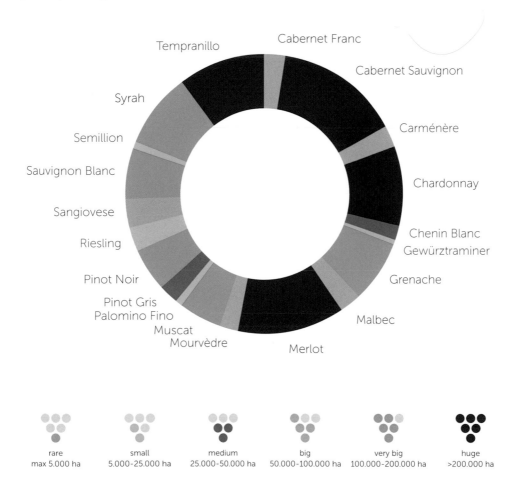

rare	small	medium	big	very big	huge
max 5.000 ha	5.000-25.000 ha	25.000-50.000 ha	50.000-100.000 ha	100.000-200.000 ha	>200.000 ha

Each G-20 grape variety has a dashboard with three counters and a few dashboard lights. The counter on the left indicates the aromatic intensity of the whites and the thickness of the skins of the reds. Both white and red wines have a right-hand counter indicating the degree of adaptation of a grape variety to different climates. The dashboard lights indicate the variety's style (dry, sweet, enhanced, and sparkling) and whether this variety is usually made into a varietal wine or a blend.

KA-br-nay frangk

Cabernet Franc: the other Cabernet

Bordo, Bouchet, Bouchy, Breton, Cabernet Franco, Cabernet Frank, Fer Servandou

big
57,383 ha (1.30%)

THIN SKIN · THICK SKIN · SPARKLING · SWEET · MONO · BLEND · FORTIFIED · DRY · HA 057,383 · MALADAPTIVE · ADAPTIVE

Cabernet Franc goes solo on the tuffeaux (limestone) slopes of Chinon-en-Bourgueil in the Loire, where the cool climate results in impressions of blackcurrant and blueberry and herbaceous aromas of green bell pepper. The New World has also discovered Cabernet Franc as a single varietal wine although, thanks to its spicy style, it is still mostly used as a blending component. That counts for Bordeaux too, where it's used as insurance in case Cabernet Sauvignon doesn't ripen completely. On the cooler clay soils of the right bank, it forms the backbone of Saint-Émilion and Pomerol, especially at Cheval Blanc. The variety is also grown in California, Argentina, Australia and New Zealand.

In warmer areas, Cabernet Franc, a distant cousin of Cabernet Sauvignon, has an attractive fragrance of blackcurrant, blueberry and blackberry, while in cooler areas it produces a much spicier wine with herbaceous aromas and more astringent tannins.

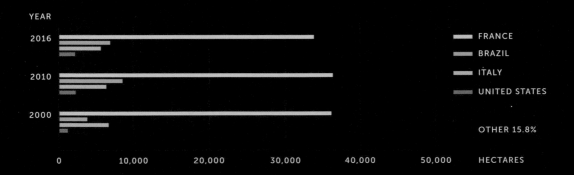

Professor Anderson's figures show that Cabernet Franc is spreading to more countries, with Brazil surprisingly in the Top 3.

The cradle of Cabernet Franc

As a wine region, Anjou encompasses a wide spectrum of wines and wine styles, including red, rosé and white, produced with varying levels of sweetness. The generic Anjou appellation extends over more than 151 municipalities. The basis for Anjou Rouge is Cabernet Franc with a maximum of 25% Cabernet Sauvignon, while some Pineau d'Aunis is also permitted. This is a spicy, fruity style preferred by many Parisians as a summer red and usually drunk slightly cooled.

BAUMARD, LE LOGIS, ANJOU, FRANCE

C	📶	Therefore: grape with a thick skin	purple		Therefore: youthful
H	📶		REDCURRANT · BLACKCURRANT · BELL PEPPER · BLACKBERRY		Therefore: Cabernet Franc / cool climate
A	📶	Therefore: reductive winemaking			
R	📶	Therefore: youthful			
A	📶	Therefore: cool climate			
C	📶	Therefore: dry wine			
T	📶	Therefore: grape with a thick skin	astringent		Therefore: Old World
E	📶		12.5 to 13%, medium body		Therefore: cool climate
R	📶	Therefore: Old World			

Tasting note: This deep purple red has medium-intense aromas of green bell pepper and blackberry and red and black currant. High acidity, medium alcohol, astringent tannins and a low relative fruit intensity.

Riedel Vinum
6416-0

 10-15 °C 0.5 hours   < $50   5-10 years

In the Anjou-style: Saumur Champigny and Bourgueil (Loire, France), Cabernet Franc (North Italy), Carménère (Maule, Curicó, Chile).

Continental Cabernet Franc

Although Mendoza is known for Malbec and then Cabernet Sauvignon, Cabernet Franc is gaining recognition. Different in style than in the Loire, riper and fuller-bodied due to the desert climate (dry and warm, with a lot of UV and with significant diurnal temperature differences), it features ripe red and black fruits, more concentration, and sweet tannins. The green bell pepper of the Loire has become grilled red bell pepper in Mendoza, with the addition of oriental spices.

TRAPICHE, BROQUEL, CABERNET FRANC, MENDOZA, ARGENTINA

C	📶	Therefore: grape with a thick skin	ruby		Therefore: 3 to 5 years old
H	📶		BLACKCURRANT BLACKBERRY BLUEBERRY PLUM BELL PEPPER		Therefore: Cabernet Franc
A	📶	Therefore: matured in oak	VANILLA TOAST CEDAR		Therefore: (partly) new French oak
R	📶	Therefore: 3 to 5 years old	WALNUT		
A	📶	Therefore: hot climate			
C	📶	Therefore: dry wine			
T	📶	Therefore: grape with a thick skin	ripe and smooth		Therefore: New World
E	📶	Therefore: lots of sunshine (high UV)	13.5 to 14.5%, full body		
R	📶	Therefore: New World			

Tasting note: This deeply-colored red has intense aromas of blackberry, blackcurrant, blueberry, black plum, grilled red pepper, vanilla, toast, cedar and walnut. Low acidity, high alcohol and lots of ripe, yes even sweet tannins. High relative fruit intensity.

Riedel Vinum
6416-0

10-15 °C   0.5 hours   < $50   5-10 years

In the Cabernet Franc Mendoza-style:
Cabernet Franc (Tuscany, Italy, Cabernet Franc (California), Blaufränkisch (Burgenland, Austria).

◀)) KA-br-nay sow-vuhn-yown

Cabernet is King

Bouchet, Bouche, Petit-Bouchet, Petit-Cabernet, Petit-Vidure, Vidure, Sauvignon Rouge

huge
313,665 ha (6.99%)

THIN SKIN　　THICK SKIN　　　　　　　　　　　　　　MALADAPTIVE　　ADAPTIVE

Cabernet Sauvignon is a natural cross between Cabernet Franc and Sauvignon Blanc and originated in Bordeaux. Cabernet Sauvignon is a small, dark-blue grape that hangs from the vine in compact clusters. Due to its thick skin, it has a lot of color and tannins. Another characteristic is that the grape, even when it ripens fully, still has a reasonable acidity. That is why the wines often have a long shelf life. Cabernet Sauvignon ripens late and therefore sometimes not completely, or not at all. This can lead to a herbaceous impression of 'green- or grilled red pepper'. But that aside, Cabernet Sauvignon retains its signature cassis flavor. In Bordeaux, in addition to cassis and blackcurrant, the grape also develops aromas of pencil shavings. Due to long macerations, Cabernet wines can show vineyard specific aromas such as eucalypt (Coonawarra and Maipo for example) and fynbos in Stellenbosch.

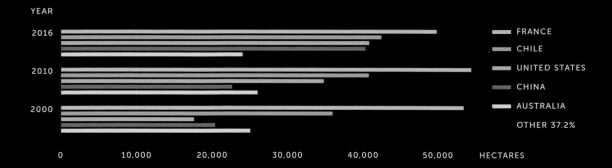

Professor Anderson's figures show that Cabernet Sauvignon is on the rise: from 221,497ha in 2000 it increased of more than 40% to 313,665ha. It is also clear that it is being planted in an increasing number of countries and that the ultimate growth country is China, followed by Chile and the United States.

The basis of the (Haut-)Médoc

As a rule, Bordeaux left bank (Médoc and Haut-Médoc) is a blend based on Cabernet Sauvignon, with Cabernet Franc, Merlot and sometimes smaller quantities Malbec and Petit Verdot. From gravelly, well-drained soils on the left bank of the Gironde between the city of Bordeaux and the Médoc in the north, comprising fifteen municipalities on a piece of land about 60 kilometers long. Chateau La Tour de By is a benchmark left bank chateau.

Riedel Vinum
6416-00

CHATEAU LA TOUR DE BY, MÉDOC, FRANCE

C	🛜	Therefore: grape with a thick skin	ruby				Therefore: 5 to 10 years old
H	🛜		BLACKCURRANT	BLACKBERRY	BLUEBERRY	BELL PEPPER	Therefore: Cabernet Sauvignon
A	🛜	Therefore: matured in oak	CEDAR	TOAST	PENCIL SHAVINGS	MOCHA	Therefore: (partly) new French oak
R	🛜	Therefore: 5 to 10 years old	TOBACCO				
A	🛜	Therefore: moderate climate					
C	🛜	Therefore: dry wine					
T	🛜	Therefore: grape with a thick skin	astringent				Therefore: long maceration/Old World
E	🛜	Therefore: lots of sunshine (long season)	13 to 14%, medium to full body				
R	🛜	Therefore: Old World					

Tasting note: This deep, ruby-colored red has a restrained nose of cassis and blackcurrant, cedar, toast, tobacco, mocha and pencil shavings. The wine is dry, with medium acidity, drying tannins and a medium to high alcohol content. Medium to full body and a low relative fruit intensity.

 10-15 °C   2 hours

 < $150

 > 10 years

In the (Haut-)Médoc-style: Bergerac (France), Madiran en Cahors (France), Cabernet blends (Hawkes Bay, New Zealand).

Coonawarra: the Médoc of Australia

Unlike Bordeaux, Cabernet Sauvignon in Coonawarra is really a single varietal produced on the famous terra rossa soil. Terra rossa is Italian for 'red earth': a red, loamy soil on a limestone subsoil, with clay and water below. Coonawarra is Aboriginal for honeysuckle. For me Coonawarra is the Bordeaux of Australia because of the dominance of Cabernet Sauvignon, very high average quality, tannic style and long aging potential.

YALUMBA, THE MENZIES, COONAWARRA, AUSTRALIA

C	📶	Therefore: grape with a very thick skin	ruby						Therefore: 5 to 10 years old
H	📶		BLACKCURRANT	BLACKBERRY	BLUEBERRY	GRILLED PEPPERS	EUCALYPT		Therefore: Australia / Cabernet (or Shiraz)
A	📶	Therefore: matured in oak	VANILLA	TOAST	CEDAR				Therefore: (partly) new French oak
R	📶	Therefore: 5 to 10 years old							
A	📶	Therefore: moderate climate							
C	📶	Therefore: dry wine							
T	📶	Therefore: grape with a thick skin	ripe						Therefore: New World
E	📶	Therefore: lots of sunshine (long season)	14%, full body						
R	📶	Therefore: New World							

Tasting note: This deep, ruby-colored red has intense aromas of blackberries, cassis and black currant, mint, eucalyptus, slightly spicy with notes of vanilla and coconut. The wine is dry, with medium acidity, ripe but firm tannins and a high alcohol content. Full body and a high relative fruit intensity.

Riedel Vinum
6416-00

 10-15 °C   0.5 hours   < $150   > 10 years

In the Coonawarra Cabernet style:
Cabernet Sauvignon (Margaret River, Australia), Cabernet Sauvignon (Cafayate, Argentina), Cabernet Franc (Mendoza, Argentina).

Maipo: the Bordeaux of Chile

Maipo is the Bordeaux of Chile and is located east of San Antonio and Casablanca and north of Cachapoal, between the Andes and the coastal area, around the capital Santiago. Maipo is known for its exceptional Cabernet Sauvignon, ripe, subtle and complex with its signature, aromatic mint and blackcurrant aromas. It amounts to more than 60% of the 10,000 hectares that comprise Maipo. Eucalyptus trees lend Maipo Cabernets their unique minty perfume.

1865, CABERNET SAUVIGNON, MAIPO, CHILE

C	Therefore: grape with a thick skin	ruby		Therefore: 3 to 5 years old
H	Therefore: Chile	BLACKCURRANT / BLACKBERRY / BLUEBERRY / MINT / BLACK CHERRY		Therefore: Cabernet (or Carménère)
A	Therefore: matured in oak	VANILLA / CEDAR / TOAST		Therefore: (partly) new French oak
R	Therefore: 3 to 5 years old			
A	Therefore: warm climate			
C	Therefore: dry wine			
T	Therefore: grape with a thick skin	ripe and soft		Therefore: New World
E	Therefore: lots of sunshine (high UV)	14 to 14.5%, full body		
R	Therefore: New World			

Tasting note: This deep, ruby-colored red has a fragrant nose of blackberry, cassis, blackcurrant and mint, including notes of vanilla, cedar and toast. The wine is dry, with low acidity, lots of ripe tannins and a high alcohol content. Full body and a high relative fruit intensity.

Riedel Vinum 6416-00

10-15 °C   0.5 hours

 < $150

 > 10 years

In the Maipo Cabernet-style: Cabernet Sauvignon (Aconcagua, Colchagua, Chile), Carménère (Maipo, Cachapoal, Colchagua, Aconcagua, Chile), Cabernet Sauvignon (Margaret River, Australia).

Mediterranean Cabernets from Napa

Although Napa Valley is only 30 miles long and a few miles wide –just a sixth the size of Bordeaux – it has a myriad of microclimates and soils. The dry, Mediterranean climate and the complex soils of volcanic and marine origin result in a pronounced intensely-fruity, ripe, Mediterranean-style Cabernet with lots of body and alcohol. Mostly (95%) small family businesses which, on average, produce very high-quality wine (priced commensurately).

ROBERT MONDAVI WINERY, CABERNET SAUVIGNON, NAPA VALLEY, CALIFORNIA

C	📶	Therefore: grape with a thick skin	ruby					Therefore: 3 to 5 years old
H	📶		BLACKCURRANT	BLACKBERRY	PLUM	BLUEBERRY	COMPOTE	Therefore: Cabernet (or Merlot)
A	📶	Therefore: matured in oak	CEDAR	TOAST	MOCHA			Therefore: (partly) new French oak
R	📶	Therefore: 3 to 5 years old						
A	📶	Therefore: warm climate						
C	📶	Therefore: dry wine						
T	📶	Therefore: grape with a thick skin	ripe and smooth					Therefore: New World
E	📶	Therefore: lots of sunshine (long season)	14 to 14.5%, full body					
R	📶	Therefore: New World						

Tasting note: This deep, ruby-colored red has an intense nose of jammy cassis, blackcurrant, blackberry jam, blueberry and blue-plum compote, including notes of cedar and toast, and mocha. The wine is dry, with low acidity, lots of smooth tannins and a high alcohol content. Full body and a high relative fruit intensity.

Riedel Vinum
6416-00

10-15 °C   0.5 hours

< $150

> 10 years

In the Napa Cabernet-style: Cabernet Sauvignon (Mendoza, Argentina), Cabernet Sauvignon (Bolgheri, Italy), Cabernet Sauvignon (Stellenbosch, South Africa).

Cape Cabernet: the best of both worlds?

Stellenbosch has a Mediterranean climate with hot, dry summers and cool, wet winters. Its soils, especially weathered granite, is very suitable for Cabernet. The presence of the mountains (which provide protection and location), the well-frained soils, the presence of fynbos, and the influence of the Cape Doctor winds, result in a unique style Cabernet Sauvignon – stylistically between Old and New World – with excellent aging potential.

BOSCHENDAL 1685, CABERNET SAUVIGNON, STELLENBOSCH, SOUTH AFRICA

C	📶	Therefore: grape with a thick skin	ruby		Therefore: 3 to 5 years old
H	📶		BLACKCURRANT · PLUM · BLUEBERRY · FYNBOS · BELL PEPPER		Therefore: South Africa because of fynbos-aromas / Cabernet
A	📶	Therefore: matured in oak	VANILLA · CEDAR · TOAST · MOCHA		Therefore: (partly) new French oak
R	📶	Therefore: 3 to 5 years old			
A	📶	Therefore: Mediterranean climate			
C	📶	Therefore: dry wine			
T	📶	Therefore: grape with a thick skin	ripe and soft		Therefore: New World
E	📶	Therefore: lots of sunshine (long season)	14 to 14.5%, full body		
R	📶	Therefore: New World			

Tasting note: This deep, ruby-colored red has an intense nose of jammy cassis, blackcurrant and blue plum, including notes of vanilla and toast, green pepper and fynbos, chocolate and mocha. The wine is dry, with low acidity, a high alcohol content, and plenty of ripe tannins. Full body and a high relative fruit intensity.

Riedel Vinum
6416-00

 10-15 °C   0.5 hours

 < $100

 > 10 years

In the Stellenbosch Cabernet-style:
Cabernet Sauvignon (Mendoza, Argentina), Cabernet Sauvignon (Napa Valley, California), Cabernet Sauvignon (Hawkes Bay, New Zealand).

140

Mendoza: Cabernet with temperament

Argentina offers three Cabernet styles from continental climates. First of all, the Primera Zona style (Maipú and Luján de Cuyo) with older vines, grown at an altitude of 700 to 900 meters, and with a good body and structure. Then there is the Uco Valley, at an altitude of 1,000 to 1,400 meters, with more acidity and freshness (as in Gualtallary). And finally, Cafayate, at 1,700 meters, with explosive, purple-fruit flavors, super-ripe tannins, and yet fresh acidity.

TRAPICHE, MEDALLA, CABERNET SAUVIGNON, MENDOZA, ARGENTINA					
C	📶	Therefore: grape with a very thick skin	ruby		Therefore: 3 to 5 years old
H	📶		BLACKCURRANT BLACKBERRY COMPOTE PLUM FIG		Therefore: Cabernet or Malbec
A	📶	Therefore: matured in oak	VANILLA CEDAR TOAST MOCHA CHOCOLATE		Therefore: (partly) new French oak
R	📶	Therefore: 3 to 5 years old			
A	📶	Therefore: warm, continental climate			
C	📶	Therefore: dry wine			
T	📶	Therefore: grape with a thick skin	ripe and soft		Therefore: New World
E	📶	Therefore: lots of sunshine (high UV)	14 to 14.5%, full body		
R	📶	Therefore: New World			

Tasting note: This deep, ruby-colored red has an intense nose of jammy cassis, black currant, blackberry jam and blue-plum compote, including notes of vanilla, cedar and toast, fig paste, chocolate and mocha. The wine is dry, with low acidity, a high alcohol content and lots of sweet, ripe tannins. Full body and a high relative fruit intensity.

Riedel Vinum
6416-00

10-15 °C   0.5 hours

< $50

> 10 years

In the Mendoza Cabernet-style:
Cabernet Sauvignon (Napa Valley, California), Cabernet Sauvignon (Bolgheri, Italy), Cabernet Sauvignon (Stellenbosch, South Africa).

8 Wine's Internationals   141

Margaret River: Australia's Maipo Valley

Margaret River is located in the extreme southwest of Australia, about three-hundred miles south of Perth. It is a peninsula in the Indian Ocean. The geography, soil and Mediterranean climate with maritime influences result in mainly winter rains, with a continuous cool sea breeze in summer and plenty of sun for a long, dry ripening season. In many ways it resembles the conditions in Chile and the Margaret River Cabernet style is closer to Maipo than to Coonawarra.

CAPE MENTELLE, CABERNET SAUVIGNON, MARGARET RIVER, AUSTRALIA

C	📶	Therefore: grape with a thick skin	ruby		Therefore: 3 to 5 years old
H	📶		 BLACKCURRANT — BLACKBERRY — PLUM — MINT — BELL PEPPER		Therefore: Cabernet (or Merlot) / Australia or Chile
A	📶	Therefore: matured in oak	VANILLA — CEDAR		Therefore: (partly) new French oak
R	📶	Therefore: 3 to 5 years old			
A	📶	Therefore: warm climate			
C	📶	Therefore: dry wine			
T	📶	Therefore: grape with a thick skin	ripe and smooth		Therefore: New World
E	📶	Therefore: lots of sunshine (long season)	14 to 14.5%, full body		
R	📶	Therefore: New World			

Tasting note: This deep, ruby-colored red has an intense nose of pure cassis, blackcurrant, blackberry and mint, including notes of vanilla, cedar and toast. The wine is dry, with medium acidity, a high alcohol content, and lots of ripe tannins. Full body and a high relative fruit intensity.

Riedel Vinum
6416-00

   10-15 °C   0.5 hours   < $100   > 10 years

In the Margaret River-style: Cabernet Sauvignon (Maipo, Aconcagua, Chile), Cabernet Sauvignon (Cafayate, Argentina), Cabernet Sauvignon (Hawkes Bay, New Zealand).

142

52,630 ha (1.17%)

🔊 KA-ri-nyan

Carignan means blending

Mazuelo, Bovale Grande, Cariñena, Carinyena, Samsó, Carignane, Carignano

THIN SKIN   THICK SKIN   MALADAPTIVE   ADAPTIVE

Despite the fact that, until the end of the twentieth century, Carignan was the most widely planted grape in France, very few enthusiasts consciously buy Carignan. That's because it is a typical blending variety due to its historically high yields (150 to 200 hl/ha is quite normal, four times as much as Cabernet Sauvignon, for example). It combines lots of tannins with good acidity and deep color, and is therefore traditionally blended with Grenache which lacks those qualities. In the 1950s it was planted en masse by returning Algerians and Tunisians. Over the past 25 years plantings have halved, at the cost of many old vines. To blunt the sharp edges of its tart tannins, carbonic maceration is often used. It is of Spanish origin (Cariñena in Aragon) and still widely planted in Catalonia (where it is known as Samsó), in Costers del Segre, Penedès, Tarragona, Terra Alta, Montsant and Priorat. In Priorat, the old gobelet-pruned vines on the llicorella-schist can yield wines of real concentration and complexity. In Rioja it's called Mazuelo.

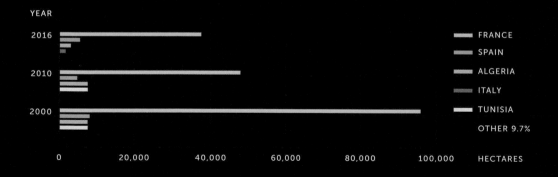

From Professor Anderson's figures it is evident that Cabernet Franc is being planted in an increasingly number of countries, with Brazil in surprisingly third position.

The cradle of Carignan

Priorat, located in Catalonia, produces intense, full-bodied reds made from old vine Cariñena and Garnacha with concentrated aromas of licorice, tar, and soaked cherries. Priorat was one of the first regions to emerge from obscurity and become world famous with some of Spain's most expensive wines. It is also one of only two wine regions in Spain to have a DOCa (the other is Rioja). Salmos is a blend of Cariñena with Garnacha and some Syrah.

Riedel Vinum 6416-30

TORRES, SALMOS, PRIORAT, SPAIN

C	Therefore: grape with a thick skin	ruby		Therefore: 3 to 5 years old
H		BLACKCHERRY, BLUEBERRY, PLUM, BLACKBERRY, ORANGE		Therefore: Spain
A	Therefore: matured in oak	TOAST, CEDAR, MOCHA		Therefore: (partly) new French oak
R	Therefore: 3 to 5 years old	TOBACCO, EARTH		
A	Therefore: warm climate			
C	Therefore: dry wine			
T	Therefore: grape with a thick skin	astringent		Therefore: Old World
E	Therefore: lots of sunshine (long season)	14 to 15%, full body		
R	Therefore: Old World			

Tasting note: This deep, ruby-colored red has medium-intense aromas of black cherry, blueberry, damson, orange peel, licorice, cocoa, mocha, cedar and toast. Low acidity, high alcohol and lots of astringent tannins. Full body and a low relative fruit intensity.

10-15 °C   2 hours

< $100

> 10 years

In the Priorat-style: Montsant (Catalunya, Spain), Canonnau (Sardinia, France), Cariñena (Cariñena, Spain).

144

Vignadores de Carignan

Vigno stands for Vignadores de Carignan and is a producers' interest group of old-vine Carignan from Maule (Secano), one of the deprived wine regions in southern Chile. Carignan is one of the original varieties planted in Chile by the Spaniards. It was in the 1990s that a number of producers, such as Gillmore, Miguel Torres and Odfjell, realized that some of these old vines, especially Carignan, could be used to make very interesting wines.

Riedel Vinum
6416-30

TORRES, CORDILLRA, CARIGNAN, MAULE, CHILE (VIGNO)				
C	📶	Therefore: grape with a thick skin	ruby	Therefore: 3 to 5 years old
H	📶		BLACKCHERRY BLUEBERRY PLUM BLACKBERRY MINT	Therefore: Chile
A	📶	Therefore: matured in oak	TOAST CEDAR MOCHA	Therefore: (partly) new French oak
R	📶	Therefore: 3 to 5 years old		
A	📶	Therefore: warm climate		
C	📶	Therefore: dry wine		
T	📶	Therefore: grape with a thick skin	ripe and smooth	Therefore: New World
E	📶	Therefore: lots of sunshine (high UV)	14%, full body	
R	📶	Therefore: New World		

Tasting note: This deep, ruby-colored red has intense aromas of black cherry, blueberry, damson, spices, mint, cocoa, mocha, cedar and toast. Low acidity, high alcohol and lots of ripe, soft tannins. Full body and a high relative fruit intensity.

 10-15 °C   0.5 hours

 < $50

 > 10 years

In the Chilean Carignan-style: Grenache (McLaren Vale, Australia), Canonnau (Sardinia, France), Priorat (Catalunya, Spain).

🔊 shar-don-nay

huge
200,148 ha (4.46%)

Chardonnay: the Chameleon

Morillon

For many people, white wine is Chardonnay. It is a brand in itself. But when you ask them what Chardonnay typically tastes like, many of them won't have an answer. That in itself is not strange because, unlike Sauvignon Blanc or Riesling, Chardonnay does not have a very distinct aroma or flavor profile, despite its popularity. That is due to the fact that the variety adapts effortlessly to various climates, resulting in a variety of styles. Add to that the fact that Chardonnay lends itself to various winemaking methods, and the result is somewhat of a chameleon. Its aromas range from apple, pear and melon to tropical fruits (such as pineapple and mango), with or without butter and vanilla, toast or other aromas caused by contact with oak. The birthplace and benchmark of the most famous white grape variety is Burgundy, but Chardonnay is now planted in virtually every wine-growing region in the world.

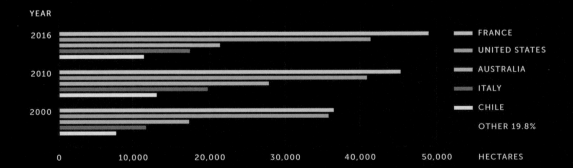

According to Professor Anderson's figures plantings of Chardonnay have increased globally consistently while stagnated in the established 'Chardonnay-countries' like France, California, Australia and Chile.

Blanc de Blancs

The term Blanc de Blancs refers to sparklings made from white grapes only (and in Champagne from Chardonnay only). As in the Côte de Blancs, a twenty kilometer long ridge of chalk and limestone running from north to south and comprising 3,313 hectares of vineyards, 90% of which is Chardonnay. Ruinart is a classic Blanc de Blancs that is understated and elegant, developing a brioche richness 'sur lattes' (on the dead yeast) in full harmony with the restrained fruit intensity.

RUINART, BLANC DE BLANCS, CHAMPAGNE, FRANCE

C			lemon	Therefore: youthful
H		Therefore: a neutral grape variety	YELLOW APPLE · PEAR · LEMON	
A			BRIOCHE · BISCUIT · BREAD · DOUGH	autolysis; therefore: méthode traditionelle
R		Therefore: youthful		
A		Therefore: cool climate	lactic acids	Therefore: malo
C		Therefore: brut	persistent mousse	Therefore: methode traditionelle
T				
E			12 to 12.5%, persistent mousse, elegant	
R		Therefore: Old World		

Tasting note: Sparkling white with restrained expression of apple, pear, citrus, brioche, biscuit and yeast. In the mouth the wine is dry with high acidity, persistent mousse, and medium alcohol. Light to medium body; elegant. Low relative fruit intensity.

Riedel
641(

Riedel Vinum
6416-58

 < 10 °C

no

 < $150

5-10 years

In the Blanc de Blancs champagne-style:
English Sparkling (England), Crémant de Bourgogne (France), Cap Classique (South Africa).

Chardonnay Down Under

'Marqs', as Australians call the Margaret River, has become one of the leading areas for top Chardonnay in Australia. Yet Chardonnay was certainly not the first grape with which they experimented here. After half a century of development, the contours of its own 'Burgundian' style are beginning to emerge. The not-very-productive Gin Gin clone (especially in terms of fruit setting) ensures low yields and a lot of concentration, while winemaking has been improved significantly.

CAPE MENTELLE, CHARDONNAY, MARGARET RIVER, AUSTRALIA				
C 📶		golden		Therefore: oxidative winemaking
H 📶	Therefore: a neutral grape variety	YELLOW APPLE, PEAR, PINEAPPLE, PEACH, DILL		
A 📶	Therefore: oxidative winemaking	BUTTER, VANILLA, TOAST		Therefore: French oak / malo
R 📶	Therefore: youthful			
A 📶	Therefore: moderate climate	lactic acids		Therefore: malo
C 📶	Therefore: dry wine	creamy texture		Therefore: sur lie
T 📶				
E 📶		13 to 13.5%, medium body		
R 📶	Therefore: New World			

Tasting note: This medium, golden-colored white has a medium-intensity nose of apple, pear, pineapple, peach and honeysuckle with a creamy mouthfeel and impressions of butter, vanilla and toast. The wine is dry, with medium acidity and a medium alcohol. Medium body and a high relative fruit intensity.

Riedel Vinum
6416-97

< 10 °C no

< $100

5-10 years

In the Margaret River-style: Reserve Chardonnay (Stellenbosch, South Africa), Reserve Chardonnay (Limarí, Chile), Reserve Chardonnay (Napa, California).

Limarí: 'Meursault meets Chile'

What sets Limarí apart from other cool areas for Chardonnay in Chile is the rare combination of cool, dry conditions and a unique soil type. Limarí has a sedimentary sea terrace (while most other soils in Chile are volcanic without any limestone). It is however exactly this limestone content of Limarí which reduces the growth of the vine, making the Chardonnays richer, with integrated acidity and longer aging potential. It also lends the resulting wines a Limarí minerality.

TORRES, CHARDONNAY, LIMARÍ, CHILE

C	📶		golden	Therefore: oxidative winemaking
H	📶	Therefore: a neutral grape variety	YELLOW APPLE · PEAR · PINEAPPLE · PEACH · MANGO	
A	📶	Therefore: oxidative winemaking	BUTTER · VANILLA · TOAST	Therefore: French oak / malo
R	📶	Therefore: youthful		
A	📶	Therefore: cool climate	lactic acids	Therefore: malo
C	📶	Therefore: dry wine	creamy texture	Therefore: sur lie
T	📶			
E	📶		13 to 13.5%, medium body	
R	📶	Therefore: New World		

Tasting note: This medium, golden-colored white has a medium-intense nose of melon, pineapple, mango, peach, and apricot with a creamy mouthfeel and impressions of butter, vanilla, toast, and lemon tart. The wine is dry, with medium acidity and alcohol. Medium body and a high relative fruit intensity.

Riedel Vinum
6416-97

 < 10 °C   no

 < $50

 5-10 years

In the Limarí-style: *Reserve Chardonnay (Casablanca, Chile), Reserve Chardonnay Penedes (Spain), Reserve Chardonnay (Margaret River, Australia).*

Napa Valley Chard

Although Napa Valley is only 30 miles long and a few miles wide, it is home to a myriad of microclimates and soils that lend themselves to a variety of grapes and styles. Including sufficient terroir possibilities for world-renowned Chardonnay. The prevailing philosophy (is there such a thing in Napa?) is to project 'the Burgundian treatment' (malo, sur lie, and oak) on the terroir of Napa Valley. This results in a ripe, intensely-fruity style with (partly) malo and (often only partly) matured on new French oak.

ROBERT MONDAVI WINERY, CHARDONNAY, NAPA VALLEY, CALIFORNIA

C	🛜		golden	Therefore: oxidative winemaking
H	🛜	Therefore: a neutral grape variety	YELLOW APPLE · PEAR · PINEAPPLE · PEACH · ZEST	
A	🛜	Therefore: oxidative winemaking	BUTTER · VANILLA · CHEESECAKE	Therefore: French oak / malo
R	🛜	Therefore: youthful		
A	🛜	Therefore: moderate climate	lactic acids	Therefore: (partly) malo
C	🛜	Therefore: dry wine	fatty texture	Therefore: sur lie
T	🛜			
E	🛜		13.5%, medium body	
R	🛜	Therefore: New World		

Tasting note: This medium, golden-colored white has a medium-intense nose of melon, pineapple, mango, peach and lemon zest with a creamy mouthfeel and impressions of butter, vanilla, and cheesecake. The wine is dry, with medium acidity and medium alcohol. Medium body and a high relative fruit intensity.

Riedel Vinum
6416-97

 < 10 °C   no

 < $100

5-10 years

In the Napa Valley-style: Reserve Chardonnay (Stellenbosch, South Africa), Reserve Chardonnay (Margaret River, Australia), Reserve Chardonnay (Limarí, Chile).

◀) SJEN-nuhn blangk

Chenin Blanc: the affordable chameleon

Chenin, Pineau, Pineau de la Loire, Pineau d'Anjou, Steen

The home of Chenin Blanc is the Loire Valley, specifically the area between Muscadet and Sancerre. Chenin Blanc is the main ingredient of Anjou Blanc, Saumur, and Vouvray, Montlouis, Savennières and Jasnières. The basic quality is understated and restrained, with citrus fruits like quince, lemon, lime, yellow apple, straw and honey. Young Chenin Blancs can be somewhat aromatic, even with a slightly floral character. However, that intensity quickly disappears in the bottle. Just like chardonnay, Chenin Blanc belongs to the neutral varieties. The grape usually retains a fresh acidity, even in South Africa. It can be produced both without oak aging (Loire) and with (South Africa) in a variety of climates.
It retains its acidity everywhere. South Africa has the most Chenin Blanc and also of the oldest vines. What sets Chenin Blanc apart from Chardonnay are the wonderful dessert wines such as Montlouis, Quarts de Chaume and Coteaux-du-Layon.

From Anderson's figures it turns out that Chenin Blanc is not growing in the classic Chenin Blanc countries including South-Africa, California and Argentina. And stalling in France.

Crémant de Loire

Crémant de Loire can be made from all terroirs in this long valley and from a variety of grape varieties, of which Chenin Blanc is often the main ingredient. That's why it comes in different styles, from floral and fruity (mainly apple-y) to flinty and minerally. Made using the *méthode traditionelle* with at least 12 months sur latte. Crémant de Loire often has more fruit intensity than champagne and less autolysis complexity.

BAUMARD, TURQUOISE, CRÉMANT DE LOIRE, FRANCE

C			lemon		Therefore: youthful
H		Therefore: a neutral grape variety	MASHED FRUITS · LEMON · QUINCE · HONEY · FLINT		Therefore: Chenin Blanc
A		Therefore: reductive winemaking			
R		Therefore: recent disgorged			
A		Therefore: cool climate	malic acids		Therefore: no malo
C		Therefore: brut	persistent mousse		Therefore: méthode traditionelle
T					
E			12 to 12.5%, light to medium body		
R		Therefore: Old World			

Tasting note: Sparkling white with restrained expression of yellow apple, lemon, quince and honey. In the mouth the wine is dry with medium to high acidity, persistent mousse, and medium alcohol. No notes of brioche or biscuit. Light to medium body and a low relative fruit intensity.

Riedel Vinum
6416-58

 < 10 °C no
 < $50
 < 5 years

In the Crémant de Loire-style: Cava (Penedes, Spain), Cap Classique (South Africa), Franciacorta (Italy).

Savennières: Chablis of the Loire Valley

Savennières is a small Anjou appellation famous for its restrained, dry, mineral-fresh Chenin Blanc from old volcanic and schist soils on the southern banks of the Loire. For me, Savennières is the Chablis of the Loire. It is located 15 kilometers southwest of Angers on the northern bank of the Loire. Almost directly opposite, on the southern bank, lie appellations such as Coteaux du Layon, Quarts de Chaume, and Bonnezeaux, which are famous for their sweet wines.

BAUMARD, CLOS SAINT YVES, SAVENNIÈRES, FRANCE				
C			lemon	Therefore: youthful
H		Therefore: a neutral grape variety	YELLOW APPLE LEMON QUINCE HONEY HAY	Therefore: Chenin Blanc
A		Therefore: reductive winemaking	BUTTER	Therefore: no contact with (new) oak / partly malo
R		Therefore: youthful		
A		Therefore: cool climate	lactic acids	Therefore: (partly) malo
C		Therefore: dry wine	fatty texture	Therefore: sur lie
T				
E			12.5 to 13%, medium body	
R		Therefore: Old World		

Tasting note: This rather neutral white has a restrained expression of quince, yellow apple, lemon, honey and hay. Refined mineral notes. In the mouth the wine is dry with high acidity, creamy mouthfeel, medium alcohol and an understated mineral taste. Medium body and a low relative fruit intensity.

Riedel Vinum
6416-05

< 10 °C   no   < $50   5-10 years

In the Savennières-style: Jasnières, Montlouis (Loire, France), Chablis (France), Muscadet de Sèvre et Maine Sur Lie (France).

Old Vines Cape Chenin

Chenin Blanc is South Africa's signature grape, even more than Pinotage. Not only it is the most planted grape in the Cape, but it also does well in a variety of climatic conditions (because of its adaptiveness). As a result, Cape Chenin has a lot of differences in style and price, from everyday simple fruit driven table wines to complex dinner wines. Most old vine Chenin is now made in a Burgundian style (so with malo, sur lie, and oak aging).

BELLINGHAM BERNARD SERIES, CHENIN BLANC, OLD VINE, SOUTH AFRICA				
C	📶		golden	Therefore: oxidative winemaking
H	📶	Therefore: a neutral grape variety	YELLOW APPLE, LIME, QUINCE, PINEAPPLE, HONEY	
A	📶	Therefore: oxidative winemaking	BUTTER, VANILLA, TOAST	Therefore: matured in oak / malo
R	📶	Therefore: youthful		
A	📶	Therefore: cool climate	lactic acids	Therefore: malo
C	📶	Therefore: dry wine	creamy texture	Therefore: sur lie
T	📶			
E	📶	Therefore: lots of sunshine (long season)	13.5 to 14.5%, full body	
R	📶	Therefore: New World		

Riedel Vinum
6416-97

Tasting note: This understated white has medium-intense harvest aromas of guava, yellow apple, lime, quince, honey and pineapple. It also exhibits some aromas of winemaking such as vanilla, toast and butter. In the mouth, the wine is dry with medium-plus acidity, creamy mouthfeel, medium to high alcohol, and mineral finish. Medium to full body and a high relative fruit intensity.

< 10 °C   no   < $50   5-10 years

In the Cape Reserve Chenin Blanc-style:
Reserve Chardonnay (Elgin, South Africa),
Reserve Chardonnay (Mendoza, Argentina),
Reserve Chardonnay (Limarí, Chile).

Between Sauternes and TBA

Quarts de Chaume is considered a leading appellation in the Loire. The name is derived from a tradition dating back to the Middle Ages, when the farmers had to pay a quarter of their harvest to the Seigneur while keeping three quarters for themselves – hence the 's' in Quarts de Chaume. The geological complexity of the area – shale and sandstone – and the south-facing position overlooking the River Layon and the morning mist is ideal for the development of *Botrytis* (noble rot).

BAUMARD, QUARTS DE CHAUME, LOIRE, FRANCE

C			golden	
H		Therefore: a neutral grape variety	MARMELADE · ZEST · QUINCE · PINEAPPLE · HONEY	honey, Therefore: Botrytis
A		Therefore: reductive winemaking		Therefore: no contact with (new) oak
R		Therefore: youthful		
A		Therefore: cool climate	malic acids	Therefore: no malo
C		Therefore: very sweet wine	more than 150 gr/L	
T				
E			14%, full body	Therefore: concentration by Botrytis
R		Therefore: Old World		

Tasting note: This medium intense, golden-colored dessert white has a restrained nose of quince and dried pineapple, lemon zest, apricot jam, apple compôte and honey. In the mouth the wine is lusciously sweet with high acidity, high alcohol and a combination of quince and dried pineapple, lemon zest, apricot jam, apple compôte and honey. Full body, long finish and a low relative fruit intensity.

Riedel Vinum
6416-33

 < 10 °C   no   < $100   > 10 years

In the Quarts du Chaume-style: *Coteaux du Layon, Bonnezeaux, Montlouis (Loire, France), Beerenauslese en Trockenbeeren- auslese (Germany), Beerenauslese, Ausbruch en Trockenbeerenauslese (Austria).*

The aromatic pinnacle: Gewürztraminer

Fromenteau, Clevener, Savagnin, Traminer

Gewürztraminer (a mutation of Savagnin Blanc) can be easily recognized by its intense aromatic nose of lychee, roses, and tropical fruits. It's exotic and intoxicating; the German prefix 'gewürz' means fragrant or spicy. Incidentally, in Germany Gewürztraminer is spelled with an umlaut and in France it is without. The grapes look unusually pink, yes, almost red, for a white variety, and their skins contain relatively a lot of pigments. As a result, they often yield golden-yellow wines. It's not unusual for Gewürztraminers to contain a few grams of residual sweetness and 14% alcohol. Like Riesling, Gewürztraminer is terroir-transparent. Marble-limestone like Hengst or Florimont produce rich and spicy wines with a lot of backbone. Granite and sandstone such as Brand and Kessler, or quartz such as Fronholz produce more aromatic and elegant wines while limestone like Furstentum or Osterberg result in full-bodied wines with lots of fruit and more acidity.

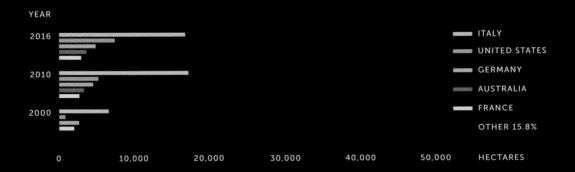

Following the figures of Professor Anderson, Gewürztraminer is steadily on the rise, almost tripled in size in the past 20 years.

At home in the Alsace

Alsace is located in the north of France, but thanks to the Vosges mountains, which absorb the westerly winds and their rain, snow, ice and hail, it's one of the driest and sunniest wine regions in the country. This means that Gewürztraminer has no problems fully maturing here and achieves a creamy, 'round' style with low acidity. Some Gewürztraminers from the Alsace even have a degree of sweetness – but not at Trimbach who prides itself in a dry style.

TRIMBACH, GEWÜRZTRAMINER, ALSACE, FRANCE

C	📶	Therefore: skin with a lot of pigments	golden	
H	📶	Therefore: aromatic grape variety	LYCHEE ROSE PINEAPPLE APRICOT	Therefore: Gewürztraminer
A	📶	Therefore: reductive winemaking		
R	📶	Therefore: youthful		
A	📶	Therefore: warm climate		
C	📶	Therefore: dry (but not bone dry)	fatty texture	Therefore: sur lie
T	📶			
E	📶	Therefore: lots of sunshine (long season)	13 to 14%, medium body	
R	📶	Therefore: Old World		

Tasting note: This medium intense, golden-colored white has an intensely aromatic scent of lychee, rose blossom, pineapple and apricot, low acidity, roundness and medium alcohol. An oily mouthfeel and medium body. Low relative fruit intensity.

Riedel Vinum 6416-33

 < 10 °C   no   < $50   5-10 years

In the Alsace-style: Muscat (Alsace, France), Gewürztraminer (Alto Adige, Italy), Torrontès (Cafayate, Argentina).

Gewürztraminer with freshness

At high altitudes, Gewürztraminer gets riper (and more alcoholic) thanks to high UV while the cool nights preserve the acidity; this is unique for Alto Adige in northern Italy (and Südost-Steiermark in Austria for instance). The altitude ensures cool conditions with high UV while the Mediterranean and the Adriatic in the south bring a Mediterranean influence. This creates the unmistakable Alto Adige Gewürztraminer style: full bodied with lots of alcohol but with high acidity and an unprecedented aromatic intensity.

TIEFENBRUNNER, GEWÜRZTRAMINER, ALTO ADIGE, ITALY

C	Therefore: skin with a lot of pigments	golden		
H	Therefore: aromatic grape variety	LYCHEE · ROSE · PINEAPPLE · APRICOT · ZEST		Therefore: Gewürztraminer
A	Therefore: reductive winemaking			
R	Therefore: youthful			
A	Therefore: cool climate			
C	Therefore: dry wine	fatty texture		Therefore: sur lie
T				
E	Therefore: lots of sunshine (high UV)	13.5 to 14.5%, medium to full body		
R	Therefore: Old World			

Tasting note: This medium intense, golden-colored white has an intensely aromatic perfume of lychee, rose blossom, pineapple and apricot, lots of alcohol but also high acidity. A lot of mouthfeel and a medium to full body and a medium relative fruit intensity.

Riedel Vinum
6416-33

< 10 °C   no

< $50

> 10 years

In the Alto Adige-style: Gewürztraminer (Alsace, France), Kerner (Alto Adige, Italy), Torrontès (Cafayate, Argentina.

Grenache likes it hot

Aragones, Alicante, Cannonau, Garnatxa negre, Garnacha Tinta, Grenache Noir

very big
156,793 ha (3.49%)

| THIN SKIN | THICK SKIN | | MONO / BLEND | MALADAPTIVE | ADAPTIVE |

HA 156,793

SPARKLING SWEET FORTIFIED DRY

Garnacha or Grenache can be recognized by its unusual combination of high alcohol and relatively light color. And, the candy-like nose of red fruit is also striking. In Provence, Grenache often picks up aromas from local herbs such as garrigue. In the bottle it develops earthy and tobacco notes. Grenache is a true blending variety as in Rioja and Priorat and in appellations in the southern Rhône, such as Châteauneuf-du-Pape. However, it is also used in the New World as a blending component, like in Australia where the 'G' of Grenache leads the GSM category (Rhône inspired blends of Grenache, Shiraz and Mourvedre/mataro). In addition, Grenache is popular as a single varietal (with extremely powerful, aromatic wines from very old vines from Barossa and McLaren Vale for example) and for rosé (as in Tavel, Lirac and Provence). Last but not least, Grenache lends itself to adding alcohol as is done in Vin Doux Naturel in Rhône, Languedoc and Roussillon.

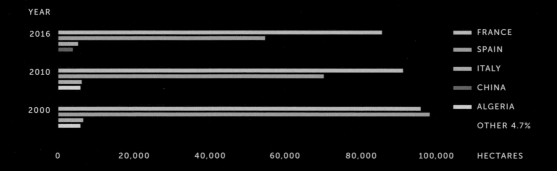

YEAR

2016

2010

2000

| 0 | 20,000 | 40,000 | 60,000 | 80,000 | 100,000 | HECTARES |

FRANCE
SPAIN
ITALY
CHINA
ALGERIA
OTHER 4.7%

The past 20 years, many hectares of Grenache have been grubbed up, especially in Spain, where the acreage under vine almost halved.

The ultimate rosé variety

The Provence is blessed with a Mediterranean climate with warm summers and mild winters. Too much sun can be a concern, although the heat is relieved by the northern Mistral. Rosé accounts for more than half of the Provençal wine production. Two techniques are used: bleeding ('saignée') and more popular: 'pressurage direct' in which the ripe grapes are only in contact with the skins during the pressing cycle. Just long enough to obtain the typical tinge of pink.

AIX, ROSÉ DE PROVENCE, FRANCE				
C	Therefore: short maceration (or direct pressing)	pink		Therefore: youthful
H		RASPBERRY STRAWBERRY PLUM RED CHERRY		
A	Therefore: reductive winemaking			
R	Therefore: youthful			
A	Therefore: warm climate			
C	Therefore: dry wine			
T				
E		13 to 13.5%, medium body		
R	Therefore: Old World			

Tasting note: A hint of pink and a restrained nose with small red fruits such as raspberry, game strawberry and red plum. Low acidity, medium alcohol, a dry style, and no tannins produce a finesse-rich rosé. Medium body and a low relative fruit intensity.

Riedel Extreme
4441-55 (AIX)

 < 10 °C   no   < $50 < 5 years

In the Rosé de Provence-style:
Languedoc (France), Tavel (Rhône, France), Garnacha Rosado (Spain).

Pinnacle of all Grenache-blends

Châteauneuf-du-Pape is the largest and most prominent appellation in the southern Rhône, with more than 3,200 hectares of vineyards and eighty growers. This appellation produces more wine than the entire northern Rhône. These rich, red wines, which remind you of the blistering heat and herb garden of the French south (garrigue), owe their complexity to the blending of up to fourteen permitted varieties – based on Grenache, which gives it its richness, mouthfeel, and jammy character.

Riedel Vinum
6416-15

CHAPOUTIER, LA BERNARDINE, CHÂTEAUNEUF-DU-PAPE, FRANCE

C	📶	Therefore: grape with a thin skin	ruby					Therefore: 3 to 5 years old
H	📶		PLUM	RED CHERRY	FIG	CINNAMON	GARRIGUE	
A	📶	Therefore: matured in oak	TOAST	MOCHA	CHOCOLATE			Therefore: (partly) new French oak
R	📶	Therefore: 3 to 5 years old	SOAKED FRUITS	PRESERVED FRUITS	DRIED FRUITS			
A	📶	Therefore: hot climate						
C	📶	Therefore: dry wine						
T	📶	Therefore: grape with a thin skin	astringent					Therefore: Old World
E	📶	Therefore: lots of sunshine (long season)	14 to 15.5%, full body					
R	📶	Therefore: Old World						

Tasting note: This medium, ruby-colored red has aromas of prunes, cherry, fig paste, spices, garrigue and toast. The wine is dry with low acidity, high alcohol, drying tannins. Full body and a low relative fruit intensity.

10-15 °C   2 hours   < $100   > 10 years

In the Châteauneuf-du-Pape-style:
Gigondas, Vacqeyras en Lirac (Rhône, France), Priorat (Spain), Canonnau (Sardinia, France).

Old Vines Grenache

In McLaren Vale, fifteen miles south of Adelaide, the first commercial vineyard (Tintara) was planted. Now there are about four thousand hectares. There is a dry and warm to hot climate, despite the cooling offered by Gulf St Vincent. McLaren Vale has soils ranging from fertile red loam on the coastal plains to hard shale and limestone in the foothills of the Lofty Ranges. Next to Shiraz and Cabernet you will find Old Vines Grenache here in an intensely-fruity, spicy (clovey) style.

YALUMBA, OLD VINE GRENACHE, MCLAREN VALE, AUSTRALIA

C	Therefore: grape with a relatively thin skin	ruby		Therefore: 3 to 5 years old
H		PLUM, RED CHERRY, BLACKCHERRY, CLOVE, EUCALYPT		Therefore: Australia of Chile
A	Therefore: oxidative winemaking	TOAST, COCONUT, MOCHA, CHOCOLATE		Therefore: partly new oak / American oak
R	Therefore: 3 to 5 years old			
A	Therefore: hot climate			
C	Therefore: dry wine			
T	Therefore: grape with a relatively thin skin	ripe and smooth		
E	Therefore: lots of sunshine (long season)	14 to 15%, full body		
R	Therefore: New World			

Tasting note: This medium ruby-colored red has jammy aromas of blue plum, red cherry, cloves, eucalyptus, toast and coconut. The wine is dry with low acidity, high alcohol, sweet, smooth tannins and a spicy finish. Full body and a high relative fruit intensity.

Riedel Vinum
6416-15

  10-15 °C   0.5 hours

 < $50

5-10 years

In the Grenache uit McLaren Vale-style:
Grenache (Barossa Valley, Australia), GSM blends (South Australia), Garnacha (Cariñena, Calatayud, Spain).

Grenache actually is Garnacha

Grenache (or rather: Garnacha) is originally from Aragon, according to the ampelographs. And Costers del Segre in Catalonia, on Spain's northeast coast, isn't far from there. In fact, the area is located on the 'Shores of the Segre' – a river that originates in the mountain ranges of the Pyrenees and flows into the river Ebro just south of the town of Lleida. Most vineyards are located in the vast river basin and the Purgatori is a legacy from the Middle Ages.

TORRES, PURGATORI, GARNACHA, COSTERS DEL SEGRE, LLEIDA, SPAIN

C	Therefore: grape with a relatively thin skin	ruby		Therefore: 3 to 5 years old
H		PLUM, RED CHERRY, FIG, WET STONE, LAUREL		Therefore: hot climate
A	Therefore: oxidative winemaking	TOAST, MOCHA		Therefore: older oak, both American and French
R	Therefore: 3 to 5 years old			
A	Therefore: hot climate			
C	Therefore: dry wine			
T	Therefore: grape with a relatively thin skin	astringent		Therefore: Old World
E	Therefore: warm climate	14 to 14.5%, full body		
R	Therefore: Old World			

Tasting note: This medium intense, ruby-colored red has aromas of prunes, cherry, fig paste, spices, and toast. The wine is dry with low acidity, high alcohol, moderate but astringent tannins. Full body and a low relative fruit intensity.

Riedel Vinum
6416-15

10-15 °C   0.5 hours

< $50

5-10 years

In the Costers del Segre-style: Priorat (Spain), Rioja Oriental (Spain), Canonnau (Sardinia, France).

Vin Doux Naturel

Due to the high sugar content and silky tannins, Grenache is quite suitable for fortification, as is done in vin doux naturels (VDN) from the Roussillon and fortified wines from Australia (port style). For VDN, after three days, eau-de-vie is added to the must, which stops the fermentation and ensures an alcohol content of 15 to 17% in the wine and about one hundred grams of residual sugars. Both for a ruby and rancio style with aromas of raisins.

CHAPOUTIER, BANYULS, FRANCE

C	Therefore: grape with a relatively thin skin	ruby		Therefore: 3 to 5 years old
H	Therefore: hot climate	PLUM, RED CHERRY, STRAWBERRY, REDCURRANT, PRESERVED FRUITS		
A	Therefore: matured in oak	CHOCOLATE		Therefore: (partly) new French oak
R	Therefore: 3 to 5 years old	TOBACCO, DRIED FRUITS		
A	Therefore: hot climate			
C	sweet	Therefore: 80 to 129 gr/l		
T	Therefore: grape with a relatively thin skin	astringent		Therefore: Old World
E	Therefore: warm climate	17%, full body		
R	Therefore: Old World			

Tasting note: This medium intense, garnet-colored, red has medium-intense aromas of prunes, game cherries and strawberry jam, chocolate and tobacco. Low acidity, very high alcohol, 80 to 129 gr/l residual sugars and soft tannins ensure a full body. And a low relative fruit intensity.

Riedel Vinum 6416-60

 10-15 °C   0.5 hours

 < $100   5-10 years

In the Banyuls-style: Rasteau (Rhône, France), Maury (Roussillon, France), Port, (Douro, Portugal).

Malbec: adopted in Argentina

Auxerrois (Cahors), Côt, Pressac

big
52,685 ha (1.17%)

THIN SKIN   THICK SKIN

SPARKLING   SWEET   MONO   BLEND   FORTIFIED   DRY

MALADAPTIVE   ADAPTIVE

HA 052,685

Originating from the Sud-Ouest and adopted in Argentina. Is a precocious variety that adapts easily to the short season at high altitudes; whether that is a thousand meters (Mendoza), two thousand meters (Cafayate) or three thousand meters (Jujuy). Malbec can cope with both the high UV as well as the extreme temperatures. The higher, the more aromatic, the deeper the color and the smoother the tannins. In Cahors, the thick skin makes for a deeply colored and tannic wine in an astringent style. Here Malbec must make up at least 70% of the blend for the appellation (supplemented with Merlot and Tannat), but often it is 100%. In Bordeaux and California, it is a typical blending grape too. In the Loire, Malbec is blended with Cabernet Franc and Gamay, sometimes as a blend of the crémants. Malbec has a thick skin and needs more sun and heat than Cabernet Sauvignon to mature. However, it then produces full, red wines with a berry fruit character.

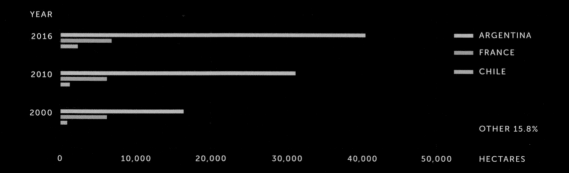

Following the statistics of Professor Anderson, Malbec is mainly growing in Argentina. Although the success in Argentina has led to modest growth elsewhere in the world.

Malbec at high altitudes

Maipú (Las Barrancas and Lunlunta) and Lujan de Cuyo (Perdriel, Agrelo, Las Compuertas, Vistalba), at seven hundred to nine hundred meters, are the Primera Zona for Malbec. Overall, this is an intensely-fruity, ripe style with full body. In the Uco Valley Malbec is sometimes planted up to fourteen-hundred meters. Varying per terroir – Tunuyán (Vistaflores, Los Arboles), Tupungato (Gualtallary) and San Carlos (La Consulta, Paraje Altamira) – the wines are juicier, more aromatic, spicy and peppery.

TRAPICHE, MEDALLA, MALBEC, MENDOZA, ARGENTINA

C	Therefore: grape with a thick skin	ruby		Therefore: 3 to 5 years old
H		REDCURRANT · BLACKCURRANT · BLUEBERRY · PLUM · BLACKBERRY		Therefore: Malbec
A	Therefore: oxidative winemaking	VANILLA · CEDAR · TOAST · CHOCOLATE · MOCHA		Therefore: (partly) new French oak
R	Therefore: 3 to 5 years old	TOBACCO		
A	Therefore: hot climate			
C	Therefore: dry wine	a lot of fruit ripeness		
T	Therefore: grape with a thick skin	ripe and soft		Therefore: New World
E	Therefore: warm climate	14 to 14.5%, full body		
R	Therefore: New World			

Riedel Vinum 6416-0

Tasting note: This deep, ruby-colored red has medium-intense aromas of red and black currant, black cherry, blue plum, vanilla, cedar, toast, tobacco and cacao. Medium acidity, high alcohol, lots of, but ripe and smooth tannins, and a high relative fruit intenstity.

 10-15 °C 0.5 hours   < $100   5-10 years

In the Malbec Mendoza-style: Bonarda (Mendoza, Argentina), Merlot (Washington State, United States), Shiraz (Stellenbosch, South Africa).

Originally from Cahors

Older than Bordeaux and the only Malbec appellation in France. Cahors is located in the southwest, bordering Bergerac in the northwest and Gaillac in South. Since the vineyards were completely destroyed by frost in 1956, it took until the late 1990s for the region to re-establish itself quality-wise. Typical Cahors is deeply colored and has a fleshy, spicy aroma, with some blackcurrant and cedar. Cahors is also tighter, more astringent and less full bodied than Mendoza.

CHÂTEAU DU CÈDRE, CAHORS, FRANCE

C	📶	Therefore: grape with a thick skin	ruby	Therefore: 3 to 5 years old
H	📶		REDCURRANT BLACKCURRANT BLACKCHERRY PLUM	Therefore: Malbec
A	📶	Therefore: oxidative winemaking	CEDAR TOAST PENCIL SHAVINGS	Therefore: (partly) new French oak
R	📶	Therefore: 3 to 5 years old	TOBACCO EARTH	
A	📶	Therefore: warm climate		
C	📶	Therefore: dry wine		
T	📶	Therefore: grape with a thick skin	astringent	Therefore: Old World
E	📶	Therefore: lots of sunshine (long season)	14%, full body	
R	📶	Therefore: Old World		

Tasting note: This deep, ruby-colored red has restrained aromas of red and black currant, black cherry, blue plum, cedar, toast and tobacco. Medium acidity, medium to high alcohol and astringent tannins. Full body and a low relative fruit intensity.

Riedel Vinum 6416-00

10-15 °C   2 hours

< $50

> 10 years

In the Cahors-style: *Madiran (France), Bandol (Provence, France), Bergerac (France).*

The ubiquitous Merlot

Picard, Langon

THIN SKIN   THICK SKIN   MALADAPTIVE   ADAPTIVE

Just as Cabernet Sauvignon dominates on the left bank of the Gironde in Bordeaux, Merlot is lord and master of the rest of Bordeaux. The question is, for how much longer? Due to climate change, Merlot is being harvested at increasingly higher sugar levels, sometimes already with enough sugar for 15% or 16% potential alcohol in the wine. That's partly because Merlot ripens earlier than Cabernet. It produces fruit-sweet wines that are not as tannin-rich as Médocs and therefore appear much rounder. If well made, they have a silky mouthfeel with an intoxicating aroma of plum and red fruit such as redcurrant, red cherries and strawberries. Merlot is planted in almost every country and can still grow and continue to enjoy great popularity. But, since the movie Sideways (2004), where Merlot was characterized as the 'anti-wine' it hasn't been easy for Merlot. And now climate change has been added to the equation.

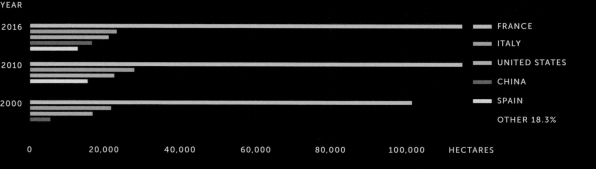

After decades of rampant growth, plantings of Merlot have stagnated and in several countries even retracted.

Right Bank Bordeaux

Saint-Émilion is one of the largest appellations of Bordeaux and produces more wine than Listrac, Moulis, Saint Estèphe, Pauillac, Saint Julien, and Margaux together. The town itself is the prettiest in Bordeaux, perched on the steep limestone cliffs slopes that house many of the region's best vineyards. The rest is situated on the flat, alluvial, sandy soils with a layer of gravel between the city and the Dordogne. Together with Pomerol, it produces the world's best Merlot-based wines.

CHÂTEAU LA TOUR FIGEAC, GRAND CRU CLASSÉ, SAINT-ÉMILION, FRANCE

C	Therefore: grape with a thick skin	ruby		Therefore: 5 to 10 years old
H		REDCURRANT · BLUEBERRY · PLUM · FLINT · BELL PEPPER		
A	Therefore: oxidative winemaking	CEDAR · TOAST · PENCIL SHAVINGS · MOCHA		Therefore: (partly) new French oak
R	Therefore: 5 to 10 years old	TOBACCO · EARTH		
A	Therefore: warm climate			
C	Therefore: dry wine			
T	Therefore: grape with a thick skin	astringent		Therefore: Old World
E	Therefore: lots of sunshine	14 to 15%, full body		
R	Therefore: Old World			

Tasting note: This deep, ruby-colored red has aromas of red currant, blueberry, red and blue plum, flint, vanilla, toast and pencil shavings. The wine is dry with low acidity, high alcohol, astringent tannins, and a low relative fruit intensity. Full body.

Riedel Vinum 6416-0

 10-15 °C   0.5 hours

 < $150

 > 10 years

In the Saint-Émilion-style: Bergerac (France), Cabernet Franc (Mendoza, Argentina), Carménère (Curicó, Chile).

Chilean Merlot

Maipo is located east of San Antonio and Casablanca and north of Cachapoal, around the capital Santiago. For a long time – and sometimes still – Merlot here is a vineyard blend of Merlot and Carménère, simply because they are sometimes planted together. But also, without Carménère, Chilean Merlot is a household name: fully ripe, intensely-fruity and with a typical Chilean perfumed nose because of the eucalyptus. From simple entry-level to complex, top-notch wine.

1865, MERLOT, MAIPO, CHILE

C	📶	Therefore: grape with a thick skin	ruby	Therefore: 3 to 5 years old
H	📶		REDCURRANT BLACKCURRANT PLUM MINT	Therefore: Chile
A	📶	Therefore: oxidative winemaking	VANILLA CEDAR TOAST MOCHA	Therefore: (partly) new French oak
R	📶	Therefore: 3 to 5 years old		
A	📶	Therefore: warm climate		
C	📶	Therefore: dry wine	a lot of fruit ripeness	
T	📶	Therefore: grape with a thick skin	ripe and smooth	Therefore: New World
E	📶	Therefore: lots of sunshine (high UV)	14 to 14.5%, full body	
R	📶	Therefore: New World		

Tasting note: This deep, ruby-colored red has aromas of red and black currant, blue and red plum, mint, vanilla and toast. The wine is dry with medium acidity, high alcohol, ripe tannins, and a intensely-fruity taste. Full body and a high relative fruit intensity.

Riedel Vinum
6416-0

 10-15 °C

 no

 < $50

> 10 years

In the Chilean Merlot-style: Carménère (Maipo, Chile), Merlot (Napa, California), Zweigelt (Burgenland, Austria).

172

Napa Valley Merlot

Napa Valley Merlot is a soft, plummy style, with velvety texture and ripe tannins. The variety is widely planted in the Napa Valley and commonly used in blends (to add body and fruit intensity). Merlot's meteoric rise in the nineties let to the variety being overplanted. The movie *Sideways* brought attention to the subsequent unfortunate downturn in quality. The impact of the movie has been difficult to pinpoint although a Sonoma State University Case Study noted a 2% decline in Merlot sales in the first three years following the movie.

DUCKHORN, MERLOT, NAPA VALLEY, CALIFORNIA

C	📶	Therefore: grape with a thick skin	ruby	Therefore: 3 to 5 years old
H	📶		REDCURRANT, BLACKCURRANT, PLUM, BLUEBERRY, BLACKBERRY	Therefore: New World
A	📶	Therefore: oxidative winemaking	VANILLA, CEDAR, TOAST, MOCHA	Therefore: (partly) new French oak
R	📶	Therefore: 3 to 5 years old		
A	📶	Therefore: warm climate		
C	📶	Therefore: dry wine	a lot of fruit ripeness	
T	📶	Therefore: grape with a thick skin	ripe and smooth	
E	📶	Therefore: lots of sunshine (high UV)	14 to 14.5%, full body	
R	📶	Therefore: New World		

Tasting note: This deep, ruby-colored red has aromas of black berry, blackcurrant, blueberry and plum, vanilla, toast, cedar and mocha. The wine is dry with low acidity, high alcohol, ripe tannins and a fruit forward palate. Full body and high relative fruit intensity.

Riedel Vinum 6416-0

 10-15 °C

 no

 < $50

> 10 years

In the Napa Valley Merlot-style: Merlot (Mendoza, Argentina), Carménère (Maipo, Chile), Merlot (Stellenbosch, South Africa).

big
52,554 ha (1.17%)

Mourvèdre as in Bandol and GSM

Mourvèdre, Mataro

THIN SKIN   THICK SKIN

SPARKLING   SWEET   MONO   BLEND   FORTIFIED   DRY

MALADAPTIVE   ADAPTIVE

HA 052,554

The variery is called Monastrell in its native Spain (Jumilla and Valencia), Mataro in Australia and California, and Mourvèdre in most other countries. Mourvèdre of Monastrell likes warm, dry climates and has small, thick-skinned grapes for a deep color and – especially in Bandol – lots of tannins. So many that it has been nicknamed Étrangle-Chien (dog strangler). These properties make the grape a suitable blending partner, especially with the rich Grenache and spicy Syrah (in GSM blend). Nevertheless, Monastrell or Mourvèdre. comes as a single varietal that is increasingly common not only in southern Spain but also in Provence and the southern Rhône valley. The reason Mourvèdre dominates so much along the coastal slopes of Bandol is that the sandy soils here did not provide a breeding ground for the grape aphid Phylloxera. The variety is also found in the Balearic Islands, in California, Washington State, South Australia, New South Wales and South Africa.

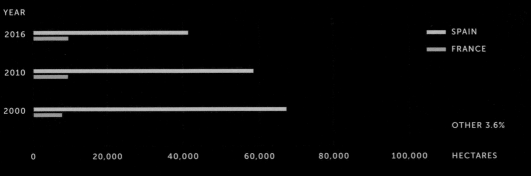

Monastrell (alas Mourvèdre) is predominantly a Spanish affair although plantings there have decreased while they have increased in France.

Mourvèdre is Monastrell

Phylloxera never had a chance in desert-like Jumilla, so the vines here remained ungrafted, until it happened in 1989. The grape aphid destroyed more than 60% of the wine acreage. Much has now been replanted (on grafted rootstock). Jumilla has broad valleys and plains crossed by gigantic mountain ridges. Monastrell feels at home in the extremely warm, long season that provides plenty of ripe tannins, jammy fruits, and a lot of alcohol.

JUAN GIL, JUMILLA, SPAIN

C	Therefore: grape with a thick skin	ruby		Therefore: 3 to 5 years old
H		PLUM, RAISINS, FIG, RED CHERRY, PRESERVED FRUITS		
A	Therefore: matured in oak	TOAST, SMOKE, MOCHA		Therefore: (partly) new French oak
R	Therefore: 3 to 5 years old	MEATY		
A	Therefore: hot climate			
C	Therefore: dry wine			
T	Therefore: grape with a thick skin	astringent		Therefore: Old World
E	Therefore: lots of sunshine (long season)	15%, full body		
R	Therefore: New World			

Tasting note: This deep, ruby-colored red has medium-intense aromas of prunes, raisins, fig paste, cherries, and earth, sometimes in a fleshy, rustic style, often with toast and smoky aromas. Low acidity, very high alcohol and medium intense but ripe tannins. Full body, and a low relative fruit intensity.

Riedel Vinum 6416-15

 10-15 °C · 0.5 hours

 < $50

 5-10 years

In the Jumilla-style: *Monastrell (Yecla, Alicante, Spain), Durif (Barossa, Australia), Zinfandel, Paso Robles (California).*

At its best in Bandol

Bandol, a small enclave bordering Côtes de Provence, gets its name from the fishing village that was once a flourishing port because of the wine trade. Mourvèdre was most resistant to Phylloxera, hence its dominance in Bandol. The vineyards are mainly located on the coast on a soil of sand and limestone. 'One vine, one bottle' is the local saying; hence the region has the lowest yields in France. The wine has a deep color and aromas of black fruits and cedar.

Riedel Vinum
6416-30

	DOMAINE TEMPIER, BANDOL, FRANCE				
C	)))	Therefore: grape with a thick skin	ruby		Therefore: 3 to 5 years old
H	)))		REDCURRANT BLACKCURRANT BLACKCHERRY PLUM GARRIGUE		
A	)))	Therefore: oxidative winemaking	CEDAR TOAST PENCIL SHAVINGS		Therefore: (partly) new French oak
R	))	Therefore: 3 to 5 years old	TOBACCO EARTH		
A	))	Therefore: warm climate			
C	)	Therefore: dry wine			
T	)))	Therefore: grape with a thick skin	ripe but astringent		Therefore: Old World
E	)))	Therefore: lots of sunshine (long season)	14%, full body		
R	))	Therefore: Old World			

Tasting note: This deep, ruby-colored red has medium-intense aromas of red and black currant and cherry, blue plum, and spices in a meaty style. Low acidity, high alcohol and lots of astringent tannins. Full body and a low relative fruit intensity.

10-15 °C   2 hours

< $100   > 10 years

In the Bandol-style: Madiran (France), Cahors (France), Bergerac (France).

Muscat: family of clones

Moscato, Moscatel, Zibibbo, Muscat Romain

NEUTRAL   AROMATIC   SPARKLING   SWEET   MONO   BLEND   FORTIFIED   DRY   MALADAPTIVE   ADAPTIVE

Theories about Muscat's origins date back to from 300 to 1000 BC in Egypt and Iran. This makes it one of the oldest grape varieties of all. Perhaps because of that long history there is not a single Muscat but a large family of clones (genetically identical offsprings of one parent, but nevertheless distinctive), each with their own regional nuance and character. Muscat Blanc à Petits Grains (Moscato Bianco in Italy) is the oldest and most famous. Another important branch of the family is Muscat of Alexandria, the second oldest member of the Muscat group, known for its light and fruity white wines. Muscat has aromas of rose blossom and grapes and is used for all types of wines, from dry whites (as in Alsace), to slightly sparkling fruity, fresh wines (such as in Moscato d'Asti and Asti Spumante), to fortified wines such as the French Vins Doux Naturals and the Australian Liqueur Muscats (from Rutherglen for example).

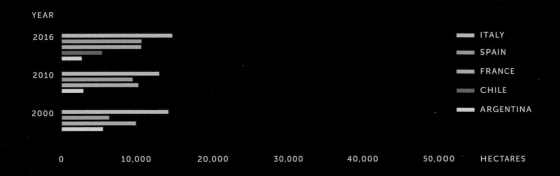

Muscat globally is modestly growing; while it is Muscat d'Alexandria in Spain and South-America, it is mainly Muscat à Petits Grains in Italy and France.

Noble variety in the Alsace

Although 50% of all wine from Alsace is still produced by cooperatives, the average quality of the (white) wines is very high. This is ensured by the clear air and abundant sun, the dry continental climate and diverse soil types, but also the culturally determined precision and dedication of the local population and the presence of noble varieties such as Muscat. Here it develops a more mineral, understated style with lower acidity, lots of alcohol and rich mouthfeel.

Riedel Vinum
6416-33

TRIMBACH, MUSCAT, ALSACE, FRANCE

C			lemon					Therefore: youthful
H		Therefore: aromatic grape variety	ROSE	BLOSSOM	GRAPE	MELON	PEAR	Therefore: Muscat
A		Therefore: reductive winemaking						
R		Therefore: youthful						
A		Therefore: warm climate						
C		Therefore: dry (but not bone dry)	rondeur, fatty texture					Therefore: sur lie
T								
E		Therefore: lots of sunshine (long season)	13.5%, medium body					
R		Therefore: Old World						

Tasting note: This pale, lemon-colored white has a strong perfume of roses, blossom, grapes, white flowers and melon, low acidity and medium plus alcohol, a creamy mouthfeel and a floral undertone. Medium body, and a low relative fruit intensity.

 < 10 °C   no   < $50 5-10 years

In the Alsace Muscat-style: Gelber Muskateller (Austria), Moscatel (Maule, Chile), Torrontes (Cafayate, Argentina).

Gelber Muskateller

Gelber Muskateller is Muscat Blanc á Petit Grains, a very old variety which dates back to the ancient world of the Mediterranean. Austria has 1,400 hectares planted, or approximately 3% of its total. It gained popularity with consumers especially at the end of the last century and since then, plantings in all wine growing regions in Austria have increased, especially in Steiermark. Gelber Muskateller is prone to rot in the vineyard and sensitive at flowering. That is why it performs best in warm sites.

WOHLMUTH, RIED STEINRIEGL, GELBER MUSKATELLER, SÜDSTEIERMARK, AUSTRIA				
C			lemon	Therefore: youthful
H		Therefore: aromatic grape variety	ROSE · BLOSSOM · GRAPE · MELON · PINEAPPLE	Therefore: Muscat
A		Therefore: reductive winemaking		
R		Therefore: youthful		
A		Therefore: moderate climate		
C		Therefore: dry		
T				
E		Therefore: moderate climate	12,5%, medium body	
R		Therefore: in between OW and NW style		

Tasting note: This pale, lemon-colored white has an intense perfume of roses, blossom, orange peel, grape and nutmeg, medium to high acidity and medium alcohol and body. Medium to high relative fruit intensity.

Riedel Vinum 6416-33

 < 10 °C   no

 < $50

 5-10 years

In the Gelber Muskateller-style:
Torrontès (Cafayate, Argentina), Muscat (Alto Adige, Italy).

Moscato d'Asti

Moscato d'Asti is a sparkling wine made from Muscat à Petits Grains from Piedmont. By law, the wine may only contain 5,5% alcohol. Using the 'Asti method', the grapes are pressed as quickly and carefully as possible to preserve harvest flavors. The must is then filtered and fermented in a pressure tank. Part of the carbon dioxide remains trapped, causing it to becomes sparkling. At about 5%, the wine is cooled back again to stop the fermentation.

LA MORANDINA, MOSCATO D'ASTI, PIEDMONT, ITALY

C	ᯤ		lemon					Therefore: youthful
H	ᯤ	Therefore: aromatic grape variety	ROSE	BLOSSOM	GRAPE	PINEAPPLE	ZEST	Therefore: Muscat
A	ᯤ	Therefore: reductive winemaking						
R	ᯤ	Therefore: youthful						
A	ᯤ	Therefore: moderate climate						
C	ᯤ	Therefore: sweet	70 to 100 gr/l, creamy mousse					Therefore: Asti-method
T	ᯤ							
E	ᯤ	Therefore: interruption fermentation	5,5%, light body					Therefore: Asti-method
R	ᯤ	Therefore: Old World						

Tasting note: This pale, lemon colored white has a strong perfume of roses, blossoms, grapes, ginger and zest, medium acidity and low alcohol (5.5%). Light body. A style unique to European wine regions with a low relative fruit intensity.

Riedel Vinum
6416-58

< 10 °C   no

< $50

< 5 jaar

In the Moscato d'Asti-style:
Asti (Piedmont, Italy).

180

Vin Doux Naturel

In the Rhône valley, it is all Muscat de Frontignan à Petit Grains. Maximum yields are thirty hectoliters per hectare with a sugar content higher than 252 grams per liter. After two days, the fermentation is interrupted by the addition of alcohol until an alcohol content of at least 15% is reached, along with at least 110 gr/l of residual sugars. A classic French dessert wine to serve with crème brûlée.

CHAPOUTIER, MUSCAT DE BEAUMES-DE-VENISE, VIN DOUX NATUREL, FRANCE				
C	🛜		lemon	Therefore: youthful
H	🛜	Therefore: aromatic grape variety	ROSE BLOSSOM GRAPE MELON PINEAPPLE	Therefore: Muscat
A	🛜	Therefore: reductive winemaking		
R	🛜	Therefore: youthful		
A	🛜	Therefore: warm climate		
C	🛜	Therefore: sweet	80 to 129 gr/l	
T	🛜			
E	🛜	Therefore: fortified wine	16 to 17%, full body	Therefore: Vin Doux Naturel
R	🛜	Therefore: Old World		

Tasting note: This pale, lemon-colored white has a strong perfume of roses, blossoms, grapes, melon, almond paste and orange peel, low acidity and, as it is fortified, high alcohol. A style unique to European wine regions. Full body, and a low relative fruit intensity.

Riedel Vinum
6416-33

 < 10 °C   no   < $50    5-10 years

In the Muscat de Beaumes-de-Venise-style: Muscat de Mireval (Languedoc-Roussillon, France), Muscat de Saint-Jean-de-Minervois (Languedoc, France), Muscat de Rivesaltes (Roussillon, France).

Passito

Originating from a small volcanic island with constant winds right in between Sicily and North Africa, better known as the Black Pearl of the Mediterranean. Made from dried Muscat of Alexandria (believed to have originated around the Nile Delta, near the Egyptian city of Alexandria). In Sicily it is called Zibibbo, meaning "raisin" in Arabic, evidence in favor of its alleged origin. Because of the winds on the island, Zibibbo has been pruned low for centuries.

DONNAFUGATA, BEN RYÉ, PASSITO DI PANTELLERIA, SICILIË, ITALY

C	📶		amber	Therefore: oxidative winemaking
H	📶	Therefore: aromatic grape variety	APRICOT BLOSSOM RAISINS ZEST GRAPE	Therefore: Muscat / passito
A	📶	Therefore: oxidative winemaking	PRESERVED FRUITS	
R	📶	Therefore: youthful		
A	📶	Therefore: warm climate		
C	📶	Therefore: luscious	200 gr/l	
T	📶			
E	📶	Therefore: concentrated (passito)	14%, full body	
R	📶	Therefore: Old World		

Tasting note: This medium intense, golden-colored white has an intense perfume of apricot jam, blossom, raisins and candied orange peel, medium acidity, and high alcohol. A style unique to European wine regions. Full body, and a low relative fruit intensity.

Riedel Vinum
6416-33

 10-15 °C   no

 < $50

 > 10 years

In the Passito di Pantelleria-style: Liqueur Muscats uit Victoria (Australia), Vin de Paille (France), Strohwein (of Schilfwein, Burgenland, Austria).

PEE-noh gree

Pinot Gris

Pinot Grigio, Ruländer, Grauburgunder, Grauer Burgunder, Malvoisie, Monemvasia, Szurkebarat, Sivi Pinot

medium
46,653 ha (1.04%)

SPARKLING SWEET MONO

FORTIFIED DRY BLEND

HA 046,653

NEUTRAL AROMATIC MALADAPTIVE ADAPTIVE

Pinot Gris is a noble variety in Alsace, where it is mainly found in the deep, clay-rich soils in the north. In Germany it is called Grauburgunder and in Italy, it is known as Pinot Grigio. Pinot Gris is a mutation within the Pinot family, a sibling of Pinot Noir and Pinot Blanc. The grapes are not white nor red but exhibit more of a pink-grey skin color (hence the *gris* and *grigio*, both of which translate to 'gray').

Pinot Gris generally has more aromas and body than Pinot Blanc and is very versatile at the dinner table. In many regions Pinot Gris is a versatile grape; it ranges from easy, entry-level quality made from high yields to minerally refined and refreshing styles with concentration and complexity, such as in Alsace, in Friuli and Alto Adige, where the grape comes into its own. Pinot Gris is also doing well in Oregon and in New Zealand. The premium qualities tend to have excellent aging potential with its higher extract, more exotic nose and distinctive spiciness.

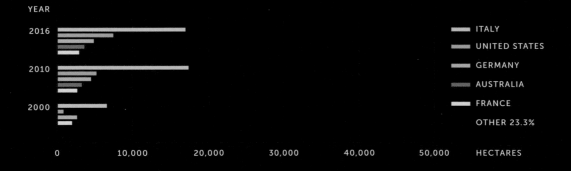

YEAR

2016

2010

2000

0   10,000   20,000   30,000   40,000   50,000   HECTARES

ITALY
UNITED STATES
GERMANY
AUSTRALIA
FRANCE
OTHER 23.3%

Pinot Gris, or should we say: Pinot Grigio, has enjoyed great popularity in the past 20 years. It has doubled in acreage in the past 10 years.

Pinot Gris in the Alsace

Pinot Gris has been present in the Alsace since at least the 16th century and produces wines in a variety of styles, from dry and off-dry to very sweet styles, from floral and fruity, fragrant and smoky, to spicy and honeyed. In 2020, new laws have been introduced which force the producers to show the perceived sweetness of the wines on the label: 'sec' (dry); 'demi-sec' (off-dry); 'moelleux' (medium-sweet) or 'doux' (sweet). Alternatively, a sweetness scale can be used.

TRIMBACH, PINOT GRIS, ALSACE, FRANCE

C	📶		lemon	Therefore: youthful
H	📶	Therefore: a neutral grape variety	YELLOW APPLE · PEAR · REINE CLAUDE · PEACH	
A	📶	Therefore: reductive winemaking		
R	📶	Therefore: youthful		
A	📶	Therefore: warm climate		
C	📶	Therefore: dry (but not bone dry)	fatty texture	Therefore: sur lie
T	📶			
E	📶	Therefore: lots of sunshine (long season)	13 to 14%, medium body	
R	📶	Therefore: Old World		

Tasting note: This medium intense, golden-colored white has a restrained scent of apple, pear and reine claude, low acidity, and high alcohol. With a creamy mouthfeel and lots of roundness. Medium body, and a low relative fruit intensity.

Riedel Vinum 6416-05

 < 10 °C   no

 < $50

 5-10 years

In the Pinot Gris-style: Pinot Blanc (Alsace, France), Pinot Gris (Willamette Valley, Oregon), Grauburgunder (Pfalz, Germany).

Pinot Grigio: Grand Cru in Alto Adige

Alto Adige became DOC in 1975 and is home to a wonderful collection of indigenous varieties (such as Lagrein, Schiava, and Gewürztraminer), Sauvignon Blanc and Pinot Noir; however, Pinot Grigio rules here. And in an exceptional style: dry, with plenty of freshness but also with body, aromatic intensity and a higher alcohol content. Above all, the wines made from Pinot Grigio are pure, as pure as the mountain air in which the grapes matured.

TIEFENBRUNNER, PINOT GRIGIO, ALTO ADIGE, ITALY

C	📶		lemon	Therefore: youthful
H	📶	Therefore: a neutral grape variety	YELLOW APPLE · PEAR · REINE CLAUDE · PEACH · MELON	
A	📶	Therefore: reductive winemaking		
R	📶	Therefore: youthful		
A	📶	Therefore: cool climate		
C	📶	Therefore: dry wine	fatty texture	Therefore: sur lie
T	📶			
E	📶	Therefore: lots of sunshine (high UV)	13 to 14%, medium to full body	
R	📶	Therefore: Old World		

Riedel Vinum 6416-05

Tasting note: This medium intense, golden-colored white has a restrained aroma of apple, pear, reine claude, peach, and melon, medium acidity, and medium alcohol. A creamy mouthfeel, medium body, and a medium relative fruit intensity.

 < 10 °C no

 < $50

 5-10 years

In the Pinot Grigio, Alto Adige-style:
Grauburgunder (Pfalz, Germany), Picpoul de Pinet, Languedoc (France), Albariño, Rias Baixas (Spain).

◀) PEE-no n'war

Pinot Noir

Pinot Nero, Pinot Negro, Spätburgunder, Blauburgunder

very big
105,724 ha (2.36%)

THIN SKIN   THICK SKIN   SPARKLING   SWEET   MONO   BLEND   FORTIFIED   DRY   MALADAPTIVE   ADAPTIVE

Pinot Noir is equivalent to Burgundy. In good years, and with the skill of a good winemaker, very exciting wines are produced there. So exciting, in fact, that they inspire winemakers around the world. But Pinot Noir is a frustrating grape. That's because with higher yields, concentration and typicity can disappear quickly. The thin skins make Pinot Noir wines light in color, medium in body, and with less prominent tannins. But, if it works out, Pinot Noirs can be among the most exciting wines in the world. Young Pinot Noir has red fruits such as raspberries, cherries and plums. With evolution in bottle the wine develops a sensual, silky mouthfeel, fleshy with a bouquet of beetroot and game. Pinot Noir also plays an important role in champagne and other sparkling wines. And it is grown all over the world, including Australia, Austria, Chile, France, New Zealand, South Africa and the USA. In Germany Pinot Noir is called Spätburgunder and in Austria Blauburgunder.

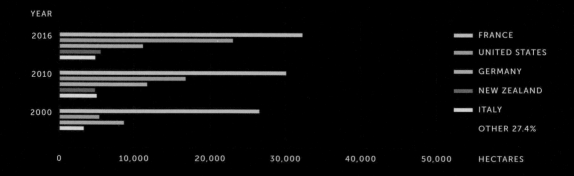

Following the statistics from Professor Anderson, Pinot Noir has enjoyed great popularity consistently in the past 20 years. Acreage actually grew more than 50% between 2016 and 2000.

Blanc de Noirs

The term Blanc de Noirs means a white wine made from red grapes. It is a term that has its origin in Champagne. If the grapes are pressed carefully enough, you will end up with a pure, white wine, even from red grapes. In the case of Gusbourne from England, it is 100% made of Pinot Noir sourced from their own vineyards in Kent and West Sussex which, just like in Champagne, enjoys a marginal, cool climate and poor soils.

GUSBOURNE, BLANC DE NOIRS, KENT, ENGLAND				
C			lemon	Therefore: youthful
H		Therefore: a neutral grape variety	YELLOW APPLE REINE CLAUDE ZEST RED CHERRY RASPBERRY	
A			BISCUIT DOUGH BREAD	autolysis, Therefore: méthode traditionelle
R		Therefore: recent disgorged		
A		Therefore: cool climate	lactic acids	Therefore: malo
C		Therefore: brut	persistent mousse	Therefore: méthode traditionelle
T				
E			12 to 12.5%	
R		Therefore: Old World		

Tasting note: This pale, lemon-colored sparkling shows a restrained expression of apple, Reine Claude, cherry and raspberry, biscuit and dough. In the mouth the wine is dry with high acidity, creamy mouthfeel, persistent mousse, and medium alcohol. Light to medium body; elegant with a low relative fruit intensity.

Riedel Vinum
6416-58

 < 10 °C   no   < $100   5-10 years

In the Blanc de Noirs-style: *Blanc de Noirs champagne (Côte des Bar, France), Blanc de Noirs (Tasmania, Australia), Blanc de Noirs Crémant de Bourgogne (France).*

Burgundy: the beating heart of Pinot Noir

The beating heart of Pinot Noir production is Burgundy, even more so in the Côte de Nuits than the Côte de Beaune. The Côte de Nuits Villages includes wines from a small number of villages, mainly in the far north and south of the Côte de Nuits: Fixin and Brochon in the north, Comblanchien, Corgoloin and Prissey in the south. Typical style, red Burgundy with restrained notes of earthy, red fruit, some oak complexity and balanced tannins.

JOSEPH DROUHIN, CHAMBOLLE-MUSIGNY, BOURGOGNE, FRANCE

C	📶	Therefore: grape with a thin skin	ruby	Therefore: 3 to 5 years old
H	📶		RED CHERRY · PLUM · BLACKCHERRY · FIG	Therefore: Pinot Noir
A	📶	Therefore: matured in oak	TOAST · CEDAR · PENCIL SHAVINGS	Therefore: (partly) new French oak
R	📶	Therefore: 3 to 5 years old	EARTH	
A	📶	Therefore: moderate climate		
C	📶	Therefore: dry wine		
T	📶	Therefore: grape with a thin skin	astringent	Therefore: Old World
E	📶		13 to 13.5%, medium body	
R	📶	Therefore: Old World		

Tasting note: This light, ruby-colored red has restrained aromas of blue and red plum, red cherry, toast and vanilla. The wine is dry with medium acidity, medium alcohol, moderate tannins and a restrained, earthy taste. Medium body and a low relative fruit intensity.

Riedel Vinum
6416-07

10-15 °C   0.5 hours

 < $150

 > 10 years

In the Burgundy-style: Pinot Noir (Alsace, France), Pinot Noir (Walker Bay, South Africa), Crus de Beaujolais (France).

Kiwi Pinots: fruit driven and spicy

I could have chosen Pinot Noirs from three different terroirs in New Zealand: from Central Otago at the southernmost tip of the South Island, and with it the world's southernmost wine region. It has a more continental style with lots of spice and fuller body. In the south of the North Island in Wairarapa (Martinborough), one finds what is perhaps the most Burgundian style in New Zealand. Then there is also Marlborough with its characteristic fruit intensity and touch of clove.

Cloudy Bay Pinot Noir bottle

CLOUDY BAY, PINOT NOIR, MARLBOROUGH, NEW ZEALAND				
C	Therefore: grape with a thin skin	ruby		Therefore: 3 to 5 years old
H		RED CHERRY, BLACKCHERRY, STRAWBERRY, RASPBERRY, CLOVE		Therefore: Pinot Noir
A	Therefore: oxidative winemaking	TOAST, CEDAR		Therefore: (partly) new French oak
R	Therefore: 3 to 5 years old			
A	Therefore: cool climate			
C	Therefore: dry wine			
T	Therefore: grape with a thin skin	ripe and soft		Therefore: New World
E	Therefore: lots of sunshine (high UV)	13.5%, medium body		
R	Therefore: New World			

Tasting note: This light, ruby-colored red has almost sweet, intensely-fruity aromas of red and black cherry, strawberry, raspberry, cloves, toast and vanilla. The wine is dry with higher acidity, higher alcohol, low tannins, medium body and a high relative fruit intensity.

Riedel Vinum
6416-07

 10-15 °C

 no

 < $50

5-10 years

In the Marlborough-style: *Pinot Noir (Central Otago, Martinborough, New Zealand), Pinot Noir (Mornington Pensinsula, Yarra, Tasmania, Australia), Pinot Noir (Casablanca, San Antonio, Costa, Chile).*

Californian Pinot

Sonoma County on the North Coast is California's Largest American Viticultural Area (AVA) with about 20,000 hectares of vineyards. Nevertheless, and completely unjustly, it has always been in the shadow of its big neighbor Napa, even though it is more picturesque with its orchards and farms. Under the influence of the cool, misty effects of the coastal climate, and a myriad of individual soil types and sites, it can become top-class Pinot Noir.

Riedel Vinum
6416-07

MARIMAR ESTATE, PINOT NOIR, SONOMA, CALIFORNIA

C	Therefore: grape with a thin skin	ruby	Therefore: 3 to 5 years old
H		RED CHERRY, BLACK CHERRY, PLUM, RASPBERRY, REDCURRANT	Therefore: Pinot Noir
A	Therefore: oxidative winemaking	TOAST, CEDAR	Therefore: (partly) new French oak
R	Therefore: 3 to 5 years old	EARTH	
A	Therefore: moderate climate		
C	Therefore: dry wine		
T	Therefore: grape with a thin skin	ripe and soft	Therefore: New World
E	Therefore: lots of sunshine (long season)	13 to 14%, medium body	
R	Therefore: New World		

Tasting note: This light, ruby-colored red has intense aromas of ripe red and black cherry, blue plum, raspberry jam, toast, and cedar. The wine is dry with medium acidity, higher alcohol, low tannins, and a more mature overall style. Medium body, and a high relative fruit intensity.

10–15 °C   no

< $100

5–10 years

In the Sonoma-style: Pinot Noir (Santa Barbara, Russian River, Monterey, California), Pinot Noir (Willamette Valley, Oregon), Pinot Noir (Walker Bay, Elgin, South Africa).

Spätburgunder

In Germany Pinot Noir is called Spätburgunder. In the past, the grape was mainly grown in the warmest areas (Pfalz, Württemberg and Baden), nowadays also in cooler areas like Nahe, Rheingau, Rheinhessen and Ahr. In their qualitative capacity, German Pinots can compete with the best of Burgundy but stylistically they are between the Old and New world. With more fruit than in Burgundy, more freshness and more consistency, but less exotic and spicy aromas of cloves than in New Zealand.

VILLA WOLF, SPÄTBURGUNDER, PFALZ, GERMANY

C		Therefore: grape with a thin skin	ruby	Therefore: 3 to 5 years old
H			RED CHERRY, CRANBERRY, PLUM, RASPBERRY, CLOVE	Therefore: Pinot Noir
A		Therefore: oxidative winemaking	TOAST, MOCIIA, CARAMEL	Therefore: (partly) new French oak
R		Therefore: 3 to 5 years old		
A		Therefore: cool climate		
C		Therefore: dry wine		
T		Therefore: grape with a thin skin	astringent	Therefore: Old World
E			13.5%, medium body	
R		Therefore: Old World		

Tasting note: This light, ruby-colored red has intense aromas of red cherry, currant, plum, raspberry, cloves, toast, coffee, and toffee. The wine is dry with high acidity, medium alcohol, moderate tannins, and a pronounced, spicy taste. Light to medium body; elegant. With a medium relative fruit intensity.

Riedel Vinum 6416-07

10-15 °C   no

< $50   5-10 years

In the Spätburgunder-style: Pinot Noir (Martinborough, New Zealand), Pinot Noir (Alto Adige, Italy), Pinot Noir (Thermenregion, Austria).

Chilean ripeness

In many ways, Chile's west coast resembles New Zealand's east coast in terms of growing conditions. In both cases, an intensely fruity Pinot Noir is created with fresh acidity and lots of pure, ripe flavors. The fruit of San Antonio (or Leyda) may be even riper, purer and more aromatic than New Zealand but lacks the spicy touch of clove with even softer tannins than in New Zealand. It cannot be compared to Burgundy because of its fruit-intensive style.

VIÑA LEYDA, PINOT NOIR, SAN ANTONIO, CHILE

C	📶	Therefore: grape with a thin skin	ruby					Therefore: 3 to 5 years old
H	📶		RED CHERRY	BLACKCHERRY	STRAWBERRY	RASPBERRY	MINT	Therefore: Pinot Noir
A	📶	Therefore: oxidative winemaking	TOAST	CEDAR				Therefore: (partly) new French oak
R	📶	Therefore: 3 to 5 years old						
A	📶	Therefore: cool climate						
C	📶	Therefore: dry wine						
T	📶	Therefore: grape with a thin skin	ripe and soft					Therefore: New World
E	📶	Therefore: lots of sunshine (high UV)	14%, medium body					
R	📶	Therefore: New World						

Tasting note: This light, ruby-colored red has almost sweet, intensely-fruity aromas of red and black cherry, strawberry, raspberry, toast and cedar. The wine is dry with higher acidity, medium alcohol, low tannins, and expressive, aromatic, pure, red fruit flavors. Medium body. High relative fruit intensity.

Riedel Vinum
6416-07

 10-15 °C no

 < $50 5-10 years

In the San Antonio-style: *Pinot Noir (Casablanca, Costa, Chile), Pinot Noir (Marlborough, Central Otago, Martinborough, New Zealand), Pinot Noir (Mornington Pensinsula, Yarra, Tasmania, Australia).*

Oregon Pinot

The Willamette Valley is protected by the Coastal Range to the west, the Cascades to the east and a series of hill ranges to the north. Named after the Willamette River, it stands on an old volcanic soil and dried up seabed covered with gravel, silt, rocks and boulders caused by flooding from Montana and Washington. A continental climate with some maritime influences, it is a large wine region (150 miles long and 60 wide) with seven appellations including Dundee Hills.

DOMAINE DROUHIN OREGON, PINOT NOIR, WILLAMETTE VALLEY, OREGON

C	Therefore: grape with a thin skin	ruby		Therefore: 3 to 5 years old
H		RED CHERRY BLACKCHERRY PLUM WET STONE		Therefore: Pinot Noir
A	Therefore: oxidative winemaking	TOAST CEDAR		Therefore: (partly) new French oak
R	Therefore: 3 to 5 years old			
A	Therefore: moderate climate			
C	Therefore: dry wine			
T	Therefore: grape with a thin skin	ripe and soft		Therefore: New World
E	Therefore: lots of sunshine (long season)	14%, medium body		
R	Therefore: New World			

Tasting note: This light, ruby-colored red has intense aromas of ripe red and black cherry, blue plum, earth, toast and cedar. The wine is dry with medium acidity, medium alcohol, low tannins, and a ripe style overall. Medium body, and a high relative fruit intensity.

Riedel Vinum
6416-07

10-15 °C   no

< $100

5-10 years

In the Willamette-style: *Pinot Noir (Santa Barbara, Russian River, Monterey, California), Pinot Noir (Alto Adige, Italy), Pinot Noir (Walker Bay, Elgin, South Africa).*

Pinot Nero

Grown at high altitudes, Pinot Noir produces a completely different style than the Pinot Noirs benefiting from cool coasts. In that regard, Pinot Noir is the best-kept secret among the red wines of Alto Adige. The perfume of red cherries and berries with notes of cloves and violets make for a very special version. As pure as the mountain air of the vineyards. Ripe yet very spicy and elegant. With higher alcohol and fuller body.

TIEFENBRUNNER, PINOT NOIR, ALTO ADIGE, ITALY				
C	Therefore: grape with a thin skin	ruby		Therefore: 3 to 5 years old
H		RED CHERRY · REDCURRANT · STRAWBERRY · CLOVE · PLUM		Therefore: Pinot Noir
A	Therefore: oxidative winemaking	TOAST · CEDAR		Therefore: (partly) new French oak
R	Therefore: 3 to 5 years old			
A	Therefore: cool climate			
C	Therefore: dry wine			
T	Therefore: grape with a thin skin	ripe and soft		Therefore: Old World
E	Therefore: lots of sunshine (high UV)	14%, medium body		
R	Therefore: Old World			

Tasting note: This light, ruby-colored red has pure intensely fruity aromas of red cherry and berry, strawberry, cloves, toast, and cedar. The wine is dry with higher acidity, high alcohol, lower tannins, and aromatic, pure, intensely-fruity flavors. Medium body and a medium relative fruit intensity.

Riedel Vinum 6416-07

 10-15 °C   no

  < $50   5-10 years

In the Alto Adige-style: Pinot Noir (Thermenregion, Austria), Spätburgunder (Pfalz, Germany), Pinot Noir (Martinborough, New Zealand).

◀) REEZ-ling

big
57,777 ha (1.33%)

German and still undervalued: Riesling

Weisser Riesling, Johannisberg Riesling, Johannisberger, Rhine Riesling, Riesling Renano

NEUTRAL   AROMATIC

SPARKLING   SWEET   MONO

FORTIFIED   DRY   BLEND

MALADAPTIVE   ADAPTIVE

The aroma of Riesling ranges from yellow to green apples, lemon to riper fruit and honey. Australian Rieslings often have an aromatic lime scent. Riesling comes in many styles: from bone dry to luscious. The sweetest Rieslings are often made with grapes affected by noble rot, late harvest or by allowing the grapes to freeze hard enough to crack (minimum -8°C). Eiswein (ice wine) mainly occurs in Germany, Austria and Canada. Riesling (with its pronounced perfume and intense acidity) has enormous aging potential. From pure harvest flavors to a bouquet that the French call *goût de pétrole* (a kerosene-like aroma). The warmer the climate, the faster Riesling develops this very grape-specific aroma. For example, Rieslings from the Australian Eden or Clare Valley often have already a kerosene-like note (harvest aroma) upon release, while in Germany, Austria and Alsace it is really a sign of age (ripening aroma).

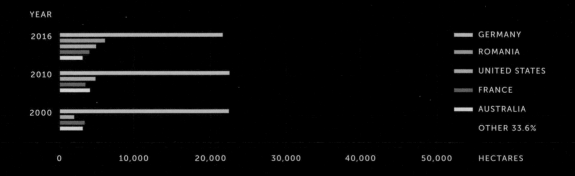

YEAR

GERMANY
ROMANIA
UNITED STATES
FRANCE
AUSTRALIA
OTHER 33.6%

It is clear from Professor Anderson's figures that Riesling has grown steadily over the past two decades. In the leading Riesling-producing countries it is stable but in countries like the United States and Austria (along with a handful of other wine countries) plantings are on the rise.

The perfect balance between acidity and sweetness

With its steep vineyards on porous slate in tight hairpin bends, the Mosel extends from Trier to Koblenz, where it flows into the Rhine. As the crow flies, it's about 120 kilometers although the river meanders for nearly 250 kilometers. With some vines planted on super-steep, almost seventy-degree slopes, mechanical harvesting is either impossible or impractical. Kabinett is made with sufficient residual sweetness to balance the very high acidity.

DR. LOOSEN, WEHLENER SONNENUHR RIESLING KABINETT, MOSEL, GERMANY

C	📶		lemon		Therefore: youthful
H	📶	Therefore: aromatic grape variety	GRANNY SMITH · LEMON · LIME · PINEAPPLE · YELLOW APPLE		Therefore: Riesling
A	📶	Therefore: reductive winemaking			
R	📶	Therefore: youthful			
A	📶	Therefore: marginal climate	malic acids		Therefore: no malo
C	📶	Therefore: off dry	20 to 50 gr/l		Therefore: kabinett
T	📶				
E	📶		8 to 9%, light body		Therefore: German signature
R	📶	Therefore: Old World			

Tasting note: This pale, lemon-colored white has intense aromas of apple, lemon and lime. The wine is off-dry; the residual sweetness balances the high acidity. The wine has low to medium alcohol and mineral, apple-y, citrusy flavors. Light body and a low relative fruit intensity.

Riedel Vinum 6416-15

 < 10 °C no < $50 · > 10 years

In the Mosel Guts/Ortswein-style: Riesling Federspiel (Wachau, Austria), Riesling (Alsace, France), Riesling (Luxemburg).

Grosses Gewächs is Grand Cru

Believing that the origin – the terroir – is the key to making great wines in Germany, the VDP (Verein Deutsche Prädikatweingüter: an elite club of about two hundred German top producers) has established its own classification. Grosses Gewächs is a fundamentally dry wine from a Grand Cru vineyard (Grosse Lage) and represents the highest quality. These wines offer the ultimate in typicity, concentration, complexity and length, and they often have a huge aging potential.

Riedel Vinum
6416-15

C	📶		lemon		Therefore: youthful
H	📶	Therefore: aromatic grape variety	YELLOW APPLE LEMON LIME PINEAPPLE FLINT		Therefore: Riesling
A	📶	Therefore: reductive winemaking			
R	📶	Therefore: youthful			
A	📶	Therefore: cool climate	malic acids		Therefore: no malo
C	📶	Therefore: trocken (but not bone dry)	rondeur		
T	📶				
E	📶		13 to 14%, medium body		
R	📶	Therefore: Old World			

DR. LOOSEN, GRAACHER HIMMELREICH, RIESLING GROSSES GEWÄCHS, MOSEL, GERMANY

Tasting note: This pale, lemon-colored white has intense aromas of apple, lemon, and lime. The wine is fundamentally dry, with medium alcohol, and mineral, concentrated flavors. Flinty. Medium body. Long finish, and a medium relative fruit intensity.

  < 10 °C   no

 < $100   > 10 years

In the Mosel Grosse Lage-style: Riesling Smaragd (Wachau, Austria), Riesling Grand Cru (Alsace, France).

Clare Riesling

An hour north of Adelaide you expect a hot climate due to the latitude. And yet it is ideal for Riesling, because of its altitude (starting at about four hundred meters), low relative humidity (40%), the high UV, the large day/night differences, a cooling sea breeze from the southwest and soil (cooling red loam over marl-like limestone and shale). Riesling is the star in a lime sorbet style with fine minerality and excellent aging potential.

GROSSET, SPRINGVALE, CLARE VALLEY RIESLING, AUSTRALIA

C	🛜		lemon		Therefore: youthful
H	🛜	Therefore: aromatic grape variety	LIME · LEMON · GRANNY SMITH · RHUBARB · PETROL		Therefore: Riesling
A	🛜	Therefore: reductive winemaking			
R	🛜	Therefore: youthful			
A	🛜	Therefore: cool climate	malic acids		Therefore: no malo
C	🛜	Therefore: dry			
T	🛜				
E	🛜	Therefore: lots of sunshine (long season)	12.5 to 13.5%, medium body		
R	🛜	Therefore: New World			

Tasting note: This pale, lemon-colored white has intense aromas of lime sorbet, lemon ice cream, rhubarb, green apple and a touch of kerosene. The wine is dry with high acidity, medium alcohol, and expressive, citrus-intense flavors. Medium body, and a high relative fruit intensity.

Riedel Vinum 6416-15

 < 10 °C   no

 < $50

 > 10 years

In the Clare Valley Riesling-style: Riesling (West-Australia, Tasmania, Eden Valley, Australia), Riesling (Finger Lakes, New York), Riesling (Costa, Chile).

198

Alsace Riesling

Riesling is the most characteristic grape variety from Alsace and perhaps even the showpiece. Due to the sunny, dry climate – and slightly more oxidative winemaking – a rich style is created with more body, slightly less acidity but more mouthfeel than the wines produced by their Eastern neighbors. Riesling in Alsace varies from bone-dry to semi-sweet. The much more concentrated Grands Crus have great aging potential. Great food wine.

Riedel Vinum
6416-15

TRIMBACH, RIESLING, ALSACE, FRANCE				
C			lemon	Therefore: youthful
H		Therefore: aromatic grape variety	YELLOW APPLE LEMON LIME PINEAPPLE FLINT	Therefore: Riesling
A		Therefore: reductive winemaking		
R		Therefore: youthful		
A		Therefore: moderate climate	malic acids	Therefore: no malo
C		Therefore: dry (but not bone dry)		
T				
E			13 to 14%, medium body	
R		Therefore: Old World		

Tasting note: This pale, lemon-colored white has intense aromas of yellow apple, lime, pineapple, green apple, and Reine Claude. The wine is usually dry with medium alcohol, high acidity, and medium body. Low relative fruit intensity.

 < 10 °C   no < $100 > 10 years

In the Alsace-style: Riesling (Luxemburg), Riesling Ortswein (Pfalz), Riesling Federspiel (Austria)

Austrian Riesling: mineral and dry

The Wachau is a UNESCO World Heritage Site with its steep, terraced vineyards in the narrow Danube valley between Melk and Krems. From harvest year 2020, the Wachau has a DAC (Districtus Austriae Controllatus, the Austrian appellation). In addition, the three style categories remain: Steinfeder, Federspiel, and most concentrated, ripe and complex: Smaragd. Austrians love their Rieslings bone-dry and use sur lie rather than residual sugar to keep the acidity in check.

DOMÄNE WACHAU, RIESLING SMARAGD, WACHAU, AUSTRIA

C			lemon	Therefore: youthful
H		Therefore: aromatic grape variety	GRANNY SMITH · LEMON · LIME · REINE CLAUDE · FLINT	Therefore: Riesling
A		Therefore: reductive winemaking		
R		Therefore: youthful		
A		Therefore: cool climate	malic acids	Therefore: no malo
C		Therefore: dry	creamy texture	Therefore: sur lie
T				
E			12.5 to 13.5%, medium body	
R		Therefore: New World		

Tasting note: This pale, lemon-colored white has intense aromas of apple, lemon and lime, Reine Claude and flint. The wine is bone dry, has medium alcohol, and mineral, concentrated flavors. Medium to full body, and a low relative fruit intensity.

Riedel Vinum
6416-15

 < 10 °C   no

 < $100

 > 10 years

In the Wachau Smaragd-style: Riesling Grosse Lage (Pfalz, Nahe, Rheingau, Germany), Riesling Grand Cru (Alsace, France).

Noble Sweet

Beerenauslese literally means: grape selection. The term is often abbreviated as 'BA' in relation to Trockenbeerenauslese, which is often referred to as 'TBA'. Both are affected by noble rot; for BA in large part, for TBA completely. This results in noble sweet wines with very high residual sugars but also very high acidity. Due to the low yields per hectare and the manual picking in 'courses' BA and especially TBA wines can be (very) expensive.

DR. LOOSEN, RIESLING BEERENAUSLESE, MOSEL, GERMANY

C	📶		golden		Therefore: youthful
H	📶		YELLOW APPLE ZEST LEMON PINEAPPLE HONEY		Therefore: Botrytis
A	📶	Therefore: reductive winemaking			
R	📶	Therefore: youthful			
A	📶	Therefore: cool climate	malic acids		Therefore: no malo
C	📶	Therefore: sweet	100 to 150 gr/l		Therefore: Beerenauslese
T	📶				
E	📶		6 to 8%, medium body		Therefore: German signature
R	📶	Therefore: Old World			

Tasting note: This pale, lemon-colored white has a perfume of apple, zest, pineapple, honey and lemon, lots of residual sugars, very high acidity and low alcohol. A mineral undertone. Unique style. Medium body and a medium relative fruit intensity.

Riedel Vinum
6416-33

< 10 °C   no

< $150

> 10 years

In the Mosel Beerenauslese-style: Ausbruch (Neusiedlersee, Austria), Trockenbeerenauslese (Mosel, Germany), Selections de Grains Nobles (Alsace, France).

Riesling 0.0

Just because the wine is non-alcoholic doesn't mean that taste or quality have to be sacrificed. The recipe of Dr. Loosen starts with a regular Kabinett Mosel Riesling with a low alcohol content and a natural balance between acidity and residual sugars. The base wine remains intact except for removing the little bit of alcohol there was – via vacuum distillation. It doesn't get any better than this when it comes to 0.0 wine!

		DR. LOOSEN, SOBR, MOSEL, GERMANY		
C			lemon	Therefore: youthful
H		Therefore: aromatic grape variety	GRANNY SMITH LEMON LIME PINEAPPLE YELLOW APPLE	Therefore: Riesling
A		Therefore: reductive winemaking		
R		Therefore: youthful		
A		Therefore: marginal climate	malic acids	Therefore: no malo
C		Therefore: off dry	20 to 50 gr/l	Therefore: kabinett sweetness
T				
E		Therefore: de-alcoholized	0.0 very light body	
R		Therefore: Old World		

Tasting note: This pale, lemon-colored white has intense aromas of yellow apple, lime, green apple, lemon, and Reine Claude. The wine is slightly sweet with high acidity, and a characteristic Mosel juiciness. Truly 0.0, very light bodied with a low relative fruit intensity.

Riedel Vinum
6416-15

 < 10 °C

 no

 < $50

> 5 years

Sangiovese: Jupiter's blood

Brunello, Sangiovese Grosso, Morellino, Prugnolo, Nielluccio

big
73,741 ha (1.64%)

THIN SKIN   THICK SKIN

SPARKLING   SWEET   MONO

FORTIFIED   DRY   BLEND

MALADAPTIVE   ADAPTIVE

Sangiovese is the most widely planted grape in Italy. Sangiovese means *sanguis Jovis*, or the 'blood of Jove'. Whether or not the wine can be compared with 'Jove's blood' depends entirely on the yields and the winemaker because Sangiovese is made in very different qualities. Nevertheless, it forms the basis of all the great Tuscan red wines: Chianti, Brunello di Montalcino and Vino Nobile di Montepulciano. The grape has a relatively high acidity and a good tannin structure. The most characteristic aromas are plum, cherry, tobacco and tea.

Outside of Tuscany, Sangiovese is widely planted in Lazio, Umbria, Le Marche and Corsica. In Corsica it has distinctive harvest aromas of *maquis* (the thicket around the vineyards composed of sage, juniper, heather, oak, and myrtle). Worldwide, Sangiovese has found its way to California and Australia, where its high acidity is an asset in hot climates.

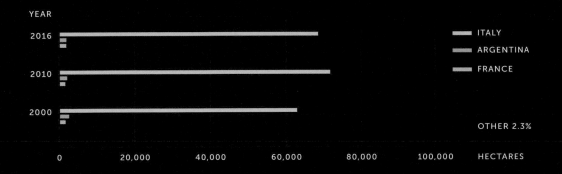

ITALY
ARGENTINA
FRANCE

OTHER 2.3%

Evident from Professor Anderson's figures is that Italy dominates the global acreage of Sangiovese. After some growth this century it has now stabilized.

Chianti Classico

Chianti Classico, a DOCG with about 7.000 hectares between Florence and Siena to the foothills of the Apennines, comprises two styles: the full, fleshy style of the lower sandy, alluvial soils and the more elegant, finer style of the higher limestone. Chianti Classico consists of a minimum of 80% Sangiovese and a maximum of 20% Canaiolo, Merlot and Cabernet Sauvignon and will not be released until October 1 of the year following the harvest.

Riedel Vinum
6416-90

VILLA ANTINORI, CHIANTI CLASSICO, TUSCANY, ITALY

C	Therefore: grape with a thick skin	ruby		Therefore: 3 to 5 years old
H		PLUM, RED CHERRY, BLACK TEA, FIG, REDCURRANT		Therefore: Sangiovese (blend)
A	Therefore: oxidative winemaking	CEDAR, TOAST		Therefore: (partly) new French oak
R	Therefore: 3 to 5 years old	TOBACCO		
A	Therefore: moderate climate			
C	Therefore: dry wine			
T	Therefore: grape with a thick skin	astringent		Therefore: Old World
E	Therefore: lots of sunshine (long season)	13.5 to 14.5%, full body		
R	Therefore: Old World			

Tasting note: This medium, ruby-colored red has medium-intense aromas of red and black cherry, plum, tea, tobacco, and leather. Medium plus acidity, medium to medium plus alcohol, and medium plus tannins provide a medium to full body, and a low relative fruit intensity.

 10-15 °C 0.5 hours

 < $100   > 10 years

In the Chianti-style: *Vino Nobile di Montepulciano (Tuscany, Italy), Brunello di Montalcino (Tuscany, Italy), Carmignano (Tuscany, Italy.*

🔊 sow-vuhn-YOWN blangk

Sauvignon Blanc: one of the most aromatic in the world

Sauvignon Jaune, Blanc Fumé, Muskat-Silvaner, Fumé blanc

Sauvignon Blanc is one of the most aromatic grapes in the world, with an intense 'green' nose: green apple, grasss, boxwood, green tomato, asparagus, gooseberry, grapefruit and passion fruit. That green smell is often also a harbinger of a fresh acidity as Sauvignon Blanc does well in particular cool climates such as the Loire, Alto Adige, Styria, Friuli, New Zealand, San Antonio and the Western Cape. And although the wines from Sancerre, Pouilly-Fumé, Quincy, Reuilly and Menetou-Salon rarely mention the grape variety on the label, this is where the most mineral, dry and understated Sauvignon Blancs in the world are produced. Sauvignon Blanc is also the basis of most white Bordeaux in a classic coalition with Semillon, often aged in oak. These are richer wines, fuller and rounder, with less acidity and more vanilla and toast. Depending on the terroir, either gooseberry, passion fruit, grass, boxwood, grapefruit, tomato leaf or granny smith is the dominating aroma.

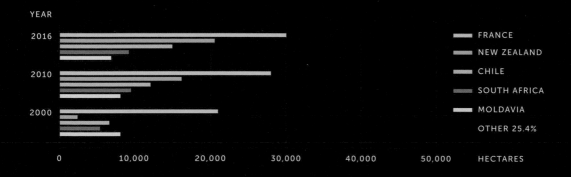

The statistics confirm the global success story of Sauvignon Blanc. It doubled in vineyard size in just 15 years. It did well in France, New Zealand and Chile, amongst other countries.

Sancerre

Sancerre is located on the left bank of the Loire opposite Pouilly-Fumé. While Pouilly-Fumé is compact and homogeneous, the fourteen municipalities of Sancerre are spread over almost 3.000 hectares in various valleys and on three different soils: silex (white flint that takes care of the fine structure and restrained perfume), terres blanches (calcareous clay that produces a lot of fruit richness), and caillottes (a soil full of large limestones).

JOSEPH MELLOT, SANCERRE, FRANCE

					Therefore:
C			lemon		youthful
H		Therefore: aromatic grape variety	GRANNY SMITH / GRAPEFRUIT / ASPARAGUS / WET STONE / GOOSEBERRY		Therefore: Sauvignon Blanc
A		Therefore: reductive winemaking			
R		Therefore: youthful			
A		Therefore: cool climate	malic acids		Therefore: no malo
C		Therefore: dry wine	creamy texture		Therefore: sur lie
T					
E			13 to 14%, medium body		
R		Therefore: Old World			

Tasting note: This pale, lemon-colored white has medium plus intense aromas of granny smith, boxwood, gooseberry, and grapefruit. In the mouth the wine is dry, with lots of acidity, medium to high alcohol, and a mineral undertone. Medium body, and a low relative fruit intensity.

Riedel Vinum 6416-33

 < 10 °C

 no

 < $50

5-10 years

In the Sancerre-style: Pouilly Fumé, Menetou-Salon, Quincy, Reuilly (Loire, France), Sauvignon Blanc de Touraine (Loire, France), Sauvignon Blanc and Verdejo (Rueda, Spain).

Marlborough Sauvignon Blanc

It was Sauvignon Blanc that put Marlborough and New Zealand on the map for wine lovers. The sunny, cool, windy north of the South Island created a unique style that could neither be ignored nor imitated. What makes Marlborough special is its unusual combination of long days, cool nights, intense sunlight and – in most years – dry autumn months. This gives the grapes a lot of time to ripen without losing their signature gooseberry-rich acidity.

CLOUDY BAY, MARLBOROUGH SAUVIGNON BLANC, NEW ZEALAND

C			lemon		Therefore: youthful
H		Therefore: aromatic grape variety	GOOSEBERRY GRAPEFRUIT GRANNY SMITH LIME PASSION FRUIT		Therefore: Sauvignon Blanc
A		Therefore: reductive winemaking			
R		Therefore: youthful			
A		Therefore: marginal climate	malic acids		Therefore: no malo
C		Therefore: dry wine	fatty texture		Therefore: sur lie
T					
E		Therefore: lots of sunshine (high UV)	12.5 to 13.5%, medium body		
R		Therefore: New World			

Tasting note: This pale, lemon-colored white has intense spicy aromas of gooseberry, grapefruit, granny smith, lime, lemon, and passion fruit. In the mouth, the wine is dry, with intense (malic) acidity, a creamy mouthfeel, and medium alcohol. Medium body, and a high relative fruit intensity.

Riedel Vinum
6416-33

 < 10 °C no

 < $50

 < 5 jaar

In the Marlborough Sauvignon Blanc-style: Sauvignon Blanc (San Antonio, Casablanca, Costa, Chile), Sauvignon Blanc de Touraine (Loire, France), Sauvignon Blanc (Tasmania, Australia).

8 Wine's Internationals   207

As pure as the mountain air

Sauvignon Blanc was introduced from France to Alto Adige at the end of the 19th century. At high altitudes, taking advantage of the cool conditions in Alto Adige at the foothills of the Alps, it has become one of the region's leading wines. That's because it retains it's beautiful acidity here, without losing its aromatic intensity and yet still builds up a lot of mouthfeel and alcohol. Unmistakably Alto Adige because of the typical notes of tomato leaf and green tomato.

TIEFENBRUNNER, SAUVIGNON BLANC, RACHTL, ALTO ADIGE, ITALY

C			lemon		Therefore: youthful
H		Therefore: aromatic grape variety	TOMATO LEAF, GRAPEFRUIT, GRANNY SMITH, LIME, PINEAPPLE		Therefore: Sauvignon Blanc
A		Therefore: reductive winemaking			
R		Therefore: youthful			
A		Therefore: marginal climate	malic acids		Therefore: no malo
C		Therefore: dry wine	fatty texture		Therefore: sur lie
T					
E		Therefore: lots of sunshine (high UV)	13.5 to 14.5%, medium body		
R		Therefore: Old World			

Tasting note: This pale, lemon-colored white has intense aromas of tomato leaf, gooseberry, grapefruit, and green apple. The wine is dry with high acidity, medium plus alcohol, and an dominant tomato-leaf aroma and flavor. Medium body, and a medium relative fruit intensity.

Riedel Vinum 6416-33

 < 10 °C   no

 < $50

5-10 years

In the Sauvignon Blanc Alto Adige-style:
Sauvignon Blanc (Steiermark, Austria),
Sauvignon Blanc (Friuli, Italy), Sauvignon
Blanc (Elim, Elgin, Constantia, Durbanville,
South Africa).

The herbaceous Cape style

The most distinctive Sauvignons of the Western Cape come from Elim, Elgin, Walker Bay, Stellenbosch and Constantia on the south coast and Durbanville and Darling (and to a lesser extent Olifants River) on the west coast. Distinctive because of the grasssy style and slightly rounder mouthfeel and also because they are available at various price points including entry level (which isn't possible in most other wine countries). The common style is reductive without any contact with oak.

BELLINGHAM HOMESTEAD, SAUVIGNON BLANC, CONSTANTIA, SOUTH AFRICA				
C			lemon	Therefore: youthful
H		Therefore: aromatic grape variety	GRASSS · GRANNY SMITH · LIME · GRAPEFRUIT · GOOSEBERRY	Therefore: Sauvignon Blanc
A		Therefore: reductive winemaking		
R		Therefore: youthful		
A		Therefore: cool climate	malic acids	Therefore: no malo
C		Therefore: dry	fatty texture	Therefore: sur lie
T				
E			12.5 to 13%, medium body	
R		Therefore: New World		

Tasting note: This pale, lemon-colored white has intense aromas of freshly cut grasss, citrus, gooseberry, and grapefruit. The wine is dry with medium to high acidity, medium alcohol, and expressive flavors dominated by grassy notes. Medium body, and a high relative fruit intensity.

Riedel Vinum
6416-33

 < 10 °C   no
 < $50
 < 5 jaar

In the Cape Sauvignon Blanc-style:
Sauvignon Blanc de Touraine (Loire, France), Sauvignon Blanc en blends (Rueda, Spain), Sauvignon Blanc (Cafayate, Argentina).

Graves Blanc

The Graves is the wine region located directly south of the city of Bordeaux, in the direction of Sauternes. The name is derived from 'gravel' and the best soils indeed are gravelly, mixed with sand and occasionally clay. Graves is bigger than the Médoc, but produces only half the amount of wine. The area has a reputation for blends of Sauvignon Blanc and Semillon, (often) supplemented with some Muscadelle, matured in barriques, with ensures a long aging potential.

CLOS FLORIDÈNE, GRAVES, FRANCE

C			golden	Therefore: youthful
H		Therefore: aromatic grape variety	GRANNY SMITH · LIME · GRAPEFRUIT · PINEAPPLE · APRICOT	Therefore: Sauvignon Blanc
A		Therefore: oxidative winemaking	TOAST · CEDAR · ALMOND	Therefore: (partly) new French oak
R		Therefore: youthful		
A		Therefore: cool climate	malic acids	Therefore: no malo
C		Therefore: dry wine	fatty texture	Therefore: sur lie
T				
E		Therefore: lots of sunshine (long season)	13 to 13.5%, medium body	
R		Therefore: Old World		

Tasting note: This medium intense, golden-colored white has medium plus aromas of granny smith, lime, grapefruit, pineapple, toast, cedar and almond. Dry in the mouth, this wine has high acidity, creamy mouthfeel and medium alcohol. Medium to full body with a low relative fruit intensity.

Riedel Vinum
6416-33

 < 10 °C   no

 < $100

 > 10 years

In the Graves-style: *Fumé Blanc (Napa Valley, California), other oak-matured Sauvignon Blancs (such as Te Koko in New Zealand).*

Costa Sauvignon Blanc

Chilean winemakers like Pablo Morandé watched the success of Marlborough in the eighties with sorrowful eyes. Shouldn't that expressive, intensely-fruity style also be possible in Chile? Casablanca would be the initial Chilean answer, followed by the even cooler San Antonio/Leyda region, and in its wake the Costas of other valleys. The fruit in Chile is riper than in New Zealand and the dominant gooseberry of Marlborough here gives way to more exotic hints of passion fruit.

VIÑA LEYDA, SAUVIGNON BLANC, SAN ANTONIO, CHILE

					Therefore:
C	📶		lemon		Therefore: youthful
H	📶	Therefore: aromatic grape variety	PASSION FRUIT · PINEAPPLE · LIME · GRAPEFRUIT · GRANNY SMITH		Therefore: Sauvignon Blanc
A	📶	Therefore: reductive winemaking			
R	📶	Therefore: youthful			
A	📶	Therefore: marginal climate	malic acids		Therefore: no malo
C	📶	Therefore: dry wine	fatty texture		Therefore: sur lie
T	📶				
E	📶	Therefore: lots of sunshine (high UV)	12.5 to 14%, medium body		
R	📶	Therefore: New World			

Tasting note: This pale, lemon-colored white has an intense and exotic aroma of passion fruit, lime, grapefruit, gooseberry, granny smith and lemon. The wine is dry in the mouth with an intense (malic) acidity, a creamy mouthfeel and medium alcohol. Medium body and a high relative fruit intensity.

Riedel Vinum 6416-33

< 10 °C   no   < $50   < 5 jaar

In the Leyda Sauvignon Blanc-style:
Sauvignon Blanc (Casablanca, Costa, Chile), Sauvignon Blanc (Marlborough, New Zealand), Sauvignon Blanc de Touraine (Loire, France).

Fumé Blanc

Fumé Blanc is a legacy of Robert Mondavi himself, who taught so many Americans to appreciate Sauvignon Blanc with oak-complexity, Californian style. Inspired by white Graves but in Napa Valley with a higher fruit intensity and more body, more alcohol and more mouthfeel. Aromatically seductive because of the very ripe fruit and the cedar and toast notes of the oak in which it ferments and matures. Often a blend of a majority Sauvignon Blanc with some Semillon.

		ROBERT MONDAVI WINERY, FUMÉ BLANC, NAPA VALLEY, CALIFORNIA		
C			lemon	Therefore: youthful
H		Therefore: aromatic grape variety	GRAPEFRUIT · LIME · PINEAPPLE · GRANNY SMITH · PASSION FRUIT	Therefore: Sauvignon Blanc
A		Therefore: oxidative winemaking	TOAST · CEDAR · CHEESECAKE	Therefore: (partly) new French oak
R		Therefore: youthful		
A		Therefore: cool climate	malic acids	Therefore: no malo
C		Therefore: dry wine	creamy texture	Therefore: sur lie
T				
E		Therefore: lots of sunshine (long season)	13 to 14%, medium to full body	
R		Therefore: New World		

Tasting note: This pale, lemon-colored white has medium plus aromas of granny smith, lime, pineapple, grapefruit and toasted oak. In the mouth the wine is dry with a lot of acidity, creamy mouthfeel, notes of vanilla, cheese cake and toasted oak, and medium alcohol. Medium to full body with a high relative fruit intensity.

Riedel Vinum 6416-33

< 10 °C   no

< $100

> 10 years

In the Fumé Blanc-style: *Graves Blanc (Bordeaux, France), other oak-matured Sauvignon Blancs (such as Te koko in New Zealand).*

Semillon: from bone dry to super sweet

Malaga, Chevrier, Columbier, Blanc Doux, Wyngrape

NEUTRAL   AROMATIC   MALADAPTIVE   ADAPTIVE

Semillon is one of the wine world's most underrated grapes. Although it is the basis of the world's most famous dessert wine, Sauternes, and the dry white wines from the Graves and Pessac-Léognan, the variety is not mentioned on the label. Fortunately, it is mentioned on the label of Australia's leading dry white: Aged Hunter Semillon from the Hunter Valley. Semillon is an easy grape in the vineyard. It flowers later (but ripens earlier) than its blending partner Sauvignon Blanc. Foggy mornings followed by sunny afternoons stimulate the development of noble rot in Sauternes with a multitude of aromas: from apricot, peach, nectarine and mango, to impressions of citrus, nuts and honey. Often Semillon lacks good acidity and is therefore blended with Sauvignon Blanc. Muscadelle is sometimes added for a little more perfume. Semillon has affinity with oak, but also does well without.

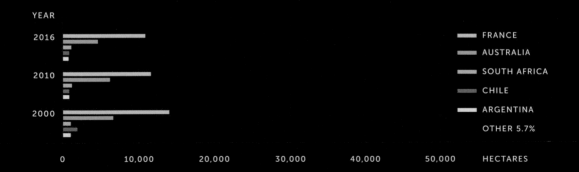

Professor Anderson's figures show that the Semillon planting is slowly but surely declining. Decreases in all of the classic countries is partly compensated by new plantings elsewhere.

Aged Hunter Semillon

On paper, the warm, humid climate of the Hunter Valley wouldn't be able to produce a Semillon with elegance and character. Yet, harvested early to retain acidity and aged for several years in the bottle, the neutral base wine develops into a flavorfull, complex nectar, with impressions of nuts, honey and wax. Low alcohol (usually about 10 to 11%), huge freshness and elegance are the most important characteristics. Long aging potential.

TYRRELL'S AGED HUNTER SEMILLON, AUSTRALIA

C			lemon			Therefore: youthful... (not really)
H			REINE CLAUDE / ZEST / LIME / GRANNY SMITH			
A		Therefore: reductive winemaking				
R		Therefore: bottle aged	WAX / MASHED FRUITS / SOAKED FRUITS			Therefore: Semillon
A		Therefore: early harvest	malic acids			Therefore: no malo
C						
T						
E		Therefore: cool climate (not really)	10,5 to 11.5%, light to medium body			Therefore: early harvest
R		Therefore: New World				

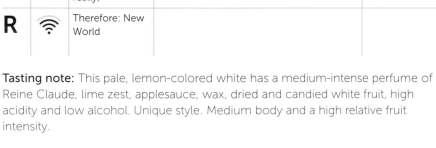

Tasting note: This pale, lemon-colored white has a medium-intense perfume of Reine Claude, lime zest, applesauce, wax, dried and candied white fruit, high acidity and low alcohol. Unique style. Medium body and a high relative fruit intensity.

Riedel Vinum
6416-33

< 10 °C   no

< $50

> 10 years

In the Aged Hunter Semillon-style: mature Anjou and Muscadet de Sèvre et Maine (both Loire, France), mature Riesling Kabinett Trocken (Germany) and mature Riesling Federspeil (Wachau, Austria).

Sauternes

The world's most famous sweet white wine, from the Sauternes, with autumn mist from the evening until well into the next morning, until the sun burns through it. The fog is caused by the cool waters of the Ciron River in combination with the warmer tidal area of the Garonne. The result is ideal for the *Botrytis cinerea* fungus. If the infection comes at the right time, the fungus feeds on the moisture in the ripe grapes, dries them out and leaves concentrated, shriveled fruit.

C			golden	Therefore: oxidative winemaking
H			YELLOW APPLE, PEACH, APRICOT, PINEAPPLE, HONEY	honey, Therefore: Botrytis
A		Therefore: oxidative winemaking	VANILLA, TOAST, ALMOND	Therefore: (partly) new French oak
R		Therefore: 3 to 5 years old	ZEST, CHEESECAKE	
A			malic acids	Therefore: no malo
C		Therefore: sweet	80 to 130 gr/l	Therefore: Sauternes
T				
E		Therefore: late harvest	13 to 14%, medium to full body	
R		Therefore: Old World		

CHÂTEAU RIEUSSEC, SAUTERNES, FRANCE

Tasting note: This medium intense, golden-colored white has a perfume of apple, pear, peach, apricot, pineapple, honey, vanilla, toast, almond paste and orange peel, high acidity and medium to high alcohol. A mineral undertone. Unique style. Medium to full body and a low relative fruit intensity.

Riedel Vinum
6416-33

 < 10 °C   no   < $150   > 10 years

In the Sauternes-style: Barsac, Cérons, Sainte-Croix-du-Mont, Cadillac en Loupiac (Bordeaux, France Monbazillac (Bergerac, France).

Qué Syrah, Shiraz?

Shiraz, Hermitage, Candive

very big
185,335 ha (4.13%)

THIN SKIN   THICK SKIN   SPARKLING SWEET   MONO   MALADAPTIVE   ADAPTIVE

FORTIFIED   DRY   BLEND

Whatever will be, will be. Syrah is for red grape varieties what Chardonnay is for the whites: planted almost all over the world and successful in both cool and warm climates – which is to say: super adaptive. Syrah and Shiraz are synonyms by the way. The character of Syrah is determined by its pure, purple fruit, firm tannins and spiciness as in black pepper. In the bottle it takes on ripening aromas of leather, cloves and laurel. In Australian Shiraz we often find eucalyptus or mint. In very warm areas like Barossa, the wine is full bodied, concentrated and mature, mouth filling and very high in alcohol. When it is aged in American oak, Australian Shiraz gets something exotic (with impressions of coconut and vanilla). But in cooler places in Australia – like in Victoria, Yarra and Mornington Peninsula – and on the Chilean Costa, the style resembles more the northern Rhône. Rest of Chile, Argentina, Washington State and South Africa is stylistically in between.

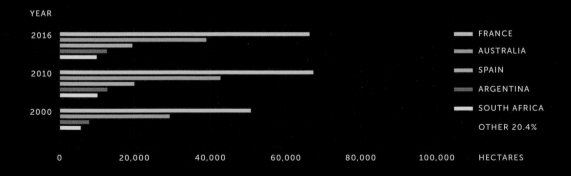

Professor Anderson's figures show an initially rambunctious growth that has leveled off since 2010. Almost simultaneously, many countries experienced similar growth and saturation curves. However, as a variety, Syrah has become increasingly popular, in an increasing number of countries.

Hermitage

Hermitage is the most famous appellation of the Northern Rhône. The Hermitage hill is located above the town of Tain and overlooks the town of Tournon, across the river. Hermitage is only one 120 hectares in size but produces powerful wines, with a deep color, excellent freshness, firm tannins and long aging potential. Syrah gains a refined mineral, peppery complexity in Hermitage. Similar in style are Cornas, Crozes-Hermitage, Saint-Joseph, and Côte-Rôtie.

HERMITAGE, RHÔNE, FRANCE

C	Therefore: grape with a thick skin	ruby		Therefore: 3 to 5 years old
H		BLACKBERRY, BLUEBERRY, PLUM, BLACK PEPPER, WET STONE		Therefore: Northern Rhône/ Syrah
A	Therefore: oxidative winemaking	TOAST, CEDAR		Therefore: (partly) new French oak
R	Therefore: 3 to 5 years old	EARTH		Therefore: (partly) new French oak
A	Therefore: moderate climate			
C	Therefore: dry wine			
T	Therefore: grape with a thick skin	astringent		Therefore: Old World
E	Therefore: lots of sunshine (long season)	14 to 14.5%, medium to full body		
R	Therefore: Old World			

Tasting note: This deep, ruby-colored red has a restrained nose of blackberry, blueberry, blue plum and pepper, with toast and cedar, slightly earthy. Dry with high alcohol, fresh acidity and ripe but firm tannins and a mineral finish. Medium to full body and a low relative fruit intensity.

Riedel Vinum
6416-30

 10-15 °C · 2 hours

 < $100

 > 10 years

In the Hermitage-style: Crozes-Hermitage, Saint-Joseph, Cornas (Rhône, France), Syrah (Ticino, Switzerland), Syrah Gimblett Gravels (Hawkes Bay, New Zealand).

8 Wine's Internationals   217

Barossa Shiraz

The Barossa Valley is the beating heart of viticulture in Australia and is particularly known for its muscular, oak-aged, long lived Shiraz. Barossa has a very warm, sunny, dry continental climate. It produces Shiraz in a very concentrated style, with full body, low acidity, high alcohol and ripe (but firm) tannins. The wine is usually matured in American oak and therefore usually gains winemaking aromas of vanilla and coconut.

YALUMBA, BAROSSA VALLEY SHIRAZ, AUSTRALIA

C	🛜	Therefore: grape with a very thick skin	ruby	Therefore: 3 to 5 years old
H	🛜		BLACKBERRY BLACKCURRANT BLACK CHERRY BLUEBERRY EUCALYPT	Therefore: Chile or Australia / Shiraz (or Cabernet)
A	🛜	Therefore: oxidative winemaking	VANILLA COCONUT TOAST	Therefore: (partly) new American oak
R	🛜	Therefore: 3 to 5 years old	WALNUT	
A	🛜	Therefore: warm climate		
C	🛜	Therefore: dry wine		
T	🛜	Therefore: grape with a thick skin	ripe and smooth	Therefore: New World
E	🛜	Therefore: lots of sunshine (long season)	14 to 14.5%, full body	
R	🛜	Therefore: New World		

Tasting note: This deep, ruby-colored red – with a pronounced nose of blackberries, blue currant, black cherry, mint, eucalyptus, vanilla and coconut – is dry, with low acidity, lots of ripe tannins and a high alcohol content. Full bodied, powerful and a high relative fruit intensity.

Riedel Vinum
6416-30

10-15 °C   0.5 hours   < $100   > 10 years

In the Barossa Valley-style: non-Costa Shiraz (Maipo, Colchagua, Cachapoal, Aconcagua, Chile), Shiraz (Washington State), Shiraz Primera Zona (Mendoza, Argentina).

Elquí: Chilean's answer to the Northern Rhône

The Atacama Desert may be the driest non-polar place on Earth, but on its southern edge one can find a wine region – Elquí. This green belt meanders inland from the Pacific Ocean, starting from the country's second oldest city, La Serena. In addition to having an estimated 70% of the world's astronomical infrastructure, thanks to its high altitude, low population density and extremely clear skies, in Elquí, Syrah has developed into a regional star.

1865, SYRAH, ELQUÍ VALLEY, CHILE

C	📶	Therefore: grape with a thick skin	ruby	Therefore: 3 to 5 years old
H	📶	Perfume: therefore: Chile	BLACKBERRY · BLUEBERRY · PLUM · BLACK PEPPER · MINT	Therefore: Syrah
A	📶	Therefore: oxidative winemaking	TOAST · CEDAR	Therefore: (partly) new French oak
R	📶	Therefore: 3 to 5 years old	EARTH	
A	📶	Therefore: moderate climate		
C	📶	Therefore: dry wine		
T	📶	Therefore: grape with a thick skin	ripe and smooth	Therefore: New World
E	📶	Therefore: lots of sunshine (high UV)	14 to 14.5%, medium to full body	
R	📶	Therefore: New World		

Tasting note: This deep, ruby-colored red with a perfume of blackberry, blueberry, blue plum and pepper, with toast and cedar, and mint. Dry with high alcohol, medium acidity, ripe tannins, and a juicy finish. Medium to full body, and a high relative fruit intensity.

Riedel Vinum
6416-30

 10-15 °C   no   < $50   5-10 years

In the Elquí-style: *Syrah (Costa, Chile), Syrah (Yarra Valley, Heathcote, Pyrenees, Canberra, Australia), Syrah (Swartland, Elgin, Elim, South Africa).*

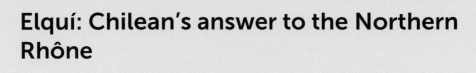

Cape Shiraz

Syrah may have come ashore on the Cape as early as the second half of the 17th century, but it has only recently become one of the Cape's most exciting red grape varieties. Especially in the cooler coastal areas on both the Atlantic and Indian Oceans (Elgin, Swartland, and Olifantsrivier for example), this results in a style that can remind you of the northern Rhône. But in general, Cape Syrah (or Shiraz) is more muscular, with a fuller body and more mouthfeel.

BOSCHENDAL 1685, SHIRAZ, STELLENBOSCH, SOUTH AFRICA

C	📶	Therefore: grape with a thick skin	ruby					Therefore: 3 to 5 years old
H	📶		BLUEBERRY	BLACKCURRANT	PLUM	BLACK PEPPER	FYNBOS	Therefore: South Africa (fynbos)
A	📶	Therefore: oxidative winemaking	VANILLA	CEDAR	TOAST	MOCHA		Therefore: (partly) new French oak
R	📶	Therefore: 3 to 5 years old	EARTH					
A	📶	Therefore: warm climate						
C	📶	Therefore: dry wine						
T	📶	Therefore: grape with a thick skin	ripe					Therefore: New World
E	📶	Therefore: lots of sunshine (long season)	14 to 14.5%, full body					
R	📶	Therefore: New World						

Tasting note: This deep, ruby-colored red has an above-average intense nose of jammy blue and black currant and blue plum, also with notes of vanilla and toast, black pepper and fynbos, and mocha. The wine is dry, with low acidity, a lot of ripe tannins, and lots of alcohol. Full body, and a high relative fruit intensity.

Riedel Vinum 6416-30

 < 10 °C   no

  < $50

< 5 jaar

In the Cape Shiraz-style: Shiraz (Mendoza, Argentina), Shiraz (Napa Valley, California), Shiraz Victoria (Australia).

220

Gimblett Gravels

Until the end of the 1980s, this gravelly strip in Hawke's Bay was considered 'worthless' as it was poor and unproductive; it took three hectares to raise one sheep and there was little hope for a decent harvest of anything. You couldn't give the land away, to illustrate how worthless it was. That is to say until, in 1982, Alan Limmer of Stonecroft rescued a few Syrah cuttings from a nursery that was going out of business and planted them here. The rest is history.

CRAGGY RANGE, SYRAH, GIMBLETT GRAVELS, HAWKES BAY, NEW ZEALAND				
C 🛜	Therefore: grape with a thick skin	ruby		Therefore: 3 to 5 years old
H 🛜		BLACKCURRANT BLUEBERRY WHITE PEPPER NUTMEG CLOVE		Therefore: Syrah / Nothern Rhône-style
A 🛜	Therefore: oxidative winemaking	TOAST CEDAR		Therefore: (partly) new French oak
R 🛜	Therefore: 3 to 5 years old	EARTH		
A 🛜	Therefore: moderate climate			
C 🛜	Therefore: dry wine			
T 🛜	Therefore: grape with a thick skin	ripe		Therefore: New World
E 🛜	Therefore: lots of sunshine (high UV)	14 to 14.5%, medium to full body		
R 🛜	Therefore: New World			

Tasting note: This deep, ruby-colored red has a scent of black and blueberry, blue plum and white pepper, with toast and cedar, minerals, and clove. Dry wine with high alcohol, medium acidity, and ripe but firm tannins as well as a juicy finish. Medium to full body, and a high relative fruit intensity.

Riedel Vinum 6416-30

 10-15 °C   no

 < $100

 > 10 years

In the Gimblett Gravels-style: Syrah (Costa, Chile), Syrah (Yarra Valley, Heathcote, Pyrenees, Canberra, Australia), Syrah (Swartland, Elgin, Elim, South Africa).

Tannat's Tannins

Tanat, Moustrou, Moustroun, Bordeleza Belcha, Harriague

THIN SKIN — THICK SKIN   SPARKLING SWEET / FORTIFIED DRY   MONO / BLEND   MALADAPTIVE — ADAPTIVE

Tannat is best known as the ruling grape variety in Madiran, the most famous red wine in the French Southwest. The grape probably originated in the Basque country. It derived its French name from its high tannin levels as Tannat is a very thick-skinned grape variety that can produce deeply colored, astringent and austere wines in Madiran. However, with aging, even in Madiran, the massive tannins will round out while the wine develops nuances of spices, mocha, cocao, and tobacco.

Because of its massive tannins in Madiran, Tannat is usually blended with Cabernet Sauvignon, Cabernet Franc and Fer (approximately 30 to 40% of the blend). The only other country where Tannat is seriously grown is Uruguay, where it was planted by Basque settlers in the 19th century. Recently plantings have spread over the border into Argentina where the grape does well, especially at very high altitudes in Cafayate and Salta, and into bordering Tarija in Bolivia.

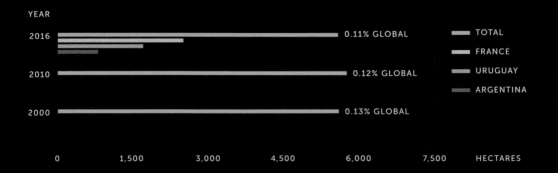

YEAR		
2016	0.11% GLOBAL	▬ TOTAL
		▬ FRANCE
2010	0.12% GLOBAL	▬ URUGUAY
		▬ ARGENTINA
2000	0.13% GLOBAL	

0   1,500   3,000   4,500   6,000   7,500   HECTARES

Tannat plantings in Uruguay increased till 2020, then started decreasing. In the meantime, acreage in France is stable and growing in Argentina, especially in Cafayate.

Originally from Madiran

Tannat comes from Madiran in southwestern France and produces robust, deeply-colored, red wines with huge tannins and excellent aging potential. In 1990, Madiran's astringency prompted winemaker Patrick Ducournau to experiment with micro-oxidation (*microbullage*). During the alcoholic fermentation micro-amounts of air are dosed into the tank or barrel to rid the wine of its unstable, most astringent tannins. *Microbullage* then also became popular in the rest of the world.

CHÂTEAU MONTUS, MADIRAN, FRANCE

C	Therefore: grape with a very thick skin	ruby		Therefore: 3 to 5 years old
H		REDCURRANT, BLACKCURRANT, BLACKCHERRY, PLUM, BELL PEPPER		
A	Therefore: matured in oak	CEDAR, TOAST, PENCIL SHAVINGS		Therefore: (partly) new French oak
R	Therefore: 3 to 5 years old	TOBACCO, WALNUT, EARTH		
A	Therefore: moderate climate			
C	Therefore: dry wine			
T	Therefore: grape with a very thick skin	very astringent		Therefore: Old World
E	Therefore: lots of sunshine (long season)	12 to 13%, medium body		
R	Therefore: Old World			

Tasting note: This deep, ruby-colored red has medium-intense aromas of red and black currant, black cherry, blue plum, blueberry, cedar, toast and tobacco. Medium acidity, medium plus to high alcohol and lots of ripe, smooth tannins. Full body and a high relative fruit intensity.

Riedel Vinum 6416-30

 10-15 °C   2 hours

 < $100

 > 10 years

In the Madiran-style: *Sagrantino di Montefalco (Umbrië, Italy), Bandol (France), Cahors (France).*

New World Tannat

In Uruguay, Tannat is considered part of the national heritage. In the middle of the 19th century, Uruguay's first oenologists, who were French, introduced Tannat and one of them, Pascual Harriague, built the first Tannat vineyard, planted in Salto. After 130 years, Tannat in Uruguay has adapted to the local conditions with riper, softer tannins. After Canalones, Colonia, and Montevideo, Viña Garzon in Maldonado proves what can be done with Tannat in Uruguay.

VIÑA GARZÓN, MALDONADO, URUGUAY

C	Therefore: grape with a very thick skin	ruby		Therefore: 3 to 5 years old
H		REDCURRANT, BLACKCURRANT, BLACKCHERRY, PLUM, BLUEBERRY		
A	Therefore: oxidative winemaking	CEDAR, TOAST, VANILLA		Therefore: (partly) new French oak
R	Therefore: 3 to 5 years old	TOBACCO		
A	Therefore: moderate climate			
C	Therefore: dry wine			
T	Therefore: grape with a very thick skin	ripe and soft		Therefore: New World
E	Therefore: lots of sunshine (long season)	14.5%, full body		
R	Therefore: New World			

Tasting note: This deep, ruby-colored red has medium-intense aromas of red and black currant, black cherry, blue plum, cedar, toast, tobacco and walnut. Medium acidity, medium plus to high alcohol, and astringent tannins with a spicy vegetal undertone. Medium body and a low relative fruit intensity.

Riedel Vinum 6416-30

 10-15 °C   0.5 hours

 < $100   > 10 years

In the Coastal Uruguay-style: Tannat Tarija (Bolivia), Tannat Cafayate (Argentina), Madiran (France).

huge
219,124 ha (4.88%)

🔊 tem-pra-NEE-oh

Tempranillo

Aragonez, Cencibel, Tinta Roriz, Tinto Fino, Tinta de Toro, Ull de Llebre, Tinta del Pais

What Pinot Noir is to Burgundy, Tempranillo is to Ribera del Duero and increasingly also for Rioja. Tempranillo is the grape that takes its name from *temprana*, Spanish for early. And indeed, Tempranillo often ripens two weeks before Garnacha, the other grape in the Rioja. Tempranillo is known as a thick-skinned grape variety that produces deeply colored wines. That thick skin also provides characteristic aromas of strawberry, tobacco and spices. The grape is also planted in Northern and Central Spain (i.e. in Navarra, Penedès, Costers del Segre, Somontano, Valdepeñas and La Mancha). In the Spanish tradition, the character of the wine – although largely made from that one grape variety – can in large part be determined in the cellar. Winemaking aromas such as vanilla, toast, spices and coconut can play a dominant role. Called Aragonez in the south and Tinta Roriz in the Douro, Tempranillo has been popular as well in Portugal, both for port and still wine.

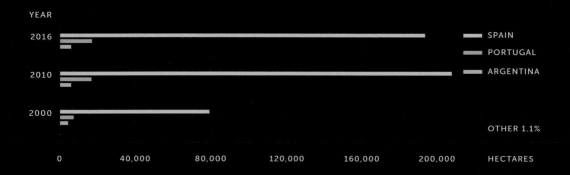

Professor Anderson's numbers show tremendous growth in the Iberian Peninsula at the beginning of this century, and a stabilization since 2010. Also, South America has begun to discover Tempranillo.

Ribera del Duero

Ribera del Duero didn't get its DO status until 1982, at a time when only nine bodegas were active. Now, there are more than 200 bodegas and 20.000 hectares of vineyards. Ribera del Duero owes its success firstly to the schist-like soils, secondly to the *gran altura* microclimate with its warm days and cool nights, which together provide ripeness while preserving freshness and aromas, and thirdly to the early-ripening mono-cépage Tempranillo.

TORRES, CELESTE, CRIANZA, RIBERA DEL DUERO, SPAIN

C	📶	Therefore: grape with a thick skin	ruby	Therefore: 3 to 5 years old
H	📶		BLACKCURRANT PLUM REDCURRANT FIG	
A	📶	Therefore: oxidative winemaking	VANILLA TOAST COCONUT	Therefore: (new) American oak
R	📶	Therefore: 3 to 5 years old	WALNUT	
A	📶	Therefore: moderate climate		
C	📶	Therefore: dry wine		
T	📶	Therefore: grape with a thick skin	slightly drying	Therefore: Old World
E	📶	Therefore: lots of sunshine (high UV)	14 to 14.5%, full body	
R	📶	Therefore: Old World		

Tasting note: This deep, ruby-colored red has a restrained nose of blackcurrant, blue plum, black cherry, fig paste, vanilla, toast and sometimes coconut. The wine is dry with moderate acidity, firm tannins, and a high alcohol content. Full body, and a low relative fruit intensity.

Riedel Vinum 6416-30

 10-15 °C   0.5 hours

 < $100

 > 10 years

In the Ribera del Duero-style: Rioja (Spain), Aragonez, Tinta Roriz (Douro, Portugal), Malbec Primera Zona (Mendoza, Argentina).

Rioja

Rioja, along with Sherry, is Spain's most famous wine. It includes more than six hundred bodegas, almost 15,000 winegrowers and the largest 'barrique collection' in the world. The wine region is located in the north of Spain, on both sides of the river Ebro. With over 65,000 hectares of vineyards, each city and terroir has its own personality, making Rioja unique. The dominant grape variety is Tempranillo, often blended with Garnacha, Mazuelo and Graciano.

Riedel Vinum
6416-31

TORRES, LAS PISADAS, RIOJA, SPAIN				
C	📶	Therefore: grape with a thick skin	ruby	Therefore: 5 to 10 years old
H	📶		REDCURRANT · PLUM · RED CHERRY · FIG	
A	📶	Therefore: oxidative winemaking	VANILLA · TOAST · COCONUT	Therefore: (new) American oak
R	📶	Therefore: 5 to 10 years old	WALNUT	
A	📶	Therefore: moderate climate		
C	📶	Therefore: dry wine		
T	📶	Therefore: grape with a thick skin	slightly drying	Therefore: Old World
E	📶	Therefore: lots of sunshine (long season)	14%, medium to full body	
R	📶	Therefore: Old World		

Tasting note: This deep, ruby-colored red has a restrained nose of red currant, red plum, red cherry, fig paste, vanilla, toast and coconut. The wine is dry, with moderate acidity, firm tannins and a high alcohol content. Full body and a low relative fruit intensity.

10-15 °C   0.5 hours   < $50   5-10 years

In the Rioja-style: *Ribera del Duero (Spain), Aragonez, Tinta Roriz (Douro, Portugal), Malbec Primera Zona Mendoza (Argentina).*

9
Local Heroes

Around the world in 80 Wines

Since we discussed the most important grape varieties across the globe in Chapter 8, now it's time to turn our attention to the varieties less widely grown. From Albariño to Zweigelt. Unlike those mentioned in the previous chapter, these grape varieties don't have an individual dashboard but we get to know them on the basis of a single benchmark wine.

We kick off with a classic wine from a classic wine country.

🔊 ayor-YEE-tee-koh

rare
3,270 ha (0.7%)

Agiorgitiko: at its best in Nemea

Aghiorghitiko, Mavro Nemeas, St. George

This is Greece's most widely planted (indigenous) red grape variety, which can offer both high yields and high quality in various styles. Mainly planted in the Peloponnese (about 3,000 hectares) and Attiki on the continent (5,000 hectares). In Nemea it is the only grape variety allowed for red wine, with impressions of very ripe black fruit and Syrah-like notes of pepper and spice. It is used for a variety of styles from rosé to deep-colored powerhouse reds.

GAIA, AGIORGITIKO, NEMEA, GREECE

C	📶	Therefore: grape with a thick skin	ruby	Therefore: 3 to 5 years old
H	📶		BLACKCHERRY · RED CHERRY · BLACKCURRANT · NUTMEG · PLUM	
A	📶	Therefore: matured in oak	CEDAR · TOAST	Therefore: (partly) new French oak
R	📶	Therefore: 3 to 5 years old	TOBACCO	
A	📶	Therefore: warm climate		
C	📶	Therefore: dry wine		
T	📶	Therefore: grape with a thick skin	astringent	Therefore: Old World
E	📶	Therefore: lots of sunshine (long season)	13.5%, medium body	
R	📶	Therefore: Old World		

Tasting note: This deep, ruby-colored red has medium intense aromas of black and red cherry, blackcurrant, nutmeg and plum, cedar and toast and tobacco. The wine is dry with medium acidity, medium to high alcohol, firm tannins, and medium flavor intensity. Medium to full body and a low relative fruit intensity.

Riedel Vinum 6416-30

 10-15 °C   2 hours   < $50   5-10 years

In the Agiorgitiko-style: Cahors (France), Madiran (France), Blaufränkisch (Burgenland, Austria).

small
9,716 ha (0.22%)

Aglianico: Barolo of the South

Gnanico, Agliatica, Ellenico, Ellanico, Uva Nera

Aglianico (Nero) is a late maturing indigenous variety which rules Basilicata. Also found in Campania and elsewhere in southern Italy. Aglianico has a deep color, ripe, jammy fruit, astringent tannins, and full body. Despite the high temperatures and excessive sunlight during the day, the grapes retain their acidity reasonably well because of the diurnal temperature differences. The best results are said to be achieved on the volcanic soils of Taurasi and Vulture (both DOCG).

RIVERA, ALGIANICO, PUGLIA, ITALY

C	📶	Therefore: grape with a very thick skin	ruby		Therefore: 3 to 5 years old
H	📶		BLACKCHERRY · BLUEBERRY · VIOLETS · CINNAMON · FLINT		
A	📶	Therefore: oxidative winemaking	TOAST · SMOKE		Therefore: partly new oak
R	📶	Therefore: 3 to 5 years old	TOBACCO · EARTH		
A	📶				
C	📶	Therefore: dry wine			
T	📶	Therefore: grape with a very thick skin	astringent		Therefore: Old World
E	📶	Therefore: lots of sunshine (long season)	13%, medium body		
R	📶	Therefore: Old World			

Tasting note: This deep, ruby-colored red has a restrained expression of jammy black cherry and blueberry fruit but also impressions of flint, violet, and cinnamon, in addition to smoky notes, toast, tobacco and earthy hints. In the mouth the wine is dry with medium acidity, medium alcohol, astringent tannins, and a mineral finish. Medium to full body and a low relative fruit intensity.

Riedel Vinum
6416-90

 10-15 °C   2 hours

 < $50

 5-10 years

In the Aglianico-style: Nebbiolo Langhe (Piedmont, Italy), Xinomavro (Greece), Agiorgitiko (Nemea, Greece).

230

small
5,545 ha (0.12%)

🔊 alba-REEN-yoh

Albariño: rules in Rias Baixas

Alvarinho

The white wines of Galicia are anything but stereotypically Spanish as they are elegant, refined and minerally complex. The decor is equally un-Spanish: fjord-like inland seas, here called *rias*, have a tempering effect on the climate both in winter and summer. Albariño wines usually are pale, oak free with impressions of pear, apricot, peach, botanical notes and a fresh zesty acidity. Most do not age well.

PAZO DAS BRUXAS, ALBARIÑO, RIAS BAIXAS, SPAIN

C	📶		lemon					Therefore: youthful
H	📶	Therefore: a neutral grape variety	YELLOW APPLE · PEAR · APRICOT · PEACH · FENNEL					
A	📶	Therefore: reductive winemaking						
R	📶	Therefore: youthful						
A	📶	Therefore: cool climate	malic acids					Therefore: no malo
C	📶	Therefore: dry wine	fatty					Therefore: sur lie
T	📶							
E	📶		12.5 to 13%, medium body					
R	📶	Therefore: Old World						

Tasting note: This pale, lemon-colored white has a restrained nose of apple, pear, apricot, peach and fennel, medium to high acidity and medium alcohol with a mineral undertone. Medium body and a low relative fruit intensity.

Riedel Vinum
6416-05

 < 10 °C

 no

 < $50

< 5 years

In the Albariño-style: Loureiro (Portugal), Vinho Verde (Portugal), Furmint (Hungary).

🔊 alva-REEN-yoh

Uruguay's 'Galicia'

Alvarinho

Maldonado (as well as the other coastal regions Canelones and Montevideo) in Uruguay resembles Rias Baixas in Spain in several aspects. First of all, it is located 15 to 25 kilometers inland from the Atlantic coast. Furthermore, the vineyards are located on a hilly terrain on the oldest granite in the world (granite soils that have eroded under their own weight). Albariño does very well here with a slightly richer style and creamier texture.

ALBARIÑO GARZON, MALDONADO, URUGUAY

C	📶		lemon		Therefore: youthful
H	📶	Therefore: non-aromatic variety	YELLOW APPLE · PEAR · APRICOT · PEACH · PINEAPPLE		
A	📶	Therefore: reductive winemaking			
R	📶	Therefore: youthful			
A	📶	Therefore: moderate climate	malic acids		Therefore: no malo
C	📶	Therefore: dry wine	creamy texture		Therefore: sur lie
T	📶				
E	📶		13.5%, medium body		
R	📶	Therefore: New World			

Tasting note: This pale, lemon-colored white has medium-intense aromas of apple, pear, apricot, peach and pineapple, medium acidity and medium alcohol. A creamy texture and a mineral undertone. Medium body and a high relative fruit intensity.

Riedel Vinum
6416-05

 < 10 °C   no   < $50   < 5 years

In the Maldonado-style: Fiano (Italy), Frappato (Italy), Albariño (Spain), unoaked Chenin Blanc (South Africa).

small
5,545 ha (0.12%)

🔊 alba-REEN-yoh

Alvariño: the Albariño of Portugal

Albariño

On the Portuguese side of the border with Spain, in the Vinho Verde, Albariño is called Alvarinho. Here, it is often blended with Loureiro, Arinto and Trajadura. Alvarinho has a distinctive floral, fruity and salty profile with notes of lime, fennel, honeysuckle, peach, grapefruit and apple; all underpinned with high acidity and low to medium alcohol. Young Alvarinhos often have a touch of CO_2 which is added prior to bottling.

CONDE VILLAR, ALVARINHO, VINHO VERDE, PORTUGAL

C		lemon		Therefore: youthful
H		Therefore: a neutral grape variety	YELLOW APPLE · LIME · LEMON · PEACH · FENNEL	
A		Therefore: reductive winemaking		
R		Therefore: youthful		
A		Therefore: cool climate	malic acids	Therefore: no malo
C			creamy texture	Therefore: sur lie
T				
E			11.5 to 12.5%, light body	
R		Therefore: Old World		

Tasting note: This pale, lemon-colored white has a restrained nose of lime, fennel, peach, grapefruit and apple, is high in acidity with medium alcohol. A mineral undertone. Light to medium body and a low relative fruit intensity.

Riedel Vinum
6416-05

< 10 °C   no   < $50   < 5 years

In the Alvarinho-style: *Loureiro (Vinho Verde, Portugal), Albariño (Rias Baixas, Spain), Furmint (Hungary).*

36,192 ha (0.81%)

🔊 allee-cante BOO-shay

Alicante Bouschet: color is key

Garnacha Tintorera

Productive southern French *teinturier* (a variety with pigments in both skin and the flesh of the fruit) that has now been planted in many countries and is doing well in Portugal, in Alentejo in particular. A cross of Grenache with Petit Bouschet done by Henri Bouschet in 1855. Particularly popular for its deep color and high yields. Used both in blends and as a single varietal for wines with a lot of color, full body and ripe, soft tannins.

HERDADE DE SÃO MIGUEL, ALICANTE BOUSCHET, ALENTEJO, PORTUGAL

C	📶	Therefore: grape with a very thick skin	ruby		Therefore: 3 to 5 years old
H	📶		PLUM, BLACKCHERRY, CLOVE, CINNAMON, BLACKCURRANT		
A	📶	Therefore: matured in oak	SMOKE, MOCHA, VANILLA		Therefore: partly new
R	📶	Therefore: 3 to 5 years old	TOBACCO, EARTH		
A	📶	Therefore: warm climate			
C	📶	Therefore: dry wine			
T	📶	Therefore: grape with a thick skin	astringent		Therefore: Old World
E	📶	Therefore: lots of sunshine (long season)	14 to 15%, full body		
R	📶	Therefore: Old World			

Tasting note: This very deep, ruby-colored red has medium-intense aromas of blue plum, black cherry, cloves, cinnamon, blackcurrant, smoky mocha and vanilla notes and impressions of tobacco and earth. Low acidity, high alcohol and firm tannins. Full body and a low relative fruit intensity.

Riedel Vinum
6416-15

 10-15 °C   2 hours

 < $50

 < 5 years

In the Alicante Bouschet-style:
Monastrell (Jumilla, Spain), Petite Sirah (California, United States), Touriga Nacional (Portugal).

234

27,000 ha (0.6%)

◀) allee-go-TAY

Aligoté: in the shadow of Chardonnay

Blanc de Troyes, Vert blanc, Chaudenet Gris, Plant Gris

Due to its neutral character and high acidity, Aligoté is mainly known as a blending wine, as in Crémant de Bourgogne. Planted from north to south, with Bouzeron a notable location, the grape ripens early with moderate yields and produces wines with high acidity and a restrained apple-y aroma and a touch of damp cloth. Traditionally, Aligoté is the basis for the cocktail kir (also known as vin blanc cassis) with crème de cassis.

DOMAINE A&P DE VILLAINE, ALIGOTÉ, BOUZERON, FRANCE

C			lemon		Therefore: youthful
H		Therefore: a neutral grape variety	YELLOW APPLE LEMON PEAR WET STONE CHALK		
A		Therefore: reductive winemaking			
R		Therefore: youthful			
A		Therefore: cool climate	malic acids		Therefore: no malo
C		Therefore: dry wine	creamy texture		Therefore: sur lie
T					
E			12.5 to 13.5%, light body		
R		Therefore: Old World			

Tasting note: This pale, lemon-colored white has a restrained nose of apple, pear and lemon, chalk and wet stones. Dry on the palate, with high acidity and medium alcohol. A creamy texture and a mineral undertone. Light to medium body and a low relative fruit intensity.

Riedel Vinum
6416-05

 < 10 °C

 no

 < $50

< 5 years

In the Aligoté-style: Chardonnay (Bourgogne, France), Chenin Blanc (Loire, France), Loureiro (Rias Baixas, Spain).

🔊 ah-REEN-toh

small
5,409 ha (0.12%)

Versatile Arinto

Pederna

Arinto (or Pederna) is an indigenous grape of the central coast of Portugal. The grape thrives here because of its naturally high acid content. Arinto aromatically varies from typical lemon and grapefruit to pome fruit and peach. In Bucelas, just north of Lisbon, Arinto is the basis (at least 75%) of the local white wine blend, and is also found in Vinho Verde, Ribatejo, Bairrada and Alentejo, where it is often blended with Fernão Pires and Loureiro.

QUINTA DA FONTE SOUTO, ALENTEJO, PORTUGAL				
C	🛜		lemon	Therefore: youthful
H	🛜	Therefore: aromatic grape variety	REINE CLAUDE · GRAPEFRUIT · LEMON · MANGO	
A	🛜	Therefore: oxidative winemaking	VANILLA · TOAST	Therefore: partly new French oak
R	🛜	Therefore: youthful		
A	🛜	Therefore: moderate climate	malic acids	Therefore: no malo
C	🛜	Therefore: dry wine	creamy texture	Therefore: sur lie
T	🛜			
E	🛜		13 to 14%, medium body	
R	🛜	Therefore: Old World		

Tasting note: This pale, lemon-colored white has a pronounced citrus perfume of *Reine Claude* (greengage), lemon, grapefruit, and mango, vanilla, toast, medium acidity and medium alcohol. A waxy mouthfeel and a ripe undertone. Medium body and a low relative fruit intensity.

Riedel Vinum
6416-15

 < 10 °C   no   < $50   < 5 years

In the Arinto, Alentejo-style: Assyrtiko (Santorini, Greece), Catarratto (Sicily, Italy), Chenin Blanc (Swartland, South-Africa).

236

rare
1,174 ha (0.03%)

🔊 ahr-NEYS

Arneis: 'Little Rascal'

Bianchetta, Bianchetto

Arneis, from the hills of Roero (northwest of Alba in Piedmont), literally means 'little rascal' in local dialect. The grapes have low acidity and a tendency to become overripe. In addition, Arneis is sensitive to mildew, which often results in low yields. On the chalky, sandy soil of Roero, the grapes retain acidity and structure, while on clay they develop a more exotic perfume with aromas of almonds, apricots, peaches, pears and star anise. Most Arneis are oak free.

MALVIRÀ, ROERO ARNEIS, PIEDMONT, ITALY

C	📶		lemon	Therefore: youthful
H	📶	Therefore: a neutral grape variety	APRICOT PEACH BLOSSOM ANISE PEAR	
A	📶		ALMOND	Therefore: foudres
R	📶	Therefore: youthful		
A	📶	Therefore: moderate climate		
C	📶	Therefore: dry wine	creamy texture	Therefore: sur lie
T	📶			
E	📶		12.5 to 13%, medium body	
R	📶	Therefore: Old World		

Tasting note: This pale, lemon-colored white has a restrained yet exotic perfume of almond, apricot, peach, blossom, star anise and pear, medium acidity and medium alcohol. A creamy texture, medium body and a low relative fruit intensity.

Riedel Vinum
6416-05

< 10 °C   no   < $50   < 5 years

In the Arneis-style: Pinot Grigio (Veneto, Italy), Soave (Veneto, Italy), Xarel 'lo (Penedes, Spain).

rare
1,770 ha (0.04%)

◀)) ah-SIR-tee-koh

Assyrtiko: Chablis of the Mediterranean

Originating from Santorini, from 60- to 250-year-old vines, often ungrafted and pruned like a basket to minimize wind damage and protect the grapes from sunburn. The only precipitation comes as fog. Viticulture is increasingly losing out to advancing tourism, but in the meantime, Assyrtiko has been planted elsewhere in Greece. Its principle style is medium to full bodied, bone-dry, high acidity and spicy-mineral impressions from the volcanic soils.

Riedel Vinum
6416-97

GAIA, ASSYRTIKO, SANTORINI, GREECE

C	🛜		lemon	Therefore: youthful
H	🛜	Therefore: a neutral grape variety	LIME YELLOW APPLE PEACH FLINT VOLCANIC	
A	🛜	Therefore: reductive winemaking		
R	🛜	Therefore: youthful		
A	🛜	Therefore: cool climate	malic acids	Therefore: no malo
C	🛜	Therefore: dry wine	creamy texture	Therefore: sur lie
T	🛜			
E	🛜		13 to 13.5%, medium body	
R	🛜	Therefore: Old World		

Tasting note: This pale, lemon-colored white has a restrained 'volcanic' perfume of lime, yellow apple, pear and flint, high acidity and medium to high alcohol. A creamy texture and a spicy-mineral undertone. Medium to full body and a low relative fruit intensity.

< 10 °C   no   < $50   5-10 years

In the Assyrtiko-style: Etna Bianco (Carricante, Italy), Grüner Veltliner (Kremstal, Austria), Chenin Blanc (Swartland, South Africa).

238

🔊 BAH-gah

Baga da Bairrada

Tinta (da) Bairrada

small
6,750 ha (0.15%)

B

Baga is known for its generous yields and is most widely planted in Beiras, especially in Bairrada and Dão. In Bairrada, Baga has a good color, structure and crisp acidity with firm but fine tannins for excellent aging potential. Typical bouquet with red cherries and berries, black plum, tobacco and mocha. The finest Baga are up with classed-growth Bordeaux in quality. Very suitable for sparkling wines too.

MARQUÊS DI MARIALVA 2015 BAIRRADA

**Riedel Vinum
6416-16**

MARQUÊS DE MARIALVA, BAGA RESERVA, BAIRRADA, PORTUGAL

C	📶	Therefore: grape with a thick skin	garnet	Therefore: approximately 5 years old
H	📶		RED CHERRY, REDCURRANT, PLUM	
A	📶	Therefore: oxidative winemaking	MOCHA, PENCIL SHAVINGS, SMOKE	Therefore: aging in (partly new) oak barrels
R	📶	Therefore: approximately 5 years old	TOBACCO	
A	📶	Therefore: moderate climate		
C	📶	Therefore: dry wine		
T	📶	Therefore: grape with a thick skin	astringent	Therefore: Old World
E	📶		13.5%, medium body	
R	📶	Therefore: Old World		

Tasting note: This deep, garnet-colored red has medium-intense aromas of red cherries and redcurrant, black plum, smokey mocha, pencil shavings and tobacco. Medium acidity, medium alcohol and firm tannins. Medium to full body and a low relative fruit intensity.

 10-15 °C | 2 hours

 < $50

 5-10 years

In the Baga-style: Xinomavro (Macedonia, Greece), Barolo Barbaresco (Piedmont, Italy), Blaufränkisch (Burgenland, Austria).

small
17,820 ha (0.4%)

🔊 bar-BAIR-ah

Barbera: Piedmont's everyday wine

In Italy, Barbera produces wines with a medium to deep color, high acidity, moderate tannins, medium to high alcohol, mouth-filling fruit and yet a dry finish. And in Piedmont, Barbera and Nebbiolo can be compared with Gamay and Pinot Noir in Burgundy, with Barbera being more fruit forward and rarely achieving the complexity of Nebbiolo. In hot climates such as the San Joaquim Valley in California and Argentina, the wine can take on a more 'raisiny' character.

PARUSSO, BARBERA D'ALBA, PIEDMONT, ITALY

C	Therefore: grape with a thick skin	ruby		Therefore: 3 to 5 years old
H		RED CHERRY · BLACK CHERRY · BLUEBERRY · BLACK PEPPER · LAUREL		
A	Therefore: oxidative winemaking	ALMOND · TOAST		Therefore: foudres
R	Therefore: 3 to 5 years old	PRESERVED FRUITS		
A	Therefore: moderate climate			
C	Therefore: dry wine			
T	Therefore: grape with a thick skin	astringent		Therefore: Old World
E	Therefore: lots of sunshine (long season)	14%, full body		
R	Therefore: Old World			

Tasting note: This medium, ruby-colored red has medium-intense aromas of red and black cherries, blueberries, black pepper and bay leaf. Medium to high acidity, high alcohol and medium but drying tannins. Medium to full body and a low relative fruit intensity.

Riedel Vinum
6416-30

10-15 °C   2 hours

💲💲
💲💲
< $50

5-10 years

In the Barbera-style: Agiorgitiko (Nemea, Greece), Blaufränkisch (Burgenland, Austria), Dolcetto (Piedmont, Italy).

🔊 blahw-FREN-keesh

Blaufränkisch is Burgenland!

Modra Frankinja, Lemberger, Blauer Limberger, Frankovka (Franconia), Kékfrankos, Gamé

Blaufränkisch is a cross between the Blauer Zimmettraube and the equally obscure Weisser Heunisch. It was originally planted throughout the Habsburg Monarchy (known in Hungary as Kékfrankos) and has emerged as the signature red of Burgenland, the finest of which have richness, class, minerality and excellent aging potential. In Germany (and Washington State) Blaufränkisch is known as Lemberger, named after the town in Lower Austria from which it was imported.

WELLANSCHITZ, NECKENMARKTER FAHNENSCHWINGER, HOCHBERG, BURGENLAND, AUSTRIA

C	📶	Therefore: grape with a thick skin	ruby	Therefore: 3 to 5 years old
H	📶		BLACKBERRY, BLACKCURRANT, PLUM, WHITE PEPPER, CLOVE	
A	📶	Therefore: oxidative winemaking	CEDAR, TOAST	Therefore: (partly) new French oak
R	📶	Therefore: 3 to 5 years old	TOBACCO	
A	📶	Therefore: moderate climate		
C	📶	Therefore: dry wine		
T	📶	Therefore: grape with a thick skin	astringent	Therefore: Old World
E	📶	Therefore: lots of sunshine (long season)	13.5%, medium body	
R	📶	Therefore: Old World		

Tasting note: This deep, ruby-colored red has medium-intense aromas of blackberry, black currant, blue plum, white pepper, cloves, cedar, toast and tobacco. Medium acidity, high alcohol and firm tannins provide a medium to full body. Low relative fruit intensity.

Riedel Vinum 6416-30

 10-15 °C 2 hours

 < $50

> 10 years

In the Blaufränkisch-style: Agiorgitiko (Nemea, Greece), (Haut) Médoc (Bordeaux, France), Chianti Classico (Tuscany, Italy).

big
59,187 ha (1.32%)

🔊 boh-BAL

Bobal: bull's blood

Bobos, Requeña

● Bobal is derived from the Latin bovale (bull) and refers to the shape of the bunches which resemble the head of a bull. Its thick skin, late ripening and drought resistance make it suitable for dry, continental climates such as Utiel-Requena, Valencia, Manchuela, Alicante and Murcia. With 90,000 hectares, it is Spain's third most planted variety. For a long time Bobal was mainly used for bulk wine but it can generate great blackberry-fruited and peppery-spiced full bodied reds.

CERROGALLINA, BOBAL, UTIEL-REQUEÑA, SPAIN

2016

C 📶	Therefore: grape with a thick skin	ruby		Therefore: 3 to 5 years old
H 📶		BLUEBERRY CINNAMON BLACKBERRY REDCURRANT CRANBERRY		
A 📶	Therefore: oxidative winemaking	TOAST VANILLA		Therefore: partly new oak
R 📶	Therefore: 3 to 5 years old	TOBACCO EARTH		
A 📶	Therefore: hot climate			
C 📶	Therefore: dry wine			
T 📶	Therefore: grape with a thick skin	astringent		Therefore: Old World
E 📶	Therefore: lots of sunshine (long season)	14 to 14.5%, full body		
R 📶	Therefore: Old World			

Tasting note: This deep, ruby-colored red has medium intense aromas of blueberries, cinnamon, blackberries, redcurrant and elderberries, toast, vanilla, tobacco and earth. Low acidity, high alcohol and firm tannins result in a full bodied red with a low relative fruit intensity.

Riedel Vinum
6416-15

 10-15 °C   2 hours

 < $50

 5-10 years

In the Bobal-style: *Zweigelt (Austria), Barbera (Piedmont, Italy), Blaufränkisch (Burgenland, Austria).*

small
5,925 ha (0.13%)

B

🔊 boh-NAR-dah

Bonarda: emigrated to Argentina

Douce Noir, Charbono, Carbeau, Plant Noir en Turca

Bonarda is an established Italian variety from Savoie (which only became part of France in 1860). Brought to Argentina by Italian immigrants, it is now the second most planted grape in Argentina behind Malbec. However, Bonarda is also grown in California, often under the name Charbono. Among them vines of 70 years and older, which still produce wonderful wines. Bonarda gives wines with a deep color featuring aromas of cassis, fennel, cherries and figs.

BROQUEL, BONARDA, MENDOZA, ARGENTINA

C	Therefore: grape with a thick skin	ruby		Therefore: 3 to 5 years old
H		BLACKBERRY, PLUM, FIG, NUTMEG, COMPOTE		Therefore: hot climate
A	Therefore: oxidative winemaking	CEDAR, TOAST, VANILLA		Therefore: (partly) new French oak
R	Therefore: 3 to 5 years old	LEATHER		
A	Therefore: hot climate			
C	Therefore: dry wine			
T	Therefore: grape with a thick skin	ripe and smooth		Therefore: New World
E	Therefore: lots of sunshine (high UV)	14.5%, full body		
R	Therefore: New World			

Tasting note: This deep, ruby-colored red has medium-intense aromas of blackberry, fig, compote, nutmeg, prune, cedar, toast, vanilla and leather. Low acidity, high alcohol and firm but ripe tannins. Full body and a high relative fruit intensity.

Riedel Vinum
6416-15

10-15 °C

no

< $50

5-10 years

In the Bonarda-style: Malbec (Malbec (San Juan, San Rafael, Argentina), Tannat (Canelones, Montevideo, Uruguay).

small
21,823 ha (0.41%)

🔊 kar-may-NAIR-uh

Carménère: reinvented

Grande Vidure, Carméneyre, Carmenelle, Cabernelle, Bouton Blanc, Carbouet, Carbonet

Carménère (from *carmine*, the raspberry-red color of the autumn leaves) was one of the components in the Médoc blend, until Phylloxera. Due to notoriously low yields (mildew) and late ripening, the grape was not replanted there after 1900. Fortunately, it had already been exported to Chile in 1850, where it was long confused with Merlot. Needs to fully ripen if it is to lose its herbaceous character, which it does in the hotter and drier parts of Cachapoal, Colchagua, Maipo and Aconcagua.

1865, CARMÉNÈRE, MAULE, CHILE

C 📶	Therefore: grape with a thick skin	ruby		Therefore: 3 to 5 years old
H 📶		BLUEBERRY · REDCURRANT · RED CHERRY · MINT · BLACKCHERRY		Therefore: Chile (due to the perfumery style)
A 📶	Therefore: oxidative winemaking	VANILLA · CEDAR · TOAST		Therefore: (partly) new French oak
R 📶	Therefore: 3 to 5 years old			
A 📶	Therefore: warm climate			
C 📶	Therefore: dry wine	a lot of fruit ripeness		
T 📶	Therefore: grape with a thick skin	ripe and soft		Therefore: New World
E 📶	Therefore: lots of sunshine (high UV)	14 to 14.5%, full body		
R 📶	Therefore: New World			

Tasting note: This deep, ruby-colored red has a perfume of cherry, redcurrant, blueberry, mint and blackcherry, vanilla, cedar and toast. Low acidity, high alcohol and soft, ripe, almost sweet tannins. Full body and a high relative fruit intensity.

Rieedel Vinum
6416-0

 10-15 °C no

  < $100

\> 10 years

In the Carménère-style: Shiraz (Aconcagua, Chile), Merlot (Maipo, Chile), Cabernet Franc (Mendoza, Argentina).

rare
149 ha (0.01%)

🔊 karree-KAN-tuh

Carricante: from the Etna

Catanese Bianco, Catarratto

Carricante is an ancient white variety indigenous to eastern Sicily, originating from the volcanic slopes of Mount Etna. Carica means 'load' in Italian because the grape naturally produces high yields (with a good acidity due to the diurnal temperature differences at higher altitudes). The resulting wines are generally characterized by refreshing citrus aromas – from green apple, lemon and lime to grapefruit – in addition to spicy notes such as mint and anise.

PLANETA, CARRICANTE, SICILY, ITALY

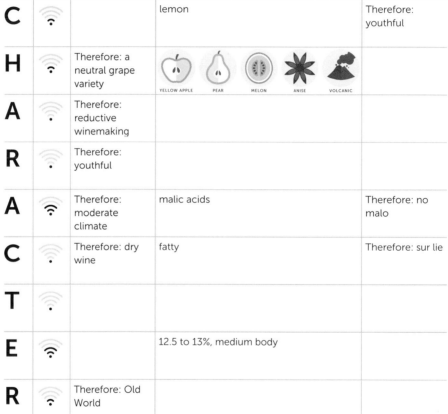

C			lemon					Therefore: youthful
H		Therefore: a neutral grape variety	YELLOW APPLE	PEAR	MELON	ANISE	VOLCANIC	
A		Therefore: reductive winemaking						
R		Therefore: youthful						
A		Therefore: moderate climate	malic acids					Therefore: no malo
C		Therefore: dry wine	fatty					Therefore: sur lie
T								
E			12.5 to 13%, medium body					
R		Therefore: Old World						

Tasting note: This pale, lemon-colored white has a restrained scent of apple, quince and melon, aniseed, medium acidity and medium alcohol. A fatty mouthfeel and a mineral, volcanic undertone. Medium body and a low relative fruit intensity.

Riedel Vinum
6416-05

 < 10 °C   no

 < $50

 5-10 years

In the Carricante-style: *Fiona (Sicily, Italy), Catarratto (Sicily, Italy), Arneis (Piedmont, Italy).*

🔊 kas-tel-LAHW

Castelão, of: Periquita

João de Santarém, Periquita

The most widely planted grape variety of Portugal. Better known as Periquita, although that name is legally owned by José Maria da Fonseca on Setubal. The grape is adaptive to different climatic conditions amd makes a variety of styles: from everyday quaffer and rosado to powerful red wines with aging potential. The grape is mainly planted in Tejo, Alentejo and Lisbon but is nevertheless identified with Setubal where it produces intense wines with aromas of red currant.

	QUINTA DA MIMOSA, CASTELÃO, PALMELA, PORTUGAL			
C	📶	Therefore: grape with a thick skin	ruby	Therefore: 3 to 5 years old
H	📶		RED CHERRY, BLACKCHERRY, REDCURRANT, BLACKBERRY, PLUM	
A	📶	Therefore: oxidative winemaking	ALMOND, VANILLA	Therefore: (partly) new French oak
R	📶	Therefore: 3 to 5 years old	MEATY	
A	📶	Therefore: warm climate		
C	📶	Therefore: dry wine		
T	📶	Therefore: grape with a thick skin	astringent	Therefore: Old World
E	📶	Therefore: lots of sunshine (long season)	14 to 14.5%, full body	
R	📶	Therefore: Old World		

Tasting note: This medium, ruby-colored red has medium intense harvest aromas of red cherry, black cherry, redcurrant, blackberries and plum, some aromas of winemaking (like almond, vanilla and smoke) and ripening (meat). Low acidity, high alcohol, astringent tannins and a low relative fruit intensity.

Riedel Vinum
6416-30

 10-15 °C 2 hours

💲 < $50

 5-10 years

In the Castelão-style: Barbera d'Asti (Piedmont, Italy), Agiorgitiko (Nemea, Greece), Blaufränkisch (Burgenland, Austria).

28,601 ha (0.64%)

Catarratto: dominant on Sicily

C

Catarratto is Sicily's predominant white grape variety; it is planted in 60% of all vineyards of white varieties on the island, and widely planted across Italy. Catarratto is genetically related to Garganega. Often used for blending (with Catarratto for Etna DOC for example) and/or for Marsala. Catarratto is a productive variety, light in style, quite neutral in terms of aromas and juicy with lemony flavors without much acidity.

DONNAFUGATA, PRIO, CATARRATTO, SICILY, ITALY

C		lemon		Therefore: youthful
H	Therefore: a neutral grape variety	LIME · YELLOW APPLE · PEACH · LEMON · PINEAPPLE		
A	Therefore: reductive winemaking			
R	Therefore: youthful			
A	Therefore: moderate climate	malic acids		Therefore: no malo
C	Therefore: dry wine	fatty		Therefore: sur lie
T				
E		12.5 to 13%, medium body		
R	Therefore: Old World			

Tasting note: This pale, lemon-colored white has a restrained scent of apple, quince and melon, pineapple, medium acidity and medium alcohol. A fatty mouthfeel and a mineral undertone. Medium body and a low relative fruit intensity.

Riedel Vinum
6416-05

 < 10 °C   no

 < $50

 5-10 years

In the Catarratto-style: Albariño (Rias Baixas, Spain), Picpoul de Pinet (Languedoc, France), Carricante (Sicily, Italy)

🔊 shass-uh-LA

Chasselas: Fendant versus Edelzwicker

(Weisser) Gutedel, Fendant

Chasselas, of Swiss origine, takes its name from a village in the Loire and indeed is used to make Pouilly-sur-Loire. It is planted worldwide, and the most widely planted grape in Switzerland with 30% of total wine production, where it is known as Fendant. Here it is reliably low to medium in alcohol, typically dry, neutral and polished. In Alsace Chasselas is blended with other grapes in Edelzwicker, although new plantings have been banned here.

BADOUX, AIGLE LES MURAILLES, VALAIS, ZWITSERLAND

C			lemon		Therefore: youthful
H		Therefore: a neutral grape variety	YELLOW APPLE · PEAR · MELON · WET STONE		
A		Therefore: reductive winemaking			
R		Therefore: youthful			
A		Therefore: cool climate	malic acids		Therefore: no malo
C		Therefore: dry wine	fatty		Therefore: sur lie
T					
E			12.5 to 13%, light to medium body		
R		Therefore: Old World			

Tasting note: This pale, lemon-colored white has a restrained scent of apple, pear and melon, medium acidity and medium alcohol. A creamy texture and a mineral finish. Light to medium body and a low relative fruit intensity.

Riedel Vinum
6416-05

< 10 °C   no   < $50   5-10 years

In the Fendant-style: Chasselas (Alsace, France), Silvaner (Franken, Germany), Savennières (Loire, France).

26,167 ha (0.58%)

 sin-SOH

Cinsau(l)t: not just for rosé

Cinsaut, Cinq Sao, Ottavianello

Cinsaut and Cinsault are interchangeable. The latter is the French spelling and refers to its southern French origin, while the former encapsulates its modern-day global renaissance. Cinsaut is disease resistant and can withstand a lot of drought and heat, yet maintain good yields. In short, a robust grape with 20,000 hectares in France (mainly Corbieres, Languedoc), 2,000 hectares in South Africa (Cinsaut) and 1,000 hectares in Itata, in the south of Chile.

LA CAUSA, CINSAULT, ITATA, CHILE

C	Therefore: grape with a thin skin	purple		Therefore: youthful
H		RED CHERRY · RASPBERRY · PLUM · MINT · CRANBERRY		Therefore: Chile (due to the perfumery style)
A	Therefore: reductive winemaking			
R	Therefore: youthful			
A	Therefore: warm climate			
C	Therefore: dry wine			
T	Therefore: grape with a thin skin	ripe and soft		Therefore: New World
E	Therefore: lots of sunshine (high UV)	14 to 14.5%; medium to full body		
R	Therefore: New World			

Tasting note: This light, purple-colored red has intense aromas of red cherry, raspberry, plum, strawberry and mint. Low acidity, high alcohol and moderate tannins provide medium to full body.

Riedel Vinum
6416-30

10-15 °C · no

< $50 · 5-10 years

In the Cinsault-style: *Schiava (Alto Adige, Italy), Beaujolais-Villages (France), Sankt Laurent (Thermenregion, Austria).*

rare
2,403 ha (0.05%)

Cortese: as Piedmontese as white truffles

Cortese dell'Alto Monferrato, Colli Tortonesi, Gavi di Gavi

Cortese is native to Piedmont and performs best in the hills between Novi and Tortona in southeastern Piedmont where it used for Gavi and Cortese dell' Alto Monferrato. It is also featured in Lombardy and Veneto's Bianco di Custoza. Usually produces wines which are light in color, have a lemon-fresh perfume with moderate alcohol, juicy acidity and a restrained, mineral taste. The best Cortese can develop a honey-like richness.

VILLA SPARINA, GAVI, PIEDMONT, ITALY

C			lemon		Therefore: youthful
H		Therefore: a neutral grape variety	REINE CLAUDE · LIME · YELLOW APPLE · PEAR · WET STONE		
A		Therefore: reductive winemaking	ALMOND		Therefore: inert oak (like foudres)
R		Therefore: youthful			
A		Therefore: cool climate	malic acids		Therefore: no malo
C		Therefore: dry wine	fatty		Therefore: sur lie
T					
E			12.5 to 13%, medium body		
R		Therefore: Old World			

Tasting note: This pale, lemon-colored white has a mineral perfume of Reine Claude (greengage), lime, apple, pear and wet stones, with medium to high acidity and medium alcohol. A fatty mouthfeel and a mineral finish. Medium body and a low relative fruit intensity.

Riedel Vinum
6416-15

< 10 °C   no   < $50   < 5 years

In the Gavi-style: Grechetto (Umbria, Italy), Pinot Grigio (Alto Adige, Italy), Arneis (Piedmont, Italy).

small
6,235 ha (0.14%)

C

Corvina: the base for Valpolicella

Cruina

Corvina is mainly planted on the shores of Lake Garda and the hills of Valpolicella in the northeast of Verona. It is blended with the deeply colored Rondinella and to a lesser extent with the pale Molinara to produce Valpolicella and Bardolino. It can be a tricky grape because it ripens late and is prone to rot. Under good confitions, it is a naturally productive grape, ideal to produce the cherry-scented and red fruit driven regular Valpolicella.

BERTANI CRU
OGNISANTI
DI NOVARE
VALPOLICELLA
CLASSICO SUPERIORE

C	📶		purple	Therefore: youthful
H	📶		RED CHERRY · REDCURRANT · PLUM · LAUREL	
A	📶	Therefore: reductive winemaking	ALMOND	Therefore: inert oak (like foudres)
R	📶	Therefore: youthful		
A	📶	Therefore: moderate climate		
C	📶	Therefore: dry wine		
T	📶	Therefore: short (or cold) maceration	astringent	Therefore: Old World
E	📶		12.5 to 13.5%, medium body	
R	📶	Therefore: Old World		

Tasting note: This medium, purple-colored red wine has medium-intense aromas of red cherry, redcurrant, plum, bay leaf and almond. Medium acidity, medium alcohol and supple tannins provide a medium body.

Riedel Vinum
6416-07

 10-15 °C

 no

 < $50

< 5 years

In the Valpolicella-style: Beaujolais-Villages (France), Zweigelt (Austria), Dolcetto (Piedmont, Italy).

Corvina: and for Amarone!

small
6,235 ha (0.14%)

Amarone della Valpolicella, or Amarone, is a full bodied red (primarily) made from Corvina which has been air-dried for some 120 days, commonly in in- or outdoor drying rooms. This process is called *appassimento* in Italian. Amarone literally means 'great bitter', to distinguish it from Recioto, which is made similarly but with lots of residual sugar. Amarone is (off) dry, high in alcohol, with distinctive raisiny aromas and a bitter-edged almond and chocolaty flavor.

BERTANI, AMARONE DELLA VALPOLICELLA, VENETO, ITALY

C 📶	Therefore: grape with a thick skin	ruby		Therefore: 3 to 5 years old
H 📶		PRESERVED FRUITS, COMPOTE, PLUM, DRIED FRUITS, RAISINS		
A 📶	Therefore: oxidative winemaking	ALMOND, CEDAR, TOAST		Therefore: inert oak (like foudres)
R 📶	Therefore: 3 to 5 years old	TOBACCO, EARTH		
A 📶	Therefore: moderate climate			
C 📶	Therefore: not bone dry			
T 📶	Therefore: grape with a thick skin	astringent		Therefore: Old World
E 📶	Therefore: concentration through raising	14 to 14.5%, full body		
R 📶	Therefore: Old World			

Tasting note: This deep, ruby-colored red has medium-intense aromas of candied red currant, fig paste, blueberry jam, prune and almond, cedar, toast, tobacco and earth. Medium acidity, high alcohol, some residual sweetness and ripe but slightly drying tannins, resulting in a full body and a low relative fruit intensity.

Riedel Vinum 6416-15

10-15 °C   2 hours   < $100   > 10 years

In the Amarone della Valpolicella-style:
Ripasso (Italy), Malbec (Mendoza, Argentina), Zinfandel (California, United States).

◆) kree-YO-yah

Criolla Grande (versus Criolla Chica)

Criolla, Criolla Grande Sanjuanina

small
15,596 ha (0.35%)

Compare Criolla Grande in Argentina with Pais (Criolla Chica) in Chile. The wines made from it are mainly drunk locally and are rarely concentrated or complex. Ampelographers believe that this is not a coincidence and that they have a common parent. Criolla Grande is assumed to be a cross of Mission and Muscat of Alexandria. The grape has a pink skin but is larger than its Chilean cousin and is mainly used to make white wine or rosé.

C

EL ESTECO, CRIOLLA GRANDE, CAFAYATE, ARGENTINA

C	Therefore: grape with a thin skin	ruby		Therefore: youthful
H		RED CHERRY · RASPBERRY · PLUM · STRAWBERRY · LAUREL		
A	Therefore: reductive winemaking	ALMOND		Therefore: no aging in oak
R	Therefore: youthful			
A	Therefore: moderate climate			
C	Therefore: dry wine			
T	Therefore: grape with a thin skin	ripe and soft		Therefore: New World
E	Therefore: lots of sunshine (high UV)	14.5%, full body		
R	Therefore: New World			

Tasting note: This light to medium, ruby-colored red has intense aromas of red cherry, raspberry, plum, strawberry and bay leaf. Low acidity, medium to high alcohol and moderate, sweet tannins result in a medium to full body and a high relative fruit intensity.

Riedel Vinum
6416-15

 10-15 °C no

 < $50

 5-10 years

In the Criolla-style: *Pais (Itata, Chile), Cinsault (Maule, Chile), Schiava (Alto Adige, Italy).*

Dolcetto: 'the little sweet one'

Dolsin, Ormeasca

rare
4,530 ha (0.10%)

Dolcetto ('little sweet one') is third in the ranking of red grapes in Piedmont. Because of this, and because Dolcetto ripens early, the grape often grows at higher altitudes where it is cooler and where Nebbiolo and Barbera struggle to ripen. Fortunately, these cooler spots also help the grape maintain its acidity. Dolcetto is fruit-intense, with mainly red and black cherry and plum along with impressions of licorice and almond and medium tannins.

Parusso
DOLCETTO D'ALBA
PIANI NOCE

PARUSSO, DOLCETTO, PIEDMONT, ITALY

C	Therefore: grape with a medium thick skin	purple		Therefore: youthful
H		RED CHERRY, BLACKCHERRY, REDCURRANT, PLUM, LAUREL		
A	Therefore: oxidative winemaking	ALMOND, TOAST		Therefore: foudres
R	Therefore: youthful			
A	Therefore: moderate climate			
C	Therefore: dry wine			
T	Therefore: grape with a medium thick skin	astringent		Therefore: Old World
E	Therefore: lots of sunshine (long season)	12.5%, medium body		
R	Therefore: Old World			

Tasting note: This medium, purple-colored red has medium-intense aromas of red cherry, redcurrant, plum, bay leaf, toast and almond. Medium acidity, medium alcohol and medium tannins result in a medium body and a low relative fruit intensity.

Riedel Vinum
6416-07

 10-15 °C   0.5 hours

 <$50

 5-10 years

In the Dolcetto-style: Beaujolais-Villages (France), Zweigelt (Austria), Valpolicella (Veneto, Italy).

small
7,869 ha (0.18%)

🔊 DORN-dell-der

Dornfelder: German pride?

This variety quickly rises to the number two position of German reds. It is productive and early-ripening with lots of color and a thick skin. Developed in Württemberg in 1955 to add a bit of color to Pinot Noir and other paler reds, it proved itself as a stand-alone variety with character, attractive aroma and sufficient complexity and freshness. Dornfelder does particularly well with (new) oak. It is mainly planted in Pfalz, Ahr and Rheinhessen.

D

Riedel Vinum
6416-30

DEUTZERHOF, DORNFELDER, AHR, GERMANY

C 📶	Therefore: grape with a very thick skin	purple	Therefore: youthful
H 📶		PLUM BLACKBERRY BLACKCHERRY BLOSSOM BLACKCURRANT	
A 📶	Therefore: oxidative winemaking	VANILLA CEDAR TOAST	Therefore: (partly) new French oak
R 📶	Therefore: youthful		
A 📶	Therefore: cool climate		
C 📶	Therefore: dry wine		
T 📶	Therefore: grape with a thick skin	slightly astringent	Therefore: Old World
E 📶		12 to 13%, medium body	
R 📶	Therefore: Old World		

Tasting note: This deep purple red has medium-intense aromas of plum, blackberry, black cherry, vanilla, cedar and toast. High acidity, medium alcohol and medium to high tannins provide freshness and soft texture, medium body, and a floral finish. A medium relative fruit intensity.

10-15 °C   0.5 hours   < $50   < 5 years

In the Dornfelder-style: Dolcetto (Piedmont, Italy), Zweigelt (Austria), Valpolicella (Veneto, Italy).

🔊 DEW-rif

rare
4,804 ha (0.11%)

Durif, alias Petite Sirah

Duriff, Plant Durif, Plant Fourchu, Pinot de Romans and Pinot de l'Hermitage, Petit Syrah

In the nursery of the French botanist François Durif, a spontaneous cross between Syrah and Peloursin happened in 1860. With this Durif accidentally discovered a new variety which was subsequently named after him. Mainly found in California, France, Australia and Israel (here it's known as Petite Sirah), Durif delivers inky wines with impressions of plums, blackberries, blueberries, black pepper, spices and licorice, lots of ripe tannins and medium to high acidity.

RIDGE, PETITE SIRAH, CALIFORNIA

C 📶	Therefore: grape with a thick skin	ruby		Therefore: 3 to 5 years old
H 📶		PLUM · BLACKBERRY · BLUEBERRY · CLOVE · CINNAMON		
A 📶	Therefore: oxidative winemaking	TOAST · VANILLA · CEDAR		Therefore: (partly) new French oak
R 📶	Therefore: 3 to 5 years old			
A 📶	Therefore: hot climate			
C 📶	Therefore: dry wine			
T 📶	Therefore: grape with a thick skin	ripe and soft		Therefore: New World
E 📶	Therefore: lots of sunshine (long season)	14 to 14.5%, full body		
R 📶	Therefore: New World			

Tasting note: This deep, ruby-colored red has medium-intense aromas of plum, blackberry, blueberry jam, cloves, cinnamon, licorice and toast. Low acidity, high alcohol, lots of ripe tannins, and a sun-baked character. Full body, and a high relative fruit intensity.

Riedel Vinum
6416-30

 10-15 °C 0.5 hours

 < $50

 >10 years

In the Petite Sirah-style: Alicante Bouschet (California, United States), Malbec (Mendoza, Argentina), Touriga Nacional (Douro, Portugal).

rare
3,534 ha (0.08%)

◀) fa-lan-GHEE-nah

Falanghina: the Janus variety

Biancozita en variaties op Falanghina

Falanghina, like the Roman god Janus, has two faces, and is actually two varieties – Falanghina Flegrea and Falanghina Beneventana. The two are often blended, together and with other native grapes. Falanghina is mainly planted in Campania in southern Italy and in neighboring regions such as Puglia and Abruzzo. The more Beneventana in the blend, the more concentrated the wine will be with impressions of citrus and yellow apple, mandarin and pineapple.

F

CRUNA DELAGO

LA SIBILLA

CAMPI FLEGREI FALANGHINA 'CRUNA DELAGO', LA SIBILLA

C	📶		lemon		Therefore: youthful
H	📶	Therefore: a neutral grape variety	YELLOW APPLE TANGERINE BLOSSOM PINEAPPLE ORANGE		
A	📶	Therefore: reductive winemaking			
R	📶	Therefore: youthful			
A	📶	Therefore: cool climate	malic acids		Therefore: no malo
C	📶	Therefore: bone dry	fatty		Therefore: sur lie
T	📶				
E	📶		12.5%, medium body		
R	📶	Therefore: Old World			

Tasting note: This pale, lemon-colored white has a restrained mineral perfume of lemon, peach blossom, pineapple, yellow apple, mandarin and medium acidity and medium alcohol. Italian almond touch in the aftertaste. Medium body and a low relative fruit intensity.

Riedel Vinum
6416-05

 < 10 °C   no   < $50   < 5 years

In the Falanghina-style: Soave Classico (Veneto, Italy), Albariño (Rias Baixas, Spain), Chenin Blanc (Loire, France).

12,211 ha (0.27%)

🔊 fair-NAHW pee-res

Fernão Pires: typical Portuguese

Maria Gomes

Fernão Pires is planted all over Portugal, especially in the Tejo, Lisboa and Bairrada, where it is also known as 'Maria Gomes'. Fernão Pires is aromatic with impressions of lime, lemon, rose and blossom, mandarin and orange peel. It's at its best when young. The grape is versatile, both made as a single varietal and as a blend, harvested early as a base wine for sparkling wines and late harvested for sweet wine. Outside of Portugal, it has been planted with some success in South Africa and Australia.

CASA ERMELINDA FREITAS, FERNÃO PIRES, ALENTEJO, PORTUGAL

									Therefore:
C	📶		lemon						Therefore: youthful
H	📶	Therefore: aromatic grape variety	LIME	LEMON	ROSE	BLOSSOM	TANGERINE		
A	📶	Therefore: reductive winemaking							
R	📶	Therefore: youthful							
A	📶	Therefore: moderate climate							
C	📶	Therefore: dry wine	fatty						Therefore: sur lie
T	📶								
E	📶	Therefore lots of sunshine (long season)	13 to 14%, medium body						
R	📶	Therefore: Old World							

Tasting note: This pale, lemon-colored white has an intense perfume of lime, lemon, rose, mandarin, blossom, citrus zest, medium acidity and medium alcohol. Medium body and a low relative fruit intensity.

Riedel Vinum 6416-33

 < 10 °C   no   < $50   < 5 years

In the Fernão Pires-style: Moschofilero (Peloponnesos, Greece), Kerner (Alto Adige, Italy), Torrontès (Cafayate, Argentina).

258

rare
3,248 ha (0.07%)

🔊 fay-tay-ES-ka nay-A-grah

Feteasca Neagra: the black virgin

Schwarze Mädchentraube

Feteasca Neagra ('black virgin' or black 'girl') is one of the best red wines in Romania. It has an Italian character with impressions of red plum, fresh acidity and ripe but drying tannins and an intriguing spicy aftertaste. It can withstand both frigid winters and very dry summers. It ripens late and has a thick skin. In the past it was primarily used as a blending grape; currently, it is increasingly used as a single varietal.

F

DAVINO, PURPURA VALAHICA, FETEASCA NEAGRA, DEALUL MARE, ROEMENIË

C	📶	Therefore: grape with a thick skin	ruby	Therefore: 5 to 10 years old
H	📶		PLUM · RED CHERRY · REDCURRANT · COMPOTE · PRESERVED FRUITS	
A	📶	Therefore: oxidative winemaking	CEDAR · TOAST	Therefore: (partly) new French oak
R	📶	Therefore: 5 to 10 years old	TOBACCO · EARTH	
A	📶	Therefore: warm climate		
C	📶	Therefore: dry wine		
T	📶	Therefore: grape with a thick skin	astringent	Therefore: Old World
E	📶	Therefore: lots of sunshine (long season)	13.5 to 14.5%, full body	
R	📶	Therefore: Old World		

Tasting note: This deep, ruby-colored red has medium-intense aromas of red plum, red cherry and red berry in a very ripe, confit style, cedar and some toast. Low acidity, high alcohol and lots of astringent tannins with an earthy finish. Full body and a low relative fruit intensity.

Riedel Vinum 6416-30

 10-15 °C 2 hours < $50 · 5-10 years

In the Feteasca Neagra-style: Chianti Classico (Toscane, Italy), Montepulciano d'Abruzzo (Italy), Negroamaro (Sicily, Italy).

rare
2,180 ha (0.05%)

🔊 fee-AH-noh

Fiano goes mainly solo

Apiano, Latino

Fiano has been in southern Italy for more than 2,000 years, especially in Campania and Sicily. Mainly made as a single varietal, it features aromas of almonds and spicy and tropical impressions such as pineapple. Most famous is Fiano di Avellino, a DOCG, from the volcanic hills of Avellino, east of Naples, but the grape is also found in Sicily, mainly also on volcanic soils. The grape is early ripening with low yields and produces fresh, balanced wines, often with a hint of honey. ●

PLANETA, COMETA, FIANO, SICILY, ITALY

C	🛜		lemon						Therefore: youthful
H	🛜	Therefore: a neutral grape variety	YELLOW APPLE	PEACH	PINE APPLE	PEAR	CHAMOMILE		
A	🛜	Therefore: reductive winemaking	ALMOND						Therefore: inert oak (like foudres)
R	🛜	Therefore: youthful							
A	🛜	Therefore: warm climate							
C	🛜	Therefore: dry wine	fatty						Therefore: sur lie
T	🛜								
E	🛜	Therefore lots of sunshine (long season)	13.5 to 14% medium to full body						
R	🛜	Therefore: Old World							

Tasting note: This pale, lemon-colored white has a perfume of apple, peach, pineapple, pear, chamomile and almond, low acidity and medium to high alcohol. A creamy texture and a medium to full body, with a low relative fruit intensity.

Riedel Vinum
6416-05

 < 10 °C   no

 < $50   < 5 years

In the Fiano-style: Côtes-du-Rhône Blanc (France), Viognier (Languedoc, France), Vermentino (Sicily, Italy).

rare
2,180 ha (0.05%)

🔊 frap-PAH-toh

Frappato: Sicilian for Beaujolais?

Frappato Nero, Frappato di Vittoria

Frappato is a light-colored grape from the southeast coast of Sicily. Historically significant because in 2005 the region of Cerasuolo di Vittoria (blend of Frappato and Nero d'Avola) received Sicily's first and only DOCG. Stylistically, Frappato is reminiscent of good Beaujolais. However, the grape is used almost exclusively in blends. Nero d'Avola is the main blending partner due to its complementary body weight and color.

F

DONNAFUGATA, BELL'ASSAI, FRAPPATO, SICILY, ITALY

C 📶	Therefore: grape with a thin skin	purple		Therefore: youthful
H 📶		RED CHERRY · RASPBERRY · PLUM · STRAWBERRY · LAUREL		
A 📶	Therefore: reductive winemaking	ALMOND		Therefore: inert oak (like foudres)
R 📶	Therefore: youthful			Therefore: youthful
A 📶	Therefore: warm climate			
C 📶	Therefore: dry wine			
T 📶	Therefore: grape with a thin skin	astringent		Therefore: Old World
E 📶	Therefore: lots of sunshine (long season)	12.5 to 13%, medium body		
R 📶	Therefore: Old World			

Tasting note: This medium, purple-colored red has intense aromas of red cherry, raspberry, plum, strawberry, almond and bay leaf. Low acidity, medium alcohol and slightly drying tannins provide a medium body with a medium relative fruit intensity.

Riedel Vinum
6416-15

 10-15 °C   no   < $50   5-10 years

In the Frappato-style: Schiava (Alto Adige, Italy), Pais (Itata, Chile), Cinsault (Maule, Chile).

🔊 free-oh-LAH-noh

Friulano: now without Tocai

Sauvignonasse, Sauvignon Vert

Friulano is most common in northeastern Italy. The wine is fruit intense with notes of citrus and almond. Originally from southwestern France where it is known as Sauvignonasse or Sauvignon Vert. The name 'Tocai' existed for centuries before it was banned due to an infringement case versus Tokaji in Hungary. Friulano is fuller and less aromatic than Sauvignon Blanc, but it has a fresh acidity with 'green' notes, just like in Sauvignon Blanc.

RONCHI DI MANZANO, FRIULANO, FRIULI COLLI, ITALY

C			lemon				Therefore: youthful
H		Therefore: aromatic grape variety	GRAPEFRUIT	LIME	PEAR	GRANNY SMITH	Sauvignon-Blanc-like aromas
A		Therefore: reductive winemaking	ALMOND				Therefore: foudres/rvs
R		Therefore: youthful					
A		Therefore: cool climate	malic acids				Therefore: no malo
C		Therefore: dry wine	fatty				Therefore: sur lie
T							
E			12.5 to 13%, light to medium body				
R		Therefore: Old World					

Tasting note: This pale, lemon-colored white has an intense scent of grapefruit, lime, pear and Granny Smith, high acidity and medium alcohol. A moderate creamy texture and a mineral undertone. Light to medium body and a low relative fruit intensity.

Riedel Vinum
6416-15

 < 10 °C   no   < $50   < 5 years

In the Friulano-style: Sauvignonasse (Curicó, Chile), Malagouzia (Macedonia, Greece), Verdejo (Rueda, Spain).

🔊 foor-MINT

rare
4,417 ha (0.10%)

Furmint from Tokaj

Mosler in Austria, Sipon in Slovenië en noordelijk Kroatië, en Zapfner in Germany

The Tokaj wine region is located 150 miles northeast of Budapest where the rivers Tisza and Bodrog meet. Tokaj enjoys long sunny summers, while the combination of a dry autumn and morning mist stimulate the development of *Botrytis cinerea*. Aszú in the name refers to the grapes affected by noble rot. A 5 Puttonyos Tokaji indicates at least 120 gr/l of residual sugar. Outside of Tokaj, Furmint is mainly found in Somlo in northwestern Hungary for dry whites.

DISZNÓKÓ, TOKAJI ASZÚ, 5 PUTTONYOS, HUNGARY

C	📶		orange	Therefore: oxidative winemaking
H	📶		APRICOT, BLOSSOM, PEACH, ACACIA, HONEY	honey, therefore: Botrytis
A	📶	Therefore: oxidative winemaking	CEDAR, ALMOND	Therefore: (partly) new French oak
R	📶	Therefore: 3 to 5 years old	ZEST, MARMELADE, WALNUT	
A	📶	Therefore: cool climate	malic acids	Therefore: no malo
C	📶	Therefore: very sweet	more than 120 gr/l	
T	📶			
E	📶		12 to 13.5%, medium to full body	
R	📶	Therefore: Old World		

Tasting note: This deep, amber-colored dessert wine has a seductive perfume of orange blossom, peach, zest, acacia, honey, orange peel and walnut and cedar, high acidity, medium alcohol and is very sweet. Classic dessert wine, one of a kind. Medium to full body with a low relative fruit intensity.

< 10 °C   no

< $100

> 10 years

Riedel Vinum
6416-33

In the Tokaji Aszú-style: Ausbruch (Neusiedlersee, Austria).

28,560 ha (0.64%)

Gamay: the essence of Beaujolais

Gamay (in full: Gamay Noir à Jus Blanc) is known for the frivolity of Beaujolais, but it certainly also has a mineral side. Gamay's aromas are fruity (especially strawberries, raspberries, and red cherries) with moderate tannins. The Dukes of Burgundy tried to stop Gamay as it spread into France from Germany. Instead, it ended up on the granite soils just north of Lyon. In retrospect, perhaps the most suitable area.

LOUIS CLAUDE DESVIGNES, MORGON, FRANCE

C	📶	Therefore: grape with a medium thick skin	purple	Therefore: youthful
H	📶	Therefore: carbonic maceration	RED CHERRY RASPBERRY PLUM STRAWBERRY	
A	📶	Therefore: carbonic maceration	PEAR DROPS	
R	📶	Therefore: youthful		
A	📶	Therefore: moderate climate		
C	📶	Therefore: dry wine		
T	📶	Therefore: carbonic maceration		
E	📶		12.5 to 14%, medium body	
R	📶	Therefore: Old World		

Tasting note: This medium intense purple-colored red has medium intense aromas of red cherry, raspberry, plum, strawberry and wine gums. Medium acidity, medium alcohol, and moderate to medium tannins provide a medium body with mineral complexity and a low relative fruit intensity.

Riedel Vinum
6416-07

10-15 °C   no

< $50

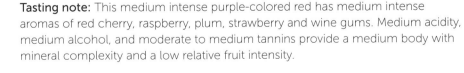

5-10 years

In the Gamay-style: Valpolicella (Veneto, Italy), Sankt Laurent (Thermenregion, Austria), Schiava (Alto Adige, Italy).

🔊 gahr-GAH-nay-gah

Garganega: the soul of Soave

Garganega ('from the town of Gargano') is indeed mainly located in the provinces of Verona and Vicenza. It is the sixth most planted white grape in Italy. It forms the basis of Soave and is also part of Gambellara and Bianco di Custoza. DNA tests in 2003 and 2008 confirmed that Sicily's Grecanico Dorato is identical to Garganega. In Soave, Garganega makes up 70 to 100% of the blend and the grape can produce a delicate wine with lemon, almond and spicy notes.

Riedel Vinum
6416-05

PIEROPAN, SOAVE CLASSICO, VENETO, ITALY

C	📶		lemon	Therefore: youthful
H	📶	Therefore: a neutral grape variety	REINE CLAUDE · LEMON · LIME · YELLOW APPLE · PEAR	
A	📶	Therefore: reductive winemaking	ALMOND	Therefore: inert oak (like foudres)
R	📶	Therefore: youthful		
A	📶	Therefore: cool climate		
C	📶	Therefore: dry wine	fatty	Therefore: sur lie
T	📶		astringent	Therefore: Old World
E	📶		13.5%, medium to full body	
R	📶	Therefore: Old World		

Tasting note: This pale, lemon-colored white has a restrained perfume of *Reine Claude* (greengage), lime, apple, pear and almond, high acidity and medium alcohol. A creamy texture and a mineral finish. Medium body and a low relative fruit intensity.

< 10 °C   no   < $50   < 5 years

In the Soave-style: *Falanghina (Campania, Italy), Albariño (Rias Baixas, Spain), Chenin Blanc (Loire, France).*

G

Goruli Mtsvane: as Georgian as it gets

Native white from Kartli in Georgia, distinct from the Kakhuri Mtsvane from Kakheti. It is one of the lightest wines in Georgia, minerally refined, with delicate citrus aromas and honey notes, slightly floral. Goruli Mtsvane is also blended with Chinuri and Budeshuri Tetri for sparkling wines. The grape has many synonyms and a lot of variability and is often blended with Rkatsiteli or Chinuri as it is prone to oxidation when used alone.

MUKHRANI, RÉSERVE ROYALE, GORULI MTSVANE, KARTLI, GEORGIA

C			lemon				Therefore: youthful
H		Therefore: a neutral grape variety	GRAPEFRUIT	PEAR	REINE CLAUDE	PEACH	
A		Therefore: reductive winemaking	ALMOND	HAZELNUT			Therefore: inert oak (like foudres)
R		Therefore: 3 to 5 years old					
A		Therefore: warm climate					
C		Therefore: dry wine	fatty				Therefore: sur lie
T							
E			12.5%, medium to full body				
R		Therefore: Old World					

CHÂTEAU MUKHRANI
RÉSERVE ROYALE
GORULI MTSVANE
2016
GRAND VIN DE GÉORGIE

Tasting note: This pale, lemon-colored white has a restrained nose of grapefruit, quince and peach, *Reine Claude* (greengage), pear, cedar, hazelnut, low acidity and medium alcohol. A fatty mouthfeel, medium body and a low relative fruit intensity.

Riedel Vinum
6416-97

< 10 °C   no

$ $ $
< $50

5-10 years

In the Goruli Mtsvane-style: *Saint-Peray (Rhône, France), Châteauneuf-du-Pape Blanc (Rhône, France).*

small
24,368 ha (0.59%)

🔊 grah-say-VEE-nah

Graševina — or Welschriesling

Riesling Italico, Grasssica, Laski Rizling, Banat Riesling, Olaszrizling, Riesler, Vojvodina, Wälschriesling, Welschrizling, Welsch Rizling, Borba en Welschriesling

Graševina (or Welschriesling) is the most widely planted variety in Croatia, but is also found throughout Central and Eastern Europe. Since it is called Welschriesling in Germany and Austria – which literally means 'foreign Riesling' – the grape most likely has been imported here (from Croatia). It is a productive grape that retains its acidity even in warmer climates and which is susceptible to Botrytis as in the Neusiedlersee in Austria.

KRACHER, WELSCHRIESLING #9, NEUSIEDLERSEE, AUSTRIA

C 📶		golden		Therefore: 3 to 5 years old
H 📶	Therefore: semi-aromatic variety	APRICOT · LYCHEE · LEMON · PINEAPPLE · HONEY		honey, therefore: Botrytis
A 📶	Therefore: reductive winemaking	ALMOND		Therefore: stainless steel (plus some oak)
R 📶	Therefore: 3 to 5 years old	DRIED FRUITS · MARMELADE · ZEST		
A 📶	Therefore: cool climate	malic acids		Therefore: no malo
C 📶	Therefore: very sweet wine	more than 250 gr/l		Therefore: TBA-style
T 📶				
E 📶	Therefore: interruption alc. fermentation	less than 10%, rich, medium body		
R 📶	Therefore: Old World			

Riedel Vinum
6416-33

Tasting note: This medium intense, golden-colored dessert wine has a medium intense nose of lychee, pineapple, lemon zest, apricot jam and honey. In the mouth the wine is lusciously sweet with high acidity, low alcohol and again that combination of pineapple, lemon zest, apricot jam, apple compote and honey. Rich but medium body and a medium relative fruit intensity.

🌡 < 10 °C   no   < $100   > 10 years

In the Welschriesling c.q. Ausbruch-style: Chenin Blancs with Botrytis In the Loire (France) BA and TBA (Germany), Sélection de Grains Nobles In the Alsace (France).

G

🔊 greh-KETT-oh

rare
1,814 ha (0.04%)

Grechetto, of Greek origin

Grechetto, Greghetto, Grechetto Spoletino, Greco Spoletino, Greco Bianco di Perugia

Grechetto (Bianco) is a white Italian grape of Greek origin. The grape is grown throughout central Italy, especially in the Umbria region, where it is mainly used for Orvieto (with Trebbiano) and blends with other varieties such as Chardonnay, Malvasia and Verdello. The thick skin allows the grape to be harvested late with high sugar levels, ideal for vin santo. There are at least two Grechetto grapes: Grechetto di Todi and Grechetto Spoletino, the former being more widely planted.

SANGIOVANNI DELLA SALA, ORVIETO, ITALY

C			lemon		Therefore: youthful
H		Therefore: a neutral grape variety	PEAR, PEACH, PINEAPPLE, ACACIA, BLOSSOM		
A		Therefore: reductive winemaking	ALMOND		
R		Therefore: youthful			
A		Therefore: warm climate			
C		Therefore: dry wine	fatty		Therefore: sur lie
T					
E		Therefore: lots of sunshine (long season)	12.5 to 13.5%, medium body		
R		Therefore: Old World			

Tasting note: This pale, lemon-colored white has a low aroma intensity of pear, peach, pineapple, acacia, blossom and almond, low acidity and medium to high alcohol. A creamy texture and medium body with a low relative fruit intensity.

Riedel Vinum
6416-05

 < 10 °C   no

 < $50   5-10 years

In the Orvieto-style: *Vermentino (Sicily, Italy), Soave (Italy).*

268

small
7,378 ha (0.16%)

🔊 GREE-yoh

Grillo for Marsala

Ariddu, Riddu, Rossese Bianco

Marsala is a fortified wine from western Sicily and was established by the British in the mid-1800s, after the port trade had come to a standstill due to the war against Bonaparte. British merchants bought Grillo, Catarratto and Inzolia from smaller producers. These producers kept their wines in casks for years, then blended them together in a solera (*perpetuo*) system and – when necessary – fortified with alcohol before starting their return journey to England.

MARCO DE BARTOLI, MARSALA SUPERIORE ORO, ITALY

C			orange	Therefore: oxidative winemaking
H			ORANGE · RAISINS · MARMELADE · ZEST · APRICOT	
A		Therefore: oxidative winemaking	HAZELNUT · ALMOND · WALNUT	Therefore: foudres
R		Therefore: 3 to 5 years in bottle	DRIED FRUITS	
A		Therefore: moderate climate	salty	
C		Therefore: medium sweet	50 to 90 gr/l	Therefore: semi-secco
T				
E		Therefore: fortified	18 to 19%, full body	
R		Therefore: Old World		

Tasting note: This fortified wine has an intense aroma of marmalade, orange peel, raisins, dates, walnut, hazelnut and almond. In the style of slightly sweet Madeira with a salty aftertaste and medium acidity. Full body and a low relative fruit intensity.

 10-15 °C no   < $100 > 10 years

Riedel Vinum
6416-33

In the Marsala-style: *Sercial and Verdelho Madeira (Portugal), Palo Cortado (sherry, Spain), Amontillado (sherry, Spain).*

and more!

Grillo is a cross of Catarratto and Zibibbo, formerly used exclusively for Marsala. However, plantings declined in the 1960s when producers opted for the more productive Catarratto. Grillo nearly went extinct but then experiments proved that it can also be appealing as a dry, white wine. Even on the warm plains around Marsala it thrives and doesn't get jammy but retains its fresh acidity and honeyed taste of citrus blossom, peach and apple along with a nutty finish.

		DONNAFUGATA, SURSUR, GRILLO, SICILY, ITALY		
C			lemon	Therefore: youthful
H		dus: semi-aromatisch druivenras	REINE CLAUDE · LIME · BLOSSOM · YELLOW APPLE · PEACH	
A		Therefore: reductive winemaking	ALMOND	
R		Therefore: youthful		
A		Therefore: moderate climate		
C		Therefore: dry wine	rich texture	Therefore: sur lie
T				
E			12.5 to 13.5%, medium body	
R		Therefore: Old World		

Tasting note: This pale, lemon-colored white has a restrained bouquet of *Reine Claude* (greengage), lime blossom, apple and peach, medium acidity and medium alcohol. A rich texture, a honeyed undertone and almond in the aftertaste. Medium body and a low relative fruit intensity.

Riedel Vinum
6416-05

 < 10 °C no

  < $50

5-10 years

In the Grillo-style: *Fiano (Sicily, Italy), Savatiano (Macedonia, Greece), Albariño (Rias Baixas, Spain).*

small
19,063 ha (0.42%)

🔊 grew-ner velt-LEE-ner

Grüner Veltliner: Austria's trump card

Weissgipfler, Grunmuskateller, Veltlin, Veltlin Zelene, Veltlinske Zelene, Zeleni Veltlinec, Zoldveltelini, Zold Veltlini

Grüner Veltliner can be found in Austria, Hungary, Slovakia and the Czech Republic, although the New World (especially Australia, New Zealand and the United States) has also discovered it. About a third of all Austrian vineyards are Grüner Veltliner, especially in Lower Austria and northern Burgenland. Recognizable by its notes of citrus, celery and white pepper. The grape reaches its highest quality in areas such as Kremstal, Kamptal and Wachau.

G

DOMÄNE WACHAU, GRÜNER VELTLINER, FEDERSPIEL, AUSTRIA

C			lemon		Therefore: youthful
H		Therefore: a neutral grape variety	REINE CLAUDE · LIME · WHITE PEPPER · YELLOW APPLE · PEAR		Citrus and white pepper, therefore: Grüner Veltliner
A		Therefore: reductive winemaking			
R		Therefore: youthful			
A		Therefore: cool climate	malic acids		Therefore: no malo
C		Therefore: dry wine	fatty		Therefore: sur lie
T					
E			12.5 to 13.5%, medium body		
R		Therefore: Old World			

Tasting note: This pale, lemon-colored white has a restrained perfume of Reine Claude (greengage), lime, apple, pear, white pepper and fennel, high acidity and medium alcohol. A creamy texture and a mineral undertone. Federspiel is a medium bodied style, while Smaragd can be full bodied.

Riedel Vinum
6416-05

 < 10 °C

 no

 < $50

5-10 years

In the Wachau Federspiel-style: Silvaner (Franken, Germany), Chenin Blanc (Loire, France), Albariño (Rias Baixas, Spain).

rare
4,713 ha (0.11%)

🔊 in-ZO-lee-ah

Inzolia (Sicily)=Ansonica (Tuscany)

Ansonica, Ansonica Bianca, Insolia, Nzolia

Inzolia is an indigenous variety planted in Sicily and Tuscany. At the end of ripening, the grape tends to lose a lot of acidity, which is what made it so suitable for Marsala. However, due to earlier picking and better vinification modern Inzolia is a fresh, dry white wine in its own right; understated in character, with nutty, citrusy impressions combined with spicy notes. In Tuscany (especially in the Maremma), the grape is known as Ansonica.

DONNAFUGATA, VIGNA DI GABRI, SICILY, ITALY

C	📶		lemon		Therefore: youthful
H	📶	Therefore: a neutral grape variety	YELLOW APPLE · LIME · PEAR · REINE CLAUDE · GARRIGUE		
A	📶	Therefore: reductive winemaking	ALMOND		Therefore: inert oak (like foudres)
R	📶	Therefore: youthful			
A	📶	Therefore: moderate climate			
C	📶	Therefore: dry wine	fatty		Therefore: sur lie
T	📶				
E	📶		12.5 to 13%, medium body		
R	📶	Therefore: Old World			

Tasting note: This pale, lemon-colored white has a subtle perfume of *Reine Claude* (greengage), lime, apple, pear, Mediterranean herbs, medium acidity and medium alcohol. A fatty mouthfeel and a low relative fruit intensity.

Riedel Vinum
6416-05

 < 10 °C   no

  < $50   5-10 years

In the Inzolia-style: Grüner Veltliner (Austria), Chenin Blanc (Swartland, South Africa), Albariño (Rias Baixas, Spain).

rare
478 ha (0.01%)

🔊 lah-GREYN

Lagrein from Süd Tirol

Originating from the northern Italian region Süd Tirol, or Alto Adige (although the name suggests the Lagarina valley of Trentino), and together with Marzemino a descendant of Teroldego and also related to Syrah, Pinot Noir and Dureza. First mentioned in the archives of the Abbey of Muri in the 17th century. Lagrein wines are powerful with plum and black cherry aromas, deeply-colored and provided with firm tannins. Lagrein has also been planted in Australia and California.

TIEFENBRUNNER, LAGREIN, ALTO ADIGE, ITALY

C	Therefore: grape with a very thick skin	ruby		Therefore: 3 to 5 years old
H		PLUM, RED CHERRY, BLACKCURRANT, BLUEBERRY, LAUREL		
A	Therefore: matured in oak	CEDAR, TOAST		Therefore: (partly) new French oak
R	Therefore: 3 to 5 years old	TOBACCO, EARTH		
A	Therefore: moderate climate			
C	Therefore: dry wine			
T	Therefore: grape with a very thick skin	astringent		Therefore: Old World
E	Therefore: lots of sunshine (long season)	13.5 to 14.5%, full body		
R	Therefore: Old World			

Tasting note: This deep, ruby-colored red has medium intense aromas of red plum, blackcurrant and amarena cherry, cedar and some toast. Medium acidity, high alcohol and lots of firm tannins and an earthy aftertaste. Full body and a medium relative fruit intensity.

Riedel Vinum
6416-30

10-15 °C   0.5 hours

< $50

5-10 years

In the Lagrein-style: Teroldego (Italy), Montepulciano d'Abruzzo (Italy), Blaufränkisch (Burgenland, Austria).

small
13,575 ha (0.31%)

Lambrusco: the comeback kid

Selvatica or Salvatica

Both grape and wine are called Lambrusco. More precisely, from a family of closely related varieties originating from four zones in Emilia-Romagna and one in Lombardy. It is an old grape with well documented history. During the 1970s and 1980s, sweet Lambrusco was the best-selling imported wine in the United States. Today's Lambruscos can be sparkling, rosé and (light) red and range from dry to sweet.

RADICE PALTRINIERI

CANTINA PALTRINIERI, RADICE, LAMBRUSCO DI SORBARA, MODENA, ITALY				
C 📶		light red to pink		Therefore: youthful
H 📶	Therefore: a neutral grape variety	BLOSSOM ORANGE GRAPEFRUIT RHUBARB LAUREL		
A 📶	Therefore: reductive winemaking			
R 📶	Therefore: youthful			
A 📶	Therefore: cool climate	malic acids		
C 📶	Therefore: dry wine	light mousse		Therefore: Charmat Method
T 📶				
E 📶		11 to 12.5%, light to medium body		
R 📶	Therefore: Old World			

Tasting note: This semi-sparkling wine has a perfume of elderflower, blood orange, grapefruit and rhubarb. Slightly spicy too. The taste is dry with high acidity, medium alcohol and impressions of red fruit, fresh herbs and a fine texture that gives the wine a pleasant roundness. Light to medium body with a low relative fruit intensity.

Riedel Vinum
4441-55

 < 10 °C   no

  < $50   5-10 years

In the Lambrusco-style: Schilcher (Steiermark, Austria).

Malagousia: a second life

Malagoussia, Malagouzia, Malaouzia, Melaouzia, Malagusiah

rare
545 ha (0.01%)

Malagousia was assumed gone but saved from extinction in the 1970s by winemaker Evangelos Gerovassiliou, first at Porto Carras and later at his own vineyard at Epanomi, on the Halkidiki peninsula. Malagousia is semi-aromatic depending on the height of the vineyard and the ripeness of the fruit and ranges from spicy, mint and citrusy to more tropical (peach). Produces wines with intensity, concentration, medium-full body with medium plus alcohol and medium acidity.

GEROVASSILIOU, MALAGOUSIA, EPANOMI, GREECE

C			lemon						Therefore: youthful
H		Therefore: aromatic grape variety	JASMIJN	BLOSSOM	LEMON	YELLOW APPLE	PEACH		
A		Therefore: reductive winemaking							
R		Therefore: youthful							
A		Therefore: warm climate							
C		Therefore: dry wine	fatty						Therefore: sur lie
T									
E		Therefore: lots of sunshine (long season)	13.5%, medium body						
R		Therefore: Old World							

Tasting note: This pale, lemon-colored white has an intense perfume of jasmine, blossom, peach, lemon and apple, moderate acidity and medium alcohol. A creamy texture and a floral undertone. Medium body and a low relative fruit intensity.

Riedel Vinum
6416-15

< 10 °C   no

< $50

5-10 years

In the Malagousia-style: *Muscat (Alsace, France), Moscatel (Maule, Chile), Torrontes (Cafayate, Argentina).*

🔊 mal-vah-SEE-ah

small
23,557 ha (0.53%)

Malvasia: originally from Crete

Malmsey, Malvasier, Malvazia, Monemvasia

Ancient variety, originally from Crete, then spread to the Balearic Islands, the Canary Islands and the island of Madeira, and now planted all over the world. With the exception of Malvasia di Candia, most species of Malvasia are closely related to Malvasia Bianca. In central Italy, Malvasia is often blended with Trebbiano and in Rioja with Viura, in both cases to add flavor and mouthfeel. Malvasia is in vogue for dry, white wine and Malmsey for the sweetest Madeira.

BLANDY'S, MALMSEY, MADEIRA, PORTUGAL

C	📶		brown		Therefore: oxidative winemaking
H	📶		ZEST · RAISINS · PLUM · PRESERVED FRUITS · CINNAMON		
A	📶	Therefore: oxidative winemaking	CARAMEL · WALNUT · HAZELNUT · CHOCOLATE		
R	📶	Therefore: 3 to 5 years old			
A	📶	Therefore: cool climate			
C	📶	Therefore: very sweet	more than 130 gr/l		
T	📶				
E	📶	Therefore: fortified	19 to 20%, full body		
R	📶	Therefore: Old World			

Tasting note: This deeply-colored, amber, fortified wine has an intense aroma of caramel, walnut, hazelnut, orange peel, raisins, prunes, cinnamon and chocolate, lots of acidity and very high alcohol. Deliberately oxidized style, very sweet. Full body and a low relative fruit intensity.

Riedel Vinum
6416-60

 10-15 °C   no

 < $100

> 10 years

In the Malmsey-style: Bual (Madeira, Portugal), Oloroso Dulce (sherry, Spain), 40 Year Old Tawny Port (Portugal).

276

rare
1,951 ha (0.04%)

🔊 mar-SAN

Marsanne: white Hermitage

Avilleran, Ermitage, Hermitage, Grosse Roussette, Marsanne Blanche, Roussette de Saint-Péray

Marsanne is the dominant white variety in the northern Rhône, where it is used for white Saint Joseph, Crozes-Hermitage and Hermitage. Marsanne is tricky because the grapes have to be picked at the right time, otherwise the wine may stay thin and uninteresting. Also prone to diseases. Sometimes blended with smaller amounts of Roussanne, which is also prone to rot and oxidation, and produces notoriously low yields.

CHAPOUTIER, CHANTE ALOUETTE, HERMITAGE BLANC, RHÔNE, FRANCE

C	📶		lemon		Therefore: youthful
H	📶	Therefore: a neutral grape variety	APRICOT PEACH PEAR REINE CLAUDE		
A	📶	Therefore: oxidative winemaking	TOAST ALMOND HAZELNUT		Therefore: (partly new) French oak barrels
R	📶	Therefore: 3 to 5 years old			
A	📶	Therefore: warm climate			
C	📶	Therefore: dry wine	fatty		Therefore: sur lie
T	📶				
E	📶	Therefore: lots of sunshine (long season)	13.5 to 14.5%, full body		
R	📶	Therefore: Old World			

Tasting note: This pale, lemon-colored white has a restrained perfume of apricot, quince and peach, *Reine Claude* (greengage), pear, vanilla, hazelnut, low acidity and high alcohol. A creamy texture, a full body and a low relative fruit intensity.

Riedel Vinum
6416-97

 < 10 °C   no

 < $100

 5-10 years

In the white Hermitage-style: Saint-Peray (Rhône, France), Châteauneuf-du-Pape Blanc (Rhône, France).

rare
4,856 ha (0.11%)

🔊 mar-suh-LAN

Marselan: from Languedoc to China

Marselan is a recent (1961) cross between Grenache and Cabernet Sauvignon; it was only registered in the French register of grape varieties in 1990 and has only been in the AOC since 2011. In the Languedoc, it is increasingly blended with Grenache, Syrah, Mourvèdre and Carignan. It has spread all over the world and is very popular in China. Marselan wines have a good color, medium body with fine tannins, and lots of black fruit.

GRACE, MARSELAN, NINGXIA, CHINA

C	📶	Therefore: grape with a thick skin	ruby	Therefore: 3 to 5 years old
H	📶		BLACKCURRANT · BLACKCHERRY · PLUM · BLUEBERRY · CLOVE	
A	📶	Therefore: oxidative winemaking	VANILLA · TOAST · MOCHA · CHOCOLATE	Therefore: (partly) new French oak
R	📶	Therefore: 3 to 5 years old	TOBACCO	
A	📶	Therefore: warm climate		
C	📶	Therefore: dry wine		
T	📶	Therefore: grape with a thick skin	astringent	Therefore: Old World
E	📶	Therefore: lots of sunshine (high UV)	14 to 14.5%, full body	
R	📶	Therefore: New World		

Tasting note: This deep, ruby-colored red has medium-intense aromas of blackcurrant and cherry, blue plum, tobacco and leather with spicy undertones. Moderate acidity, high alcohol and firm tannins provide a full body and a low relative fruit intensity.

Riedel Vinum 6416-00

 10-15 °C   0.5 hours

 < $100

 > 10 years

In the Ningxia Marselan-style: Cabernet Franc (Washington State, United States), Malbec (Mendoza, Argentina), Saperavi (Khaketi, Georgia).

small
10,227 ha (0.23%)

🔊 muh-lon de boor-GON-yuh

Melon de Bourgogne: sur Lie

Melon, Muscadet

In keeping with its name, Melon originated from Burgundy where it lost its competition to Chardonnay in the 16th century. Its resistance to frost made it attractive to Dutch distillers as a base wine for brandy. They planted it near Nantes in the 17th century, to ship the wine from there to the Netherlands. The frost resistant Melon survived the harsh winter of 1709 which destroyed all other vineyards in the Nantais and stayed around ever since then.

LE MASTER, MUSCADET DE SÈVRE ET MAINE SUR LIE, FRANCE

C	📶		lemon	Therefore: youthful
H	📶	Therefore: a very neutral grape variety	REINE CLAUDE · PEAR · LIME · GRANNY SMITH · WET STONE	
A	📶	Therefore: reductive winemaking		
R	📶	Therefore: youthful		
A	📶	Therefore: very cool climate	malic acids	Therefore: no malo
C	📶	Therefore: dry wine	fatty	Therefore: sur lie
T	📶			
E	📶		12.5 to 13%, light body	
R	📶	Therefore: Old World		

Tasting note: This pale, lemon-colored white has an almost neutral scent of Reine Claude (greengage), lime, green apple and green pear, high acidity and medium alcohol. Signature 'sur lie' creamy texture to keep the acidity in check and a mineral undertone. Neutral and light bodied with a low relative fruit intensity.

Riedel Vinum
6416-05

< 10 °C   no   < $50   5-10 years

In the Muscadet-style: Chablis (Bourgogne, France), Chenin Blanc (Loire, France), Silvaner (Franken, Germany).

M

🔊 men-SEE-yah

Mencía: the boss in Bierzo

Jaen

Originating from Bierzo in the northwest of Spain. Traditionally made in a light style (due to high yields on fertile plains), but increasingly becoming intense and concentrated (due to lower yields on schist soils). This has led to a renewed interest in Mencía and the DOs that use it (such as Bierzo, Valdeorras, Ribeira Sacra and Liébana). Mencía usually has something earthy, spicy and mineral with impressions of red currant, blackberry and pomegranate.

VILLA DE CORULLÓN, MENCÍA, BIERZO, SPAIN

C	📶	Therefore: grape with a thick skin	ruby	Therefore: 3 to 5 years old
H	📶		REDCURRANT · PLUM · PEACH · STRAWBERRY · RASPBERRY	
A	📶	Therefore: oxidative winemaking	TOAST · SMOKE	Therefore: (partly) new French oak
R	📶	Therefore: 3 to 5 years old	EARTH	
A	📶	Therefore: moderate climate		
C	📶	Therefore: dry wine		
T	📶	Therefore: grape with a thick skin	astringent	Therefore: Old World
E	📶	Therefore: lots of sunshine (long season)	14%, medium to full body	
R	📶	Therefore: Old World		

Tasting note: This medium, ruby-colored red has medium-intense aromas of red cherry, raspberry, plum, peach, strawberry, earth and toast. Medium acidity, medium alcohol, firm tannins, and a mineral undertone provide a medium to full body, and a low relative fruit intensity.

Riedel Vinum
6416-30

 10-15 °C 0.5 hours

  < $50

5-10 years

In the Mencía Bierzo-style: Cru de Beaujolais (France), Bourgeuil (Loire, France), Dolcetto (Piedmont, Italy).

32,914 ha (0.73%)

🔊 mon-tuh-pool-TJAH-noh

Montepulciano d'Abruzzo

Cordisco, Morellone, Primaticcio, Uva Abruzzo, Violone

Montepulciano is an indigenous Italian grape variety, widely planted in central and southern Italy. Allowed in 20 DOCs of the 95 Italian provinces. Because it is a late ripening variety and can be (very) 'green' if not fully ripe, it is hardly found in Northern Italy. But once ripe, Montepulciano can produce deeply-colored wines, with medium acidity and high extract and alcohol content. In Abruzzo it can be aromatic with earthy notes and blackcurrant with a deep color.

GAROFOLI
PIANCARDA
2016

GAROFOLI, MONTEPULCIANO D'ABRUZZO, ITALY				
C 🛜	Therefore: grape with a thick skin	ruby		Therefore: 3 to 5 years old
H 🛜		BLACKCURRANT BLACKCHERRY PLUM BLUEBERRY BLACK PEPPER		
A 🛜	Therefore: oxidative winemaking	ALMOND CEDAR		Therefore: foudres
R 🛜	Therefore: 3 to 5 years old	TOBACCO		
A 🛜	Therefore: warm climate			
C 🛜	Therefore: dry wine			
T 🛜	Therefore: grape with a thick skin	astringent		Therefore: Old World
E 🛜	Therefore: lots of sunshine (long season)	14%, full body		
R 🛜	Therefore: Old World			

Tasting note: This deep, ruby-colored red has medium-intense aromas of blackcurrant and cherry, plum, blueberries, almond and some toast. Medium acidity, high alcohol and medium tannins. Medium to full body and a low relative fruit intensity.

Riedel Vinum
6416-30

  10-15 °C 0.5 hours

 < $50

5-10 years

In the Montepulciano d'Abruzzo-style:
Bonarda (Mendoza, Argentina), Chianti Classico (Toscane, Italy), Negroamaro (Sicily, Italy).

M

rare
1,047 ha (0.02%)

Moschofilero: exotic but delicate

Fileri Trigoleos, Fileri Tripoleos, Phileri Tripoleos, Moscofilero, Mosxofilero

A Greek native variety with a pinkish-purple skin whose epic center is the Peloponnese, especially the Mantineia Plateau. There, high on the cold, mountainous terrain, it combines a delicate and exotic perfume (lychees, rose petals and lemon blossom), a light, frivolous body and a moderate acidity with a spicy finish. These impressions typically remain true to Moschofilero, whether it be a rosé, a sparkling wine or a grappa.

GAIA, MOSCHOFILERO, MANTINEIA, PELOPONESSOS, GREECE

C			lemon		Therefore: youthful
H		Therefore: aromatic grape variety	ROSE LYCHEE BLOSSOM GRAPE MELON		Therefore Muscat-alike
A		Therefore: reductive winemaking			
R		Therefore: youthful			
A		Therefore: moderate climate			
C		Therefore: dry wine	fatty		Therefore: sur lie
T					
E			13%, medium body		
R		Therefore: Old World			

Tasting note: This pale, lemon-colored white has an intense perfume of roses, lychee, blossom, grapes, white flowers and melon, medium acidity and medium alcohol. A creamy texture and a floral undertone. Medium body and a low relative fruit intensity.

Riedel Vinum
6416-33

 < 10 °C   no   < $50   < 5 years

In the Moschofilero-style: Gelber Muskateller (Austria), Moscatel (Maule, Chile), Torrontes (Cafayate, Argentina).

small
18,752 ha (0.42%)

🔊 mew-ler TOOR-gahw

Müller-Thurgau: promising

Rivaner, Riesling-Sylvaner, Riesling-Silvaner, Rizlingszilvani

A cross of Riesling and Madeleine Royale from 1882. With the economy in tatters, post-war Germany needed a productive grape variety to revive viticulture. Müller-Thurgau was that grape, though it led to four decades of Liebfraumilch; a slightly sweet, white quaffer. Müller-Thurgau was such a promising grape that it started the New Zealand wine industry (though it was dug up with equal enthusiasm three decades later when Sauvignon Blanc entered the scene).

TIEFENBRUNNER, MÜLLER-THURGAU, ALTO ADIGE, ITALY

C	📶		lemon					Therefore: youthful
H	📶	Therefore: a neutral grape variety	YELLOW APPLE	REINE CLAUDE	PEAR	PEACH	MELON	
A	📶	Therefore: reductive winemaking						
R	📶	Therefore: youthful						
A	📶	Therefore: cool climate						
C	📶	Therefore: dry wine	fatty					Therefore: sur lie
T	📶		ripe and soft					Therefore: New World
E	📶	Therefore: lots of sunshine (high UV)	13.5%, medium body					
R	📶	Therefore: Old World						

Tasting note: This pale, lemon-colored white has a restrained scent of apple, pear, peach, melon and *Reine Claude* (greengage), high acidity, medium alcohol and a creamy texture. Medium body and a low relative fruit intensity.

 < 10 °C   no

 < $50

 5-10 years

Riedel Vinum 6416-15

In the Müller-Thurgau, Alto Adige-style:
Silvaner (Alsace, France), Savagnin (Savoie, France), Auxerrois (Alsace, France).

small
7,973 ha (0.18%)

🔊 nebbee-OH-loh

Nebbiolo: purely Piedmontese

Spanna, Picoutener, Chiavennasca

Nebbiolo is derived from nebbia, the fog or autumn mist in which the vineyards at the feet of the Alps in Piedmont can be surrounded. However, the thick skin of the Nebbiolo is resistant to this and produces tannin-rich wines with lots of acidity and high alcohol. In the bottle, flavors of tar, truffles, roses, violets, plums and chocolate emerge. Partly due to the variety and due to the long, legally required aging in wooden vats, Barolo does not have a deep color.

PARUSSO, BAROLO, PIEDMONT, ITALY

C	📶		ruby	Therefore: 5 to 10 years old
H	📶		SOAKED FRUITS, ROSE, PLUM, VIOLETS, REDCURRANT	
A	📶	Therefore: oxidative winemaking	ALMOND, TOAST, CEDAR	Therefore: foudres
R	📶	Therefore: 5 to 10 years old	TEER, TRUFFLE, LEATHER, EARTH	
A	📶	Therefore: moderate climate		
C	📶	Therefore: dry wine		
T	📶	Therefore: grape with a thick skin	very astringent	Therefore: Old World
E	📶	Therefore: lots of sunshine (long season)	14.5%, full body	
R	📶	Therefore: Old World		

Tasting note: This medium-intense colored, ruby red has restrained aromas of cherry, rose, plum, violet, almond, toast, tar, truffles, earth and leather. High acidity, high alcohol and astringent tannins. Full body and a low relative fruit intensity.

Riedel Vinum
6416-90

 10-15 °C   2 hours

 < $150

 > 10 years

In the Barolo-style: Barbaresco *(Piedmont, Italy), Nebbiolo Langhe (Piedmont, Italy), Xinomavro (Macedonia, Greece).*

small
11,414 ha (0.25%)

🔊 nay-groh ah-MAH-roh

Negroamaro: pitch-black

Nigramaro, Negro Amaro

Indigenous variety from Puglia (such as in DOC Salice Salentino) that can withstand drought well and is especially popular as a blending grape due to its deep color, smooth tannins and blackcurrant fruit, especially with Primitivo, Malvasia Nera, Sangiovese and Montepulciano. The name could come from the Italian *negro* (black) and *amaro* (bitter), or from the Latin-Greek 'pitch black'. The better Negroamaros can develop complex aromas with cloves, cinnamon and allspice as they age.

RIVERA, SALICE SALENTINO, PUGLIA, ITALY

C	📶	Therefore: grape with a thick skin	ruby		Therefore: 3 to 5 years old
H	📶		BLACKCHERRY PLUM CLOVE CINNAMON WHITE PEPPER		
A	📶	Therefore: oxidative winemaking	ALMOND CEDAR		Therefore: foudres
R	📶	Therefore: 3 to 5 years old	LEATHER		
A	📶	Therefore: hot climate			
C	📶	Therefore: dry wine			
T	📶	Therefore: grape with a thick skin	astringent		Therefore: Old World
E	📶	Therefore: lots of sunshine (long season)	13 to 13.5%, medium body		
R	📶	Therefore: Old World			

N

Tasting note: This deep, ruby-colored red has medium intense aromas of black cherry, plum, cloves, cinnamon, allspice and almond. Low acidity, high alcohol and firm but smooth tannins ensure a full body and a low relative fruit intensity.

Riedel Vinum
6416-15

 10-15 °C   0.5 hours

 < $50

 5-10 years

In the Salice Salentino-style: Nero d'Avola (Sicily), Montepulciano d'Abruzzo (Italy).

rare
1,796 ha (0.04%)

Nerello Mascalese: the Barolo of Sicily

Niureddu, Negrello

Quickly growing in popularity, Nerello Mascalese is at its best on the volcanic slopes of Mount Etna in Sicily. The name Mascalese comes from the Mascali plain between Etna and the coast and the prefix Nerello refers to the black color of the grapes. Nerello Mascalese is a variety which displays its terroir well with a Barolo-like perfume featuring fruity and spicy aromas, earthy nuances and firm tannins. Recent DNA testing seems to point to Sangiovese as a parent though.

PLANETA, NERELLO MASCALESE, SICILY, ITALY

C	📶	Therefore: grape with a thick skin	ruby		Therefore: 3 to 5 years old
H	📶		PLUM · RED CHERRY · BLACKCURRANT · LAUREL · VOLCANIC		
A	📶	Therefore: oxidative winemaking	ALMOND		Therefore: foudres
R	📶	Therefore: 3 to 5 years old	TOBACCO · EARTH		
A	📶	Therefore: warm climate			
C	📶	Therefore: dry wine			
T	📶	Therefore: grape with a thick skin	astringent		Therefore: Old World
E	📶	Therefore: lots of sunshine (long season)	14%, full body		
R	📶	Therefore: Old World			

Tasting note: This deep, ruby-colored red has medium-intense aromas of plum, red cherry, bay leaf, almond, tobacco, and a volcanic minerality with earthy notes. Low acidity, high alcohol and firm but ripe tannins provide a full body and a low relative fruit intensity.

Riedel Vinum
6416-30

 10-15 °C   2 hours

  < $50

5-10 years

In the Nerello Mascalese-style: Barolo (Piedmont), Nebbiolo Langhe (Piedmont), Montepulciano d'Abruzzo (Italy).

nAY-ro DA-voh-lah

Nero d'Avola: the Shiraz of Sicily?

Calabrese

Nero d'Avola is the most important red grape variety in Sicily. Literally called the 'black of Avola' because of its deep color. In addition to being a traditional blending component and increasingly used as a single varietal, it is also an ingredient in Marsala. Nero d'Avola has been called the (Barossa) Shiraz of the Old World because of its ripe tannins and full body. Varies in style from a smooth, fruity, drinking wine and rosé to a muscular powerhouse with complexity and length.

PLANETA, NERO D'AVOLA, SICILY, ITALY

C	Therefore: grape with a thick skin	ruby		Therefore: 3 to 5 years old
H		PLUM, RASPBERRY, BLACKBERRY, BLACKCHERRY, BLACK PEPPER		
A	Therefore: oxidative winemaking	ALMOND, CEDAR, CHOCOLATE		Therefore: foudres
R	Therefore: 3 to 5 years old	TOBACCO		
A	Therefore: warm climate			
C	Therefore: dry wine			
T	Therefore: grape with a thick skin	astringent		Therefore: Old World
E	Therefore: lots of sunshine (long season)	13.5%, medium to full body		
R	Therefore: Old World			

Tasting note: This deep, ruby-colored red has medium intense aromas of plum, raspberry, blackberry, black cherry, black pepper, chocolate, allspice, almond and tobacco. Low acidity, high alcohol and firm but ripe tannins provide a medium to full body and a low relative fruit intensity.

Riedel Vinum
6416-30

10-15 °C   0.5 hours   < $50   5-10 years

In the Nero d'Avola-style: Negroamaro (Puglia), Bonarda (San Juan, Argentina), Montepulciano d'Abruzzo (Italy).

Nero di Troia: late ripening

Uva di Troia, Barlettana, Canosa, Sumarello, Uva della Marina

rare
2,493 ha (0.06%)

Nero di Troia is the third indigenous variety in Puglia, after Negroamaro (Brindisi and Lecce) and Primitivo (Taranto), and dominates in the north of Bari and Foggia. It is a late-ripening grape (from mid to late October), while Primitivo ripens at the end of August and Negroamaro in mid-September. Nero di Troia wine is a variety with small berries, perfumed bouquet with impressions of violets, low acidity but with a lot of color and firm tannins.

RIVERA, IL FALCONE, CASTEL DEL MONTE, PUGLIA, ITALY				
C 📶	Therefore: grape with a thick skin	ruby		Therefore: 3 to 5 years old
H 📶		PLUM, RED CHERRY, RASPBERRY, VIOLETS, LAUREL		
A 📶	Therefore: oxidative winemaking	ALMOND, CEDAR, VANILLA, PENCIL SHAVINGS		Therefore: (partly) new French oak
R 📶	Therefore: 3 to 5 years old	TOBACCO, EARTH		
A 📶	Therefore: warm climate			
C 📶	Therefore: dry wine			
T 📶	Therefore: grape with a thick skin	astringent		Therefore: Old World
E 📶	Therefore: lots of sunshine (long season)	13.5%, medium to full body		
R 📶	Therefore: Old World			

Tasting note: This deep, ruby-colored red has medium-intense aromas of plum, raspberry, red cherry, violet, bay leaf, almond and tobacco. Earthy finish. Medium acidity, high alcohol and firm but ripe tannins provide a medium to full body and a low relative fruit intensity.

Riedel Vinum
6416-30

 10-15 °C 0.5 hours

 < $50

 5-10 years

In the Nero di Troia-style: Aglianico (Campania), Nerello Mascalese (Sicily), Montepulciano d'Abruzzo (Italy).

small
10,267 ha (0.23%)

🔊 pah-EES

Pais on earth

Criolla Chica, Negra Corriente, Negra Peruana

Pais was the first *Vitis vinifera* to be exported from Spain to the New World. It is a genetic match with Listán Prieto, an ancient variety that has disappeared from Castilla-La Mancha. There are still several hectares left on the Canary Islands. But then it was the early 21st century, it was Chile's most widely planted grape until it was overtaken by Cabernet Sauvignon. Now mainly used for bulk wine in Bío-Bío, Maule and Itata. There, Pais produces a thin, rustic red wine with not much extract.

Riedel Vinum
4441-55

TORRES, ESTELADO, PAIS, MAULE, CHILE

C	📶	Therefore: grape with a thin skin / korte inweking	rosé		Therefore: youthful
H	📶		RED CHERRY · RASPBERRY · PLUM · STRAWBERRY · LAUREL		
A	📶	Therefore: reductive winemaking			Therefore no autolysis, but probably Charmat Method
R	📶	Therefore: youthful			
A	📶	Therefore: moderate climate			
C	📶	Therefore: brut			
T	📶	Therefore: very short maceration			
E	📶		12.5%, medium body		
R	📶	Therefore: New World			

Tasting note: This medium, pink-colored sparkling wine has medium-intense aromas of red cherry, raspberry, plum, strawberry and bay leaf. Moderate acidity, medium alcohol and low tannins provide a medium body and a high relative fruit intensity.

 10-15 °C   no   < $50   < 5 years

In the Pais-style: Criolla Grande (Argentina and Canary Islands), Cinsault (Maule, Chile), Schiava (Alto Adige, Italy).

23,148 ha (0.52%)

🔊 pah-loh-MEE-noh FEE-noh

Palomino Fino for Fino

Listan Blanco, Listan de Jerez, Fransdurif, Manzanilla de Sanlucar, Perrum

Of all sherries, fino ("refined" in Spanish) is the driest and the lightest. Intended for direct consumption and made reductively in the solera, and thus, unlike the oxidative oloroso, has a limited shelf life (especially when the bottle is opened). Two variations: Manzanilla is aged in San Lucar de Barrameda and Fino in Jerez de la Frontera. Both Palomino Fino base wine fortified to approximately 15%, aged in soleras from small to large (Tio Pepe's is 30,000 botas).

GONZALEZ BYASS, TIO PEPE, FINO, SHERRY, SPAIN

C			lemon	Therefore: youthful
H		Therefore: a neutral grape variety	YELLOW APPLE · FENNEL · DILL · REINE CLAUDE	
A		Therefore: reductive winemaking	ALMOND · DOUGH	acetaldehyde, Therefore: flor (yeast on the wine)
R		Therefore: youthful		
A		Therefore: warm climate		
C		Therefore: bone dry		
T				
E		Therefore: fortified wine	15%, medium body	Therefore: fino or manzanilla
R		Therefore: Old World		

Tasting note: This pale, lemon-colored white has a medium intense nose of yellow apple, fennel, dill and Reine Claude with impressions of almond and dough (or yeast). Dry wine with moderate acidity and high alcohol. Medium body and a low relative fruit intensity.

Riedel Vinum
6416-05

< 10 °C   no   < $50   < 5 jaar

In the Fino sherry-style: *Manzanilla Sherry (Andalusië, Spain), Vin Jaune (Savoie, France).*

23,148 ha (0.52%)

🔊 pah-loh-MEE-noh FEE-noh

Palomino Fino for Oloroso

Listan Blanco, Listan de Jerez, Fransdurif, Manzanilla de Sanlucar, Perrum

Oloroso is also made from Palomino Fino base wines but now fortified to at least 17% to prevent flor formation in the solera. After more than eight years of solera maturation and gradual blending, this fortified wine develops an amber to deep mahogany color (the darker, the longer matured) and aromas of walnuts, licorice, almond, hazelnut, raisin, leather and tobacco. Since these wines are already oxidized, they can be kept for a long time. Oloroso is a dry sherry.

GONZALEZ BYASS, ALFONSO, OLOROSO, SHERRY, SPAIN

C	🛜		amber		Therefore: oxidative winemaking
H	🛜	Therefore: a neutral grape variety	RAISINS, FIG, PLUM, CINNAMON, LAUREL		
A	🛜	Therefore: oxidative winemaking	MOCHA, ALMOND, HAZELNUT		
R	🛜		TOBACCO, COMPOTE, WALNUT		Therefore: oxidative winemaking
A	🛜	Therefore: warm climate			
C	🛜	Therefore: bone dry			
T	🛜				
E	🛜	Therefore: fortified wine	17 to 19%, full body		Therefore: oloroso
R	🛜	Therefore: Old World			

P

Tasting note: This deeply-colored, amber fortified wine has a medium intense bouquet of raisins, figs, plum, cinnamon and bay leaf, mocha, tobacco, almond and various nuts. Dry wine, low acidity and very high alcohol. Full body and a very low relative fruit intensity.

Riedel Vinum
6416-33

 10-15 °C   no

 < $50

 > 10 years

In the Oloroso sherry-style: Sercial (Madeira, Portugal), Palo Cortado (Andalucië, Spain), Marsala Vergine Stravecchio (Sicilië, Italy).

small
7,137 ha (0.16%)

Parellada: backbone of Cava

Parellada originates from the hills of Catalonia and is hardly planted anywhere else; of the 20,000 hectares in total, only 5% are outside Catalonia. The same also goes for its application: cava accounts for more than 95% of all Parellada. In the blend, Parellada brings aromas of blossom and green apple, making it the ideal complement to the honeyed grapefruit notes of Macabeo and the more outspokenfennel and anise flavors of Xarel-lo.

PARES BALTA, CAVA DO, SPAIN

C		lemon		Therefore: youthful
H	Therefore: a neutral grape variety	YELLOW APPLE · PEAR · LEMON · FENNEL · ANISE		
A	Therefore: reductive winemaking	BREAD · DOUGH		Therefore: méthode traditionelle
R	Therefore: recent disgorgement			
A	Therefore: moderate climate	malic acids		
C	Therefore: brut			
T				
E		12 to 12.5%, persistent mousse, light body		
R	Therefore: Old World			

Tasting note: Sparkling wine with restrained expression of apple, pear, lemon, anise and fennel. In the mouth the wine is dry with high acidity, creamy texture, persistent mousse and medium alcohol. Light to medium body and a low relative fruit intensity.

Riedel Vinum
6416-68

 < 10 °C   no   < $50   5-10 years

In the Cava champagne-style: Clairette de Die (France), Crémant de Loire (France), Crémant d'Alsace (France).

🔊 pekko-REE-noh

Pecorino: almost extinct

rare
745 ha (0.02%)

Pecorino ('little sheep') is dry and mineral with subdued floral aromas of acacia and jasmine, sometimes spiced with some licorice. Due to low yields, it was replaced by Trebbiano in the mid-20th century and later even considered extinct. In the 1980s, a local producer investigated a rumor about some forgotten vines in an overgrown vineyard. And yes, yes! Pecorino is now being grown again in Le Marche, Abruzzo, Umbria and Tuscany.

GAROFOLI, GALE, PECORINO, LE MARCHE, ITALY

C	📶		lemon	Therefore: youthful
H	📶	Therefore: a neutral grape variety	YELLOW APPLE · ACACIA · JASMIJN · LIME · WET STONE	
A	📶	Therefore: reductive winemaking	ALMOND	Therefore: foudres/rvs
R	📶	Therefore: youthful		
A	📶	Therefore: moderate climate		
C	📶	Therefore: dry wine	fatty	Therefore: sur lie
T	📶			
E	📶		12 to 13%, light to medium body	
R	📶	Therefore: Old World		

Tasting note: This pale, lemon-colored white has a restrained nose of apple, lime, acacia and jasmine, and medium acidity and alcohol. The wine has a moderate creamy texture and a mineral undertone. Light to medium body and a low relative fruit intensity.

Riedel Vinum
6416-05

< 10 °C   no   < $50   5-10 years

In the Pecorino-style: *Trebbiano d'Abruzzo (Italy), Soave (Veneto, Italy).*

P

small
8,551 ha (0.19%)

🔊 pay-droh hee-MAY-nez

PX

Pedro Jimenez, Perrum, Don Bueno

Simple recipe: take a Pedro Ximénez vineyard (usually in Montilla-Moriles) and let the grapes dry under the blistering heat and sun. This creates a concentrated, viscous must with intense aromas and flavors of apple syrup and raisins, which is then fortified and matured in the solera. What comes out after years of maturing is darker than night and richer than Onassis. Nevertheless, there is nothing wrong with casually adding this nectar to your vanilla ice cream.

GONZALEZ BYASS, NECTAR, PX, SPAIN

C	🛜		crude oil						Therefore: PX
H	🛜		YELLOW APPLE	RAISINS	PLUM	DRIED FRUITS	PRESERVED FRUITS		Therefore: raisining
A	🛜	Therefore: oxidative winemaking	CHOCOLATE	MOCHA					
R	🛜								
A	🛜	Therefore: concentration by raisining							
C	🛜	Therefore: very sweet (by raisining)	more than 250 gr/l						Therefore: PX
T	🛜								
E	🛜	Therefore: fortified	17 to 18%, full body						
R	🛜	Therefore: Old World							

Tasting note: This inky black fortified wine has an intense aroma of apple syrup and raisins, prunes, mocha and dark chocolate, medium acidity and very high alcohol. Dried, fortified and very sweet. Full body and a low relative fruit intensity.

Riedel Vinum
6416-60

10-15 °C   no

< $50

> 10 years

In the PX sherry-style: PX, Montilla-Moriles (Spain), PX, Malaga (Spain), PX, Valencia (Spain).

294

🔊 p'tee vair-DOH

Petit Verdot: for seasoning

Verdot, Petit Verdau

small
8,104 ha (0.18%)

Petit Verdot is known as a seasoning in Bordeaux. Because the grape ripens late – often too late for Bordeaux – it fell out of favor there last century, but is now gaining popularity again. Also in the rest of the world, particularly as a blending grape, especially in arid and warm climates. In Bolivia, at an altitude of 2,000 meters, it develops silky tannins. Petit Verdot has aromas of purple fruit in its youth, spice and pencil shavings, vanilla and walnuts.

CAMPOS DE SOLANA, ESTHER ORTIZ, PETIT VERDOT, TARIJA, BOLIVIA

C 📶	Therefore: grape with a thick skin	ruby		Therefore: 3 to 5 years old
H 📶		BLACKCURRANT · BLACKCHERRY · PLUM · BLACKBERRY · TOMATO LEAF		
A 📶	Therefore: oxidative winemaking	VANILLLE · TOAST · CEDAR · PENCIL SHAVINGS		Therefore: (partly) new French oak
R 📶	Therefore: 3 to 5 years old	WALNUT		
A 📶	Therefore: warm climate			
C 📶	Therefore: dry wine			
T 📶	Therefore: grape with a thick skin	ripe and soft		Therefore: New World
E 📶	Therefore: lots of sunshine (high UV)	14 to 14.5%, full body		
R 📶	Therefore: New World			

Tasting note: This deep, ruby-colored red has a medium-intense perfume of blackcurrant and cherry, plum, pencil shavings, spices, mint, vanilla and toast. Medium acidity, high alcohol and firm but ripe, smooth tannins provide a full body. Nutty finish and a medium relative fruit intensity.

Riedel Vinum
6416-00

 10-15 °C   0.5 hours

 < $100

 > 10 years

In the Petit Verdot-style: Cabernet Franc (Mendoza, Argentina), Tannat (Cafayate, Argentina), Malbec (Colchagua, Chile).

🔊 peek-POOL

rare
1,669 ha (0.04%)

Picpoul, de Pinet

Piquepoul, Picapoll, Avello, Languedocien

Picpoul is one of the oldest varieties in Languedoc. Although the grape comes in three colors (white, gray and black), white is the most common. Picpoul thrives best in a dry climate. The grapes grow in loose bunches, are oval-shaped and come off easily. Picpoul as a wine always has something of blossom and citrus with refreshing acidity. Because of the freshness and modest style you would not initially think of the Languedoc.

DOMAINE DE LAURELS, PICPOUL DE PINET, LANGUEDOC, FRANCE

C			lemon	Therefore: youthful
H		Therefore: a neutral grape variety	REINE CLAUDE · LIME · YELLOW APPLE · BLOSSOM · WET STONE	
A		Therefore: reductive winemaking		
R		Therefore: youthful		
A		Therefore: moderate climate		
C		Therefore: dry wine	fatty	Therefore: sur lie
T				
E			12.5 to 13%, medium body	
R		Therefore: Old World		

Tasting note: This pale, lemon-colored white has a mineral perfume of *Reine Claude* (greengage), lime, apple and blossom, medium acidity and medium alcohol. A moderate creamy texture and a mineral undertone. Medium body and a low relative fruit intensity.

Riedel Vinum
6416-05

 < 10 °C

 no

 < $50

5-10 years

In the Picpoul de Pinet-style: *Vinho Verde (Portugal), Pinot Grigio (Alto Adige, Italy), Albariño (Rias Baixas, Spain).*

🔊 pee-noh-TAH-juh

small
7,132 ha (0.16%)

Pinotage: as South African as a Springbok

The cross between Pinot Noir and Cinsault was called Pinotage, because the Cape synonym for Cinsault in 1920 was Hermitage. But the Pinotage resembles neither: deep purple in its youth with the aromatic fruit of red and blackcurrant, black cherry, plum (and banana). The thick skin almost always provides powerful, firm tannins and sometimes a bitter aftertaste characteristic of Pinotage. The higher the quality, the longer the aging potential.

BELLINGHAM, BERNARD SERIES, BUSH VINE PINOTAGE, SOUTH AFRICA

C	📶	Therefore: grape with a thick skin	ruby	Therefore: 3 to 5 years old
H	📶		BLACKCURRANT · BLACKCHERRY · PLUM · FYNBOS · BANANA	
A	📶	Therefore: matured in oak	VANILLA · TOAST · CEDAR	Therefore: (partly) new French oak
R	📶	Therefore: 3 to 5 years old	TOBACCO · GAME	
A	📶	Therefore: warm climate		
C	📶	Therefore: dry wine		
T	📶	Therefore: grape with a thick skin	astringent, bitter	Therefore: Pinotage
E	📶	Therefore: lots of sunshine (high UV)	13.5 to 14.5%, full body	
R	📶	Therefore: New World		

Tasting note: This deep, ruby-colored red has medium-intense aromas of red and black currant, black cherry, plum, banana, fynbos, vanilla, tobacco and toast. Low acidity, high alcohol and firm tannins ensure a full body and a high relative fruit intensity.

Riedel Vinum
6416-0

10-15 °C   0.5 hours

< $100

> 10 years

In the Pinotage-style: Cabernet Sauvignon (Stellenbosch, South Africa), Malbec (Mendoza, Argentina), Merlot (Washington State, United States).

🔊 pee-noh blahnk

Pinot Blanc: with white asparagus

Pinot Bianco, Weissburgunder, Weisser Burgunder, Beli Pinot, Klevner (Alsace), Blanc Vrai (Champagne)

Think of Pinot Blanc (Pinot Bianco in Italy and Weissburgunder in Germany) as Chardonnay's timid cousin. The grapes come from the same family. Pinot Blanc is the most productive and the least characteristic. Most Alsace Pinots are neutral in character with moderate acidity. As such, they are a perfect accompaniment with asparagus and mussels. At lower yields though, Pinot Blanc can represent different terroirs, just like Chardonnay.

TRIMBACH, PINOT BLANC, ALSACE, FRANCE

C	〰		lemon		Therefore: youthful
H	〰	Therefore: a neutral grape variety	YELLOW APPLE REINE CLAUDE PEAR MELON		
A	〰	Therefore: reductive winemaking			
R	〰	Therefore: youthful			
A	〰	Therefore: moderate climate			
C	〰	Therefore: dry wine	fatty		Therefore: sur lie
T	〰				
E	〰		12.5 to 13%, light body		
R	〰	Therefore: Old World			

Tasting note: This pale, lemon-colored white has a restrained scent of apple, pear and Reine Claude (greengage), medium acidity and medium alcohol. A creamy texture. Light body and a low relative fruit intensity.

Riedel Vinum
6416-05

< 10 °C   no   < $50   5-10 years

In the Pinot Blanc-style: Soave (Veneto, Italy), Silvaner (Alsace, France), Auxerrois (Limburg, The Netherlands and Belgium).

298

🔊 pree-mee-TEE-voh

Primitivo, originally Croatian

Zinfandel, Crljenak Kastelanski, Pribidrag, Tribidrag, Kratosija

medium
33,511 ha (0.75%)

Primitivo is a thick-skinned variety known for producing inky, tannin-rich wines in Puglia, most notably as Primitivo di Manduria. Its geographical origin is debated, though there is little doubt that the grape got to Italy through vineyards on the coast of Croatia (across the Adriatic). Here the grape is called Tribidrag and Crljenak Kasteljanski. In the 19th century, the breed was introduced to the United States under the name Zinfandel.

RIVERA, PRIMITIVO, SALENTO, ITALY				
C 📶	Therefore: grape with a thick skin	ruby		Therefore: 3 to 5 years old
H 📶		PLUM RASPBERRY BLACKBERRY CHOCOLATE BLACK PEPPER		
A 📶	Therefore: oxidative winemaking	ALMOND CEDAR		Therefore: foudres
R 📶	Therefore: 3 to 5 years old	TOBACCO		
A 📶	Therefore: warm climate			
C 📶	Therefore: dry wine			
T 📶	Therefore: grape with a thick skin	astringent		Therefore: Old World
E 📶	Therefore: lots of sunshine (long season)	14%, full body		
R 📶	Therefore: Old World			

Tasting note: This deep, ruby-colored red has medium-intense aromas of plum, raspberry, blackberry, chocolate, allspice, almond and tobacco. Low acidity, high alcohol and firm but ripe tannins provide a medium to full body and a low relative fruit intensity.

Riedel Vinum
6416-15

10-15 °C   0.5 hours

< $50   5-10 years

In the Primitivo-style: Negroamaro (Puglia, Italy), Nero d'Avola (Sicily, Italy).

33,511 ha (0.75%)

🔊 zinfan-DELL

Zin: California's own Primitivo

Some call Zinfandel California's signature variety. Often abbreviated to Zin. It is a descendant of Tribidrag and Crljenak and genetically identical to Primitivo. Zinfandel is available in various styles: from white and rosé to deep purple, from dry to semi-sweet, from light to fully bodied. The dry, full-bodied red wine is somewhere between a Barossa Shiraz and an Amarone di Valpolicella with high alcohol levels (15 to 16% is not unusual).

RIDGE, LYTTON SPRINGS, ZINFANDEL, CALIFORNIA

C	Therefore: grape with a thin skin	ruby		Therefore: 3 to 5 years old
H		PLUM, RASPBERRY, BLACK TEA, CINNAMON, BLUEBERRY		
A	Therefore: matured in oak	VANILLA, TOAST, CEDAR		Therefore: (partly) new French oak
R	Therefore: 3 to 5 years old	TOBACCO, DRIED FRUITS, PRESERVED FRUITS		
A	Therefore: warm climate			
C	Therefore: dry (but not bone dry)			
T	Therefore: grape with a thin skin	ripe and soft		Therefore: New World
E	Therefore: lots of sunshine)	14.5%, full body		
R	Therefore: New World			

Tasting note: This medium, ruby-colored red has medium-intense aromas of plum and raspberry jam, tobacco, tea, cinnamon, vanilla and toast. Low acidity, very high alcohol and moderate tannins ensure a full body and a high relative fruit intensity.

Riedel Vinum
6416-30

 10-15 °C   no   < $50   5-10 years

In the Zinfandel-style: Amarone della Valpolicella (Veneto, Italy), Mataro (McLaren Vale, Australië), Primitivo (Puglia, Italy).

small
21,000 ha (0.46%)

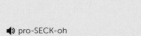

🔊 pro-SECK-oh

Prosecco: variety and wine

Glera, Serprina, Prosecco Bianco, Proseko Sciprina

Prosecco can produce high yields, but the higher the yield, the more neutral the wine. When properly made, Prosecco can have a seductive perfume of melon, peach, pear and blossom. Depending on the style, the alcohol content ranges from 8.5% to 12.5% for a Brut. Since Prosecco is both the grape and the region, the Italian authorities adopted the name Glera for Prosecco in early 2000 as they sought legal protection for the provenance name.

BISOL, PROSECCO, VALDOBBIADENE, ITALY

C	📶		lemon		Therefore: youthful
H	📶	Therefore: a neutral grape variety	MELON PEACH PEAR BLOSSOM WHITE BEER		
A	📶	Therefore: reductive winemaking			Therefore: no autolysis, likely Charmat Method
R	📶	Therefore: youthful			
A	📶	Therefore: moderate climate			
C	📶	Therefore: brut			
T	📶				
E	📶		11.5 to 12.5%, light body		
R	📶	Therefore: Old World			

Tasting note: This pale, lemon-colored sparkling white has a mineral perfume of melon, peach, pear, blossom and sometimes candy, medium acidity and medium alcohol. The wine is dry but usually not bone dry. Light body and a low relative fruit intensity.

Riedel Vinum
6416-58

< 10 °C   no   < $50   < 5 years

In the Prosecco-style: *Sekt (Germany), Vonkelwyn (South Africa).*

P

🔊 ruh-gehnt

Regent

Geilweilerhof 67-198-3

rare
1,972 ha (0.04%)

Regent is a thick-skinned, hybrid variety that was developed in 1967 in the Palatinate in Germany from Chambourcin, Silvaner, and Müller-Thurgau, among others. The grape produces wines with sufficient body and color (it is a teinturier), sufficient tannins and aromas of red fruit. Regent's resistance to disease is an advantage in cool and wet climates, such as Germany, Switzerland, England, the Netherlands and in cooler parts of the United States.

WIJNGOED DE COLONJES, REGENT, THE NETHERLANDS

C	Therefore: grape with a thick skin	ruby		Therefore: 3 to 5 years old
H			RED CHERRY · CRANBERRY · PLUM · FIG · REDCURRANT	
A	Therefore: oxidative winemaking	TOAST · CEDAR · SMOKE		Therefore: (partly) new French oak
R	Therefore: 3 to 5 years old			
A	Therefore: cool climate			
C	Therefore: dry wine			
T				Therefore: Old World
E		12 to 13%, light to medium body		
R	Therefore: Old World			

Tasting note: This deep, ruby-colored red has medium intense aromas of red cherry, currant, blue plum, fig, toast and cedar. The wine is dry with high acidity, medium alcohol, moderate tannins, medium body and a low relative fruit intensity.

Riedel Vinum
6416-30

10-15 °C   no   < $150   5-10 years

In the Regent-style: Regent (Pfalz, Germany), Cru de Beaujolais (France), Schiava (Alto Adige, Italy).

big
55,903 ha (1.25%)

🔊 kat-see-TELL-ee

Rkatsiteli: the Pinot Grigio of the Caucasus

Rkatziteli, Baiyu, Corolioc

Rkatsiteli is an ancient white variety from Georgia. At the other side of the Black Sea, Rkatsiteli also plays an important role in Ukraine, Bulgaria, Romania, Moldova and Armenia. Rkatsiteli's popularity is due to its resistance to frost, its ability to retain acids (even in the hottest summers) and its versatility (suitable for sparkling, dry, sweet and spirits). In style, it is understated with crisp green apple, quince and white peach.

MUKHRANI, RKATSITELI, KAKHETI, GEORGIA				
C	📶		lemon	Therefore: youthful
H	📶	Therefore: a neutral grape variety	YELLOW APPLE PEAR PEACH APRICOT	
A	📶	Therefore: reductive winemaking	ALMOND	Therefore: (used) oak
R	📶	Therefore: youthful		
A	📶	Therefore: warm climate		
C	📶	Therefore: dry wine	fatty	Therefore: sur lie
T	📶			
E	📶	Therefore: lots of sunshine (long season)	13.5 to 14%, medium to full body	
R	📶	Therefore: Old World		

Tasting note: This pale, lemon-colored neutral white has a restrained scent of apple, quince and white peach, apricot, pear and almonds. Low acidity and high alcohol. A creamy texture. Medium to full body and a low relative fruit intensity.

Riedel Vinum
6416-05

 < 10 °C

 no

 < $50

5-10 years

In the Rkatsiteli-style: *Pinot Grigio (Veneto, Italy), Soave (Veneto, Italy), Silvaner (Alsace, France).*

R

small
8,460 ha (0.19%)

🔊 roh-DEE-tees

Roditis

Rhoditis

Roditis is not one variety but several closely related clones of one variety found throughout Greece. The grape colors pink, light red during ripening and retains its acidity well, even in the warmer parts of Greece. Because of its versatility, the grape is used as a single varietal (Patras) and in regional blends (Peloponnese), including in Retsina together with Savatiano. Roditis knows how to display differences in terroir well and produces the best results at high altitudes.

GAIA, RITINITIS NOBILIS, PELOPONNESOS, GREECE

C	📶		lemon	Therefore: youthful
H	📶	Therefore: a neutral grape variety	REINE CLAUDE · PEACH · LIME · YELLOW APPLE	
A	📶	Therefore: reductive winemaking	RESIN	Resin added, therefore: Restsina
R	📶	Therefore: youthful		
A	📶	Therefore: moderate climate		
C	📶	Therefore: dry wine	fatty	Therefore: sur lie
T	📶			
E	📶		12 to 13%, medium body	
R	📶	Therefore: Old World		

Tasting note: This pale, lemon-colored white has a mineral perfume of *Reine Claude* (greengage), lime, peach, yellow apple and pine tree resin, medium acidity and medium alcohol. A moderate creamy texture and a resin dominated finish. Medium body and a low relative fruit intensity.

In the Retsina-style: other Retsinas.

Riedel Vinum
6416-05

 < 10 °C   no

 < $50

 5-10 years

304

rare
994 ha (0.02%)

🔊 sa-gran-TEEN-oh

Sagrantino: astringent yet juicy

Sagrantino Rosso

The name Sagrantino could come from *sagra* (feast) or *sacrestia* (sacristy or communion) as the first written record of this wine is from the 16th century, where it is mentioned as communion wine in Montefalco (Umbria). Sagrantino is a disease-resistant, low-yielding, late-ripening grape variety that needs a long, hot season. The grape is the most tannic in the world, more so than Aglianico, Tannat or Nebbiolo! Produces inky black wines with aromas of prunes, cinnamon and earth.

ARNALDO CAPRAI, SAGRANTINO DI MONTEFALCO, UMBRIË, ITALY

C	📶	Therefore: grape with a very thick skin	ruby	Therefore: 3 to 5 years old
H	📶		REDCURRANT · RED CHERRY · PLUM · BLACK TEA · LAUREL	
A	📶	Therefore: matured in oak	CEDAR · TOAST · PENCIL SHAVINGS	Therefore: (partly) new French oak
R	📶	Therefore: 3 to 5 years old	TOBACCO · EARTH	
A	📶	Therefore: warm climate		
C	📶	Therefore: dry wine		
T	📶	Therefore: grape with a very thick skin	very astringent	Therefore: Old World
E	📶	Therefore: lots of sunshine (long season)	14%, full body	
R	📶	Therefore: Old World		

Tasting note: This deep, ruby-colored red has medium-intense aromas of red currant, red cherry, plum, black tea, cedar, toast, pencil shavings, earth and tobacco. Medium acidity, high alcohol and astringent tannins provide a full body with a low relative fruit intensity.

Riedel Vinum
6416-30

 10-15 °C   2 hours

 < $100

 > 10 years

In the Sagrantino di Montefalco-style:
Madiran (France), Barbaresco/Barolo (Piedmont, Italy), Aglianico (Campania, Italy).

S

🔊 sankt LAHW-rent

Sankt Laurent

St. Laurent, Svatovavrinecke, Vavrinecke

Native Austrian variety mainly found in the Thermenregion and in Burgenland, and the most widely planted red grape in the Czech Republic (10% of the total), especially in Moravia and Bohemia. Sankt Laurent is a cross of Pinot Noir with an unknown other parent, has a thick skin and produces deeply-colored wines with characteristic aromas of cherry and plum and spicy impressions (just like Pinot Noir). The wines have affinity with oak and have good aging potential.

UMATHUM, SANKT LAURENT, THERMENREGION, AUSTRIA

C	Therefore: grape with a thick skin	ruby		Therefore: 3 to 5 years old
H		RED CHERRY, BLACKCHERRY, STRAWBERRY, RASPBERRY, CLOVE		Therefore: Pinot Noir style
A	Therefore: oxidative winemaking	TOAST, CEDAR		Therefore: (partly) new French oak
R	Therefore: 3 to 5 years old			
A	Therefore: moderate climate			
C	Therefore: dry wine			
T		astringent		Therefore: Old World
E	Therefore: lots of sunshine (long season)	12.5 to 13.5%, medium body		
R	Therefore: Old World			

Tasting note: This deep, purple-colored red has intensely-fruity aromas of red and black cherry, strawberry, raspberry, cloves, toast and cedar. The wine is dry with medium acidity, medium alcohol, moderate tannins and medium to full body. Medium relative fruit intensity.

Riedel Vinum
6416-07

10-15 °C

no, unless young and complex

< $50

5-10 years

In the Sankt Laurent-style: Zweigelt (Austria), Pinot Noir (California, United States), Cru de Beaujolais (France).

🔊 sah-pair-A-vee

small
7,328 ha (0.16%)

Saperavi means color!

Smallberiger, Nerki Khagog, Saparavi, Saperavi De Kakhetie

Saperavi is the Georgian word for dye and that is not without reason, because it is a *teinturier* (a grape with pigments in both the skin and the flesh of the fruit). Saperavi is common in the Caucasus and other former Soviet republics. It combines color and acidity and is also reasonably productive, making it an ideal ingredient for (cheaper) blends. However, in the Kakheti region of Georgia on the eastern border with Azerbaijan, it can produce high quality varietal wines.

MUKHRANI, SAPERAVI, KAKHETI, GEORGIA

C 📶	Therefore: grape with a thick skin	ruby		Therefore: 3 to 5 years old
H 📶		BLACKCURRANT BLUEBERRY PLUM CRANBERRY LAUREL		
A 📶	lagering op eiken	CEDAR TOAST PENCIL SHAVINGS		Therefore: (partly) new French oak
R 📶	Therefore: 3 to 5 years old	TOBACCO PRESERVED FRUITS MEATY		
A 📶	Therefore: warm climate			
C 📶	Therefore: dry wine			
T 📶	Therefore: grape with a thick skin	astringent		Therefore: Old World
E 📶		12.5 to 13.5%, medium body		
R 📶	Therefore: Old World			

Tasting note: This deep, ruby-colored red has medium-intense aromas of confit blackcurrant and blueberry, prune, currant, bay leaf, cedar, toast, pencil shavings and tobacco. Low acidity, medium alcohol and astringent tannins. Medium body and a low relative fruit intensity.

Riedel Vinum
6416-30

 10-15 °C 0.5 hours

 < $50

 > 10 years

In the Saperavi-style: Marselan (Ningxia, China), Shiraz (Washington State, United States), Bandol (France).

S

Savagnin for Vin Jaune

Savagnin, Traminer, Heida, Paien, Nature, Gelber Traminer

rare
2,266 ha (0.05%)

Savagnin is a neutral, white grape from the Traminer family, traditionally used for vin jaune in the Jura. After fermentation, the wine goes into wooden barrels which are not topped up. In one or two years, a yeast layer develops on top called *voile* but which is similar to *flor* of Fino and Manzanilla sherry. After aging the wine for 6 years and 3 months, about 62% of the original wine remains, which is then bottled in clavelins (bottles that hold 62cl).

HENRI MAIRE, VIN JAUNE, JURA, FRANCE

C			lemon	
H		Therefore: a neutral grape variety	YELLOW APPLE, LEMON, APRICOT, DILL, REINE CLAUDE	
A			ALMOND, BREAD, DOUGH, WHITE BEER	Therefore: flor or voile
R		Therefore: 5 to 10 years old	WALNUT, HAZELNUT	
A		Therefore: moderate climate		
C		Therefore: bone dry		
T				
E			13 to 13.5%, medium body	Therefore: no Fino but Vin Jaune
R		Therefore: Old World		

Tasting note: This pale, lemon-colored white has a restrained scent of apple, lemon, apricot, almonds, bread, dough, gueuze Lambik, walnuts and hazelnuts. Medium acidity and medium to high alcohol. Medium body and a low relative fruit intensity.

Riedel Vinum 6416-15

 < 10 °C   no

 < $50

 < 5 years

In the Vin Jaune-style: *Manzanilla sherry (Spain), Fino sherry (Spain).*

◀) sah-vah-tee-ah-NOH

Savatiano

Stamatiano, Perachoritis, Kountoura Aspri, Domdrania

Savatiano is the most widely planted grape variety in Greece, mainly in Attica (Central Greece). The variety is best known for its role in Retsina although more and more beautiful dry Savatiano are being made these days.

Savatiano is resistant to drought and diseases. The variety's name probably refers to the Greek word for 'Sabbath'. With low yields, Savatiano can produce intense, dry wines with herbaceous citrus and white flower characteristics.

DOMAINE PAPAGIANNAKOS, SAVATIANO, MARKOPOULO, GREECE

C	📶		lemon		Therefore: youthful
H	📶	Therefore: a neutral grape variety	REINE CLAUDE · LIME · GRAPEFRUIT · BLOSSOM · WET STONE		
A	📶	Therefore: reductive winemaking			
R	📶	Therefore: youthful			
A	📶	Therefore: cool climate			
C	📶	Therefore: dry wine	fatty		Therefore: sur lie
T	📶				
E	📶		12 to 13%, medium body		
R	📶	Therefore: Old World			

Tasting note: This pale, lemon-colored white has a medium-intense nose of Reine Claude (greengage), lime, grapefruit and blossom, medium acidity and medium alcohol. Medium body with a mineral undertone and again clear, but well integrated resin notes dominate also the finish.

Riedel Vinum 6416-33

 < 10 °C   no

 < $50

 5-10 years

In the Savatiano-style: Assyrtiko (Santorini, Greece), Pinot Grigio (Alto Adige, Italy), Albariño (Rias Baixas, Spain).

S

rare
2,197 ha (0.05%)

Schiava c.q. Vernatsch

Grauvernatsch, Smallvernatsch, Grossvernatsch, Schiava Grigia, Schiava Gentile, Schiava Grossa, Frankenthaler Blau, Koelner Blau, Vernatsch, Trollinger

Schiava (Slavic) is a collective name for several grape families in Trentino and Alto Adige in northern Italy. The grape has many synonyms; of these, most are derived from Vernatsch (which is "vernacular" in German) similar to Vernaccia. Schiava is the most widely planted grape of Alto Adige and is mainly used for everyday fruit-intense wines, in the style of Beaujolais-Villages. Schiava is also mixed with Lagrein for Santa Maddalena DOC.

TIEFENBRUNNER, VERNATSCH, ALTO ADIGE, ITALY

C	📶	Therefore: grape with a thin skin	purple					Therefore: youthful
H	📶		RED CHERRY	RASPBERRY	PLUM	STRAWBERRY	LAUREL	
A	📶	Therefore: reductive winemaking	ALMOND					Therefore: inert oak (like foudres)
R	📶	Therefore: youthful						
A	📶	Therefore: moderate climate						
C	📶	Therefore: dry wine						
T	📶	Therefore: grape with a thin skin	astringent					Therefore: Old World
E	📶	Therefore: lots of sunshine (long season)	12.5 to 13.5%, medium body					
R	📶	Therefore: Old World						

Tasting note: This medium, purple-colored red has medium-intense aromas of red cherry, plum, game strawberry, raspberry, bay leaf and almonds. Medium acidity, medium alcohol, low level of tannins, medium body, and a medium relative fruit intensity.

Riedel Vinum
6416-16

 10-15 °C   no

 < $50

 5-10 years

In the Schiava-style: Valpolicella, Veneto (Italy), Sankt Laurent, Thermenregion (Austria), Beaujolais-Villages (France).

🔊 shaf-kah-PEE-toh

Shavkapito

rare
59 ha (0.001%)

The 'vine with the black trunk' comes from Kartli, eastern Georgia. The grape ripens in late September and has naturally low yields. Shavkapito is a light colored grape with medium alcohol (12% is normal) and primary aromas of (sour) cherry, berry and spicy notes. Shavkapito is regularly vinified in oak as well as in traditional buried Qvevri – 800-liter, egg-shaped, earthenware amphorae without ears which are used for fermentation and maturation.

CHATEAU MUKHRANI, RÉSERVE ROYALE, SHAVKAPITO, KARTLI, GEORGIA

C	Therefore: grape with a thin skin	ruby	Therefore: 3 to 5 years old
H		RED CHERRY, PLUM, PEACH, STRAWBERRY, LAUREL	
A	Therefore: matured in oak	TOAST	Therefore: (partly) new French oak
R	Therefore: 3 to 5 years old	EARTH, WALNUT	
A	Therefore: moderate climate		
C	Therefore: dry wine		
T	Therefore: grape with a thin skin	astringent	Therefore: Old World
E		12 to 12.5%, medium body	
R	Therefore: Old World		

Tasting note: This medium, ruby-colored red has medium-intense aromas of red cherry, plum, game strawberry, peach, bay leaf, toast, walnut and earth. Medium acidity, medium alcohol, medium tannins and a mineral undertone provide a medium body and a low relative fruit intensity.

Riedel Vinum
6416-30

 10-15 °C

 no, unless young and complex

< $50

 5-10 years

In the Shavkapito-style: Cru de Beaujolais (France), Lagrein (Alto Adige, Italy), Marzemino (Trentino, Italy).

S

small
6,099 ha (0.14%)

🔊 sil-VAH-nair

Silvaner, or: Sylvaner?

Sylvaner, Silvaner, Grüner Silvaner, Sylvaner Verde, Johannisberg, Gros Rhin, Sylvánské Zelené, Zeleni Silvanec

Silvaner does not belong to the four noble varieties in Alsace (where it is spelled Sylvaner, just as in Austria), but it can be used in Alsace Grands Crus. Silvaner lends itself to high yields and, in combination with the neutral style, can lead to rather simple wines (as it was in Liebfraumilch in Rheinhessen). However, with limited yields, Silvaner can develop the complexity of a Chablis and Savennières. Mainly planted in Germany (Franken in particular) and Alsace.

RAINER SAUER, SILVANER, FRANKEN, GERMANY

C	📶		lemon			Therefore: youthful
H	📶	Therefore: a neutral grape variety	YELLOW APPLE / PEAR / LEMON / WET STONE / REINE CLAUDE			
A	📶	Therefore: reductive winemaking				
R	📶	Therefore: youthful				
A	📶	Therefore: cool climate				
C	📶	Therefore: dry (but not bone dry)	residual sugar-acidity balance			Therefore: German
T	📶					
E	📶		12 to 13%, light to medium body			
R	📶	Therefore: Old World				

Tasting note: This pale, lemon-colored white has a mineral perfume of apple, pear and lemon, high acidity and medium alcohol. A creamy texture and a mineral undertone. Light to medium body and a low relative fruit intensity.

Riedel Vinum
6416-05

 < 10 °C

 no

 < $50

> 10 years

In the Silvaner Franken-style: Chablis (France), Neuburger (Niederösterreich, Austria), Savennières (Loire, France).

small
13,168 ha (0.29%)

🔊 toh-ron-TESS

Torrontés: as Argentinean as the tango

Torontel, Moscatel de Austria

This cross of Moscatel with Criolla Negra is uniquely Argentinean. Three clones exist: Riojano, Sanjuanino, and Mendocino of which Torrontés Riojano the most aromatic is, reminiscent of Muscat and Gewürztraminer. The least aromatic – and least planted – is Torrontés Mendocino, while Torrontés Sanjuanino is in between. Torrontés achieves the best results at high altitude, especially in Cafayate and Salta in northern Argentina.

EL ESTECO, TORRONTÉS, CAFAYATE, ARGENTINA				
C	📶		lemon	Therefore: youthful
H	📶	Therefore: aromatic grape variety	LYCHEE BLOSSOM PINEAPPLE GRAPEFRUIT GEMBER	Aromas suggest Gewürztraminer, Muscat or Torrontés
A	📶	Therefore: reductive winemaking		
R	📶	Therefore: youthful		
A	📶	Therefore: cool climate		
C	📶	Therefore: dry wine	fatty	Therefore: sur lie
T	📶			
E	📶	Therefore: lots of sunshine (high UV)	13 to 14%, medium body	
R	📶	Therefore: New World		

Tasting note: This pale, lemon-colored white has an exotic, intense perfume of pineapple, blossom, lychee, grapefruit, ginger and fennel, high acidity and medium alcohol. Creamy texture, medium body and a high relative fruit intensity.

Riedel Vinum
6416-33

< 10 °C   no   < $50   5-10 years

In the Cafayate-style: Gewürztraminer (Alto Adige, Italy), Gelber Muskateller (Steiermark, Austria), Muscat (Alsace, France).

small
14,220 ha (0.32%)

🔊 too-REE-gah fran-kah

Touriga Franca

Touriga Francesa, Mortagua, Preto de Mortagua, Azal Espanhol

Touriga Franca and Touriga Nacional cannot be seen separatedly from each other, not least because they are often blended together. That is why the two benchmark wines in this book are also blends; a dry wine and a fortified one. Touriga Franca is the most widely planted grape in the Douro and the main grape for both port and dry red wines. It's popular because it is frost hardy and has good yields. Touriga Franca displays delicate but intense aromas of blackcurrant and blossom, a full body and a deep color.

PRATS SYMINGTON, DOURO, PORTUGAL

C	📶	Therefore: grape with a thick skin	ruby	Therefore: 3 to 5 years old
H	📶		BLACKCURRANT BLACKCHERRY PLUM BLOSSOM CINNAMON	
A	📶	Therefore: matured in oak	VANILLA TOAST PENCIL SHAVINGS CEDAR	Therefore: (partly) new French oak
R	📶	Therefore: 3 to 5 years old	WALNUT EARTH	
A	📶	Therefore: warm climate		
C	📶	Therefore: dry wine		
T	📶	Therefore: grape with a thick skin	astringent	Therefore: Old World
E	📶	Therefore: lots of sunshine (long season)	14.5%, full body	
R	📶	Therefore: Old World		

Tasting note: This deep, ruby-colored red has medium-intense aromas of blackcurrant and black cherry, plum, blossom, oriental spices, vanilla, toast, pencil shavings, cedar and walnuts. Low acidity, high alcohol and firm, nutty tannins with an earthy aftertaste provide a full body and a medium relative fruit intensity.

Riedel Vinum 6416-0

 10-15 °C 0.5 hours

 < $50

 > 10 years

In the Touriga Franca-style: Touriga Nacional (Douro, Portugal), Zinfandel (Paso Robles, California), Cahors (France).

small
11,710 ha (0.26%)

🔊 too-REE-gah nassee-oh-NAL

Touriga Nacional: present in port

Mortagua, Preto de Mortagua, Azal Espanhol

Touriga Nacional is Portugal's answer to Cabernet Sauvignon. It is grown in the northern regions of Dão and Douro and is an important ingredient in both dry reds and the fortified wines of Porto. Touriga Nacional has a lot of color, firm tannins, plenty of black fruit, a spicy intensity and therefore very good aging potential. In blends (especially with Touriga Franca, the equivalent of Cabernet Franc), Touriga Nacional provides structure and body.

GRAHAMS, QUINTA DOS MALVEDOS, DOURO, PORTUGAL

C	Therefore: grape with a thick skin	ruby		Therefore: 5 to 10 years old
H		BLACKCURRANT BLACKCHERRY PLUM CINNAMON PRESERVED FRUITS		
A	Therefore: matured in oak	VANILLA TOAST		Therefore: (partly) new French oak
R	Therefore: 5 to 10 years old	TOBACCO		
A	Therefore: warm climate			
C	Therefore: sweet	80 to 129 gr/l		
T	Therefore: grape with a thick skin	astringent		Therefore: Old World
E	Therefore fortified	20%, full body		Therefore: Port of Vin Doux Naturel
R	Therefore: Old World			

Tasting note: This deep, ruby-colored red has medium-intense aromas of blackcurrant and black cherry, plum, blackberry, all confit, oriental spices such as cinnamon, vanilla, toast and tobacco. Low acidity, very high alcohol, approximately 100 gr/L residual sugars and firm tannins ensure a full body and a medium relative fruit intensity.

Riedel Vinum
6416-60

 10-15 °C

 no, unless young and complex

 < $150

> 10 years

In the Quinta-style: Vintage Port (Douro, Portugal), Maury (France), Banyuls (France).

trebb-ee-AH-noh

Trebbiano

Procanico, Brucanico,

very big
147,906 ha (3.29%)

One of the most planted grape varieties in the world thanks to its high yields. The grape moved to France with the papal court from Rome to Avignon in the 14th century. There it came to be known as Ugni Blanc. From the French southeast it moved to the Charentais (Cognac) and Gascony (Armagnac) on the Atlantic coast. It gives high yields of light, fresh, rather neutral-tasting white wine, most of which is distilled.

TENUTA ROVEGLIA, LUGANA LIMNE, VENETO, ITALY

C			lemon	Therefore: youthful
H		Therefore: a neutral grape variety	YELLOW APPLE PEAR LEMON	
A		Therefore: reductive winemaking	ALMOND	Therefore: inert oak (like foudres)
R		Therefore: youthful		
A		Therefore: moderate climate		
C		Therefore: dry wine		
T				
E			12 to 13%, medium body	
R		Therefore: Old World		

Tasting note: This pale, lemon-colored white has a neutral nose of apple, pear and lemon, medium acidity and medium alcohol. A creamy texture and a mineral undertone. Almond note in the finish. Medium body and a low relative fruitintensity.

Riedel Vinum
6416-05

< 10 °C   no   < $50   5-10 years

In the Trebbiano-style: Pinot Blanc (Alsace, France), Savatiano (Attica, Greece), Neuburger (Austria).

316

small
10,510 ha (0.23%)

🔊 treen-kah-DAIR-ah

Trincadeira is Tinta Amarela

Tinta Amarela, Espadeiro, Rabo de Ovelha Tinto, Crato Preto, Murteira, Mortagua, Portugal Malbec

Trincadeira is officially called Tinta Amarela but everyone uses the name Trincadeira. Mainly planted in the Douro, Dao and Alentejo. Is prone to rot and must be harvested just in time. If you pick too early, the wine will be lean with little taste. Pick too late, the grape is overripe with jammy, raisiny flavors. However, if you pick on time, you will get a rich taste with spicy aromas of black fruit and black tea.

Riedel Vinum
6416-16

	HERDADE DE SÃO MIGUEL, PÉ DE MÃE, PORTUGAL			
C 📶	Therefore: grape with a thick skin	ruby		Therefore: 3 to 5 years old
H 📶		BLACKCURRANT BLACKCHERRY BLACKBERRY LAUREL		
A 📶	Therefore: oxidative winemaking	VANILLA TOAST CEDAR		Therefore: (partly) new French oak
R 📶	Therefore: 3 to 5 years old	ALMOND		
A 📶	Therefore: warm climate			
C 📶	Therefore: dry wine			
T 📶	Therefore: grape with a thick skin	astringent		Therefore: Old World
E 📶	Therefore: lots of sunshine (long season)	13.5%, medium body		
R 📶	Therefore: Old World			

Tasting note: This deep, ruby-colored red has medium intense harvest aromas (blackcurrant, black cherry, blackberry and mint), medium aromas of winemaking (such as vanilla, toast and cedar) and a touch of almond. Low acidity, medium alcohol and astringent tannins as well as a low relative fruit intensity.

10-15 °C   0.5 hours   < $50   > 10 years

In the Trincadeira-style: Touriga Nacional (Douro, Portugal), Touriga Franca (Douro, Portugal), Cahors (France).

T

Verdejo: Rueda's own

Planta Fina

Inextricably linked to Rueda in Spain. The name Verdejo (*verde* means green) is inspired by its bright green grapes. However, the grape was unknown until Marqués de Riscal from Rioja made beautiful fresh wines from it in the late 1960s. Verdejo is recognizable by its fennel, grasss and citrus notes, and hints of white peach. The spicy citrus character has much in common with Sauvignon Blanc, and sometimes the two are blended.

TORRES, VERDEJO, RUEDA, SPAIN

C		lemon		Therefore: youthful
H	Therefore: aromatic grape variety	 GRASS · FENNEL · GRANNY SMITH · LIME · GRAPEFRUIT		Sauvignon-Blanc-like aromas
A	Therefore: reductive winemaking			
R	Therefore: youthful			
A	Therefore: cool climate	malic acids		
C	Therefore: dry wine	fatty		Therefore: sur lie
T				
E		12.5%, medium body		
R	Therefore: Old World			

Tasting note: This pale, lemon-colored white has intense aromas of Granny Smith, grasss, fennel, grapefruit and lime. In the mouth the wine is dry, with lots of acidity, medium alcohol and a mineral undertone. Medium body and a medium relative fruit intensity.

Riedel Vinum
6416-33

< 10 °C   no   < $50   < 5 years

In the Verdejo-style: *Sauvignon Blanc (Rueda, Spain), Sancerre (Loire, France), Sauvignon Blanc (Coastal, South Africa).*

rare
4,677 ha (0.10%)

🔊 vair-DEE-kee-oh

Verdicchio!

Trebbiano di Soave, Trebbiano di Lugana, Trebbiano Valtanesi, Marchigiano, Turbiana

Verdicchio is mainly planted in the Marche where it is used for a variety of wine styles, from sparkling to sweet wine (made from dried grapes). According to insiders, Verdicchio is one of the largest indigenous white grape varieties in Italy. There are two DOCs for Verdicchio in Marche: Verdicchio dei Castelli di Jesi, and Verdicchio di Matelica. While Verdicchio is likely native to the Marches, there appears to be a genetic relationship between Trebbiano and Greco.

Riedel Vinum
6416-05

GAROFOLI, PODIUM, VERDICCHIO DEI CASTELLI DI JESI CLASSICO SUPERIORE, LE MARCHE, ITALY

C	🔉		lemon	Therefore: youthful
H	🔉	Therefore: a neutral grape variety	YELLOW APPLE · PEACH · LIME · LEMON · WET STONE	
A	🔉	Therefore: reductive winemaking	ALMOND	Therefore: inert oak (like foudres)
R	🔉	Therefore: youthful		
A	🔉	Therefore: moderate climate		
C	🔉	Therefore: dry wine	fatty	Therefore: sur lie
T	🔉			
E	🔉		12 to 13%, light to medium body	
R	🔉	Therefore: Old World		

Tasting note: This pale, lemon-colored white has a restrained perfume of yellow apple, peach, lime, lemon, peach and almonds with medium acidity and medium alcohol. A creamy texture and a mineral undertone. Light to medium body and a low relative fruit intensity.

 < 10 °C

no

  < $50

5-10 years

In the Verdicchio dei Castelli di Jesi-style: Verdicchio di Matelica (Le Marche, Italy), Trebbiano d'Abruzzo (Italy), Soave (Veneto, Italy).

V

🔊 vair-men-TEEN-oh

Vermentino: absolutely Mediterranean

Rolle, Rollo, Pigato, Favorita, Malvoisie de Corse

Vermentino is planted in northwestern Italy, southern France and the neighboring islands of Corsica and Sardinia. Vermentino has a refreshing acidity and attractive aromas of peach, lemon zest, herbes de Provence, and minerality. Bolgheri, on the coast in Tuscany, is the richest version of Vermentino (in Italy). This is partly due to the warmer Tuscan climate, but also to the winemaking method (including cold maceration, sur lie, malo and oak aging).

GUADO AL TASSO, VERMENTINO, TOSCANE, ITALY

C	📶		lemon		Therefore: youthful
H	📶	Therefore: a neutral grape variety	REINE CLAUDE · PEACH · ZEST · GARRIGUE · WET STONE		
A	📶	Therefore: reductive winemaking	ALMOND		Therefore: inert oak (like foudres)
R	📶	Therefore: youthful			
A	📶	Therefore: moderate climate			
C	📶	Therefore: dry wine	fatty		Therefore: sur lie
T	📶				
E	📶		12 to 13%, medium body		
R	📶	Therefore: Old World			

Tasting note: This pale, lemon-colored white has a restrained perfume of *Reine Claude* (greengage), peach, lemon zest and garrigue, medium acidity and medium alcohol. A creamy texture and a mineral undertone. Medium body. Almond note in aftertaste and a low relative fruit intensity.

Riedel Vinum
6416-05

 < 10 °C   no   < $50   5-10 years

In the Vermentino-style: *Picpoul de Pinet (Languedoc, France), Trebbiano d'Abbruzzo (Italy), Verdicchio (Le Marche, Italy).*

small
13,510 ha (0.30%)

Viognier

Viogné, Vionnier, Viognier Jaune, Viognier Vert

Viognier has an intoxicating aroma of apricot and peach. If Viognier aromatically hadn't been so intriguing, it might not even have gotten a page in this book, as the total surface planted is small. Even in the Mecca of Viognier, in the town of Condrieu and at Château Grillet in the northern Rhône, barely 50 hectares are planted with this grape variety. However, we're seeing Viognier slowly starting to conquer the world.

CHAPOUTIER, CONDRIEU, RHÔNE, FRANCE

C			lemon		Therefore: youthful
H		Therefore: aromatic grape variety	PEACH APRICOT PEAR MANGO ZEST		
A		Therefore: reductive winemaking			
R		Therefore: youthful			
A		Therefore: warm climate			
C		Therefore: dry wine	fatty		Therefore: sur lie
T					
E		Therefore: lots of sunshine (long season)	13 to 14.5%, medium to full body		
R		Therefore: Old World			

Tasting note: This pale, lemon-colored white has a pronounced exotic perfume of peach, apricot, mango, lemon zest and pear, low acidity and high alcohol. A rich and creamy texture and a medium to full body and a medium relative fruit intensity.

Riedel Vinum
6416-33

 < 10 °C   no

 < $100

 5-10 years

In the Condrieu-style: Château Grillet (Rhône, France), Witte Hermitage (Rhône, France), Viognier (Languedoc, France).

V

small
9,503 ha (0.21%)

🔊 VRAHN-ats

Vranac: Black Stallion

Vranec

Vranac ('black stallion') is more than half of Montenegro's plantings and also popular in Macedonia and Croatia. Vranac produces deeply-colored red wines with aromas of sour cherry, blackberry and blackcurrant, to chocolate, mint and vanilla. The grape has adapted well to the dry and continental Central European conditions, produces small clusters, a lot of alcohol, lots of tannins and a bitter aftertaste. Related to Primitivo: one would be the parent of the other.

PLANTAŽE, VRANAC, MONTENEGRO

C	Therefore: grape with a thick skin	ruby		Therefore: 3 to 5 years old
H		RED CHERRY, BLACKBERRY, BLACKCURRANT, LAUREL, MINT		
A	Therefore: oxidative winemaking	CEDAR, TOAST, CHOCOLATE		Therefore: (partly) new French oak
R	Therefore: 3 to 5 years old	TOBACCO, LEATHER		
A	Therefore: warm climate			
C	Therefore: dry wine			
T	Therefore: grape with a thick skin	astringent		Therefore: Old World
E	Therefore: lots of sunshine (long season)	13.5%, medium body		
R	Therefore: Old World			

Tasting note: This deep, ruby-colored red has medium-intense aromas of sour cherry, blackberry, blackcurrant, chocolate, mint, tobacco, cedar, bay leaf, leather and tobacco. Moderate acidity, medium alcohol and firm tannins provide a medium body and a low relative fruit intensity.

Riedel Vinum 6416-30

10-15 °C   2 hours

< $50   > 10 years

In the Vranac-style: Baga (Portugal), Primitivo (Italy), Nerello Mascalese (Sicily, Italy).

322

small
8,534 ha (0.19%)

🔊 chah-REL-loh

Xarello; the Cava grape

Pansa Blanca, Xarello (Catalaans: Xarel•lo, maar elders: Xarel-lo of niets: Xarello).

Xarello is one of the most widely planted grape varieties in Catalonia where it is mainly mixed with Perellada and Macabeu for Cava. In addition, Xarello is also used for still wines, usually as part of a blend as well, but sometimes also as mono-varietal. Xarello is especially appreciated by winemakers for its fresh acidity, outspoken citrus and anise aromas and creamy mouthfeel. The grape has a thick skin and contains many polyphenols with a good balance between sugars and acids.

Riedel Vinum
6416-05

JEAN LEON, XARELLO, PENEDES, SPAIN

C	📶		lemon		Therefore: youthful
H	📶	Therefore: a neutral grape variety	YELLOW APPLE / LIME / LEMON / FENNEL / ANISE		
A	📶	Therefore: reductive winemaking			
R	📶	Therefore: youthful			
A	📶	Therefore: cool climate	malic acids		Therefore: no malo
C	📶	Therefore: dry wine	fatty		Therefore: sur lie
T	📶				
E	📶		12 to 13%, medium body		
R	📶	Therefore: Old World			

Tasting note: This pale, lemon-colored white has a restrained perfume of yellow apple, lime, lemon, fennel and anise, high acidity and medium alcohol. A rich and creamy texture and a medium body and a low relative fruit intensity.

< 10 °C   no   < $50   < 5 years

In the Xarello-style: Loureiro (Vinho Verde, Portugal), Albariño (Rias Baixas, Spain), Furmint (Hungary).

X

9 Local Heroes   323

rare
2,128 ha (0.05%)

Xinomavro: acid and black?

Black Naousa, Xynomavro of Naousa, Xynomavro Naousis, Mavro Naoussis, Mavro Naoustino, Niaoussa, Popolka, Pipolka, Xyno Mavro

Xinomavro is at the top of the hierarchy of Greek grape varieties. The name comes from *xino* (sour) and *mavro* (black). The grape is planted all over central and northern Greece, especially in Naoussa, Amynteo, Goumenissa and Rapsani. From the right terroir and with low yields, it can produce great wines. Xinomavro has stringent tannins, high acidity with characteristic aromas of red fruit, tomatoes, olives, dried plums, tobacco and nuts. It has an affinity with oak.

TSANTALI, XINOMAVRO, NAOUSSA, GREECE

C	📶	Therefore: low pigment variety	ruby					Therefore: 3 to 5 years old
H	📶		BLACKCURRANT	REDCURRANT	BLOSSOM	TEER	PLUM	
A	📶	Therefore: matured in oak	CEDAR	TOAST	PENCIL SHAVINGS			Therefore: (partly) new French oak
R	📶	Therefore: 3 to 5 years old	TRUFFLE	LEATHER	EARTH	TOBACCO		
A	📶	Therefore: moderate climate						
C	📶	Therefore: dry wine						
T	📶	Therefore: grape with a thick skin	astringent					Therefore: Old World
E	📶	Therefore: lots of sunshine (long season)	13 to 13.5%, medium body					
R	📶	Therefore: Old World						

Tasting note: This medium, ruby-colored red has medium-intense aromas of redcurrant, blossom, tomatoes, olives, prunes, tar, tobacco and nuts. Also cedar and toast. Medium acidity, high alcohol and astringent tannins provide a medium body and a low relative fruit intensity.

Riedel Vinum
6416-30

10-15 °C   2 hours

< $100

> 10 years

In the Xinomavro-style: Baga (Portugal), Barolo (Piedmont, Italy), Nerello Mascalese (Sicily, Italy).

🔊 TSWHY-gelt

Zweigelt: an Austrian crossing

Blauer Zweigelt, Rotburger, Zweigeltrebe

Dr. Fritz Zweigelt created Blauer Zweigelt by crossing Blaufränkisch with Sankt Laurent in the 1920s. But the grape would only really gain recognition after the Second World War. Today Zweigelt is the most common red grape in Austria and is planted all over the country. It produces purplish-red wines with soft tannins and impressions of morello, red cherry and spices. Produces good results in stainless steel as well as in barrique.

ZWEIGELT, BURGENLAND, AUSTRIA

C 📶	Therefore: grape with a thick skin	ruby		Therefore: 5 to 10 years old
H 📶		RED CHERRY, PLUM, REDCURRANT, CLOVE, LAUREL		
A 📶	Therefore: oxidative winemaking	CEDAR, TOAST, PENCIL SHAVINGS		Therefore: (partly) new French oak
R 📶	Therefore: 3 to 5 years old			
A 📶	Therefore: moderate climate			
C 📶	Therefore: dry wine			
T 📶	Therefore: lots of sunshine (long season)	astringent		Therefore: Old World
E 📶	Therefore: lots of sunshine (long season)	12.5 to 13.5%, medium body		
R 📶	Therefore: Old World			

Tasting note: This deep, ruby-colored red has medium-intense aromas of red berry, plum red cherry, clove and bay leaf. Also cedar, pencil shavings and toast. Medium acidity, medium to high alcohol and moderate tannins provide a medium to full body and a low relative fruit intensity.

Riedel Vinum
6416-30

10-15 °C   0.5 hours

< $50

5-10 years

In the Zweigelt-style: Sankt Laurent (Austria), Cru de Beaujolais (France), Kekfrankos (Hungary).

Epilogue

Recommendations
Acknowledgments
Index
Bibliography

This brief chapter contains some
recommendations to help you make
even more of your tasting experience.

1   Chose wines with sufficient quality to ensure typicity

The benchmark wines featured in chapters 8 and 9 have been chosen to help you train your palate. They all have good quality and typicity — exactly what is needed when improving your wine tasting skills. So, you might ask what is good quality and typicity? And what relationship do they have with price?

Well, in general, 'more expensive' doesn't necessarily equal 'better' but, please don't buy cheap and waste your money! This subject deserves some explanation. The lower the price, the less wine you get. That may sound logical but it is more dramatic than you think.

In the US, like any other market, the costs for the bottle, the label, the closure and the transport are more or less fixed. Margins are variable and are relatively high in the US, but still the fixed costs affect the ratio of wine versus the price for the bottle. Let me illustrate in the next graph.

Purchase a bottle of $4.99 and you might just get 75 cents worth of wine (or 15% of the retail price). This is because the fixed costs are weighing heavy on the price.

Purchase a bottle of $9.99 and the ratio is already improving as you can see from the figure. At $9.99 you get approximately $3.40 worth of wine (or one third of the retail price) as the fixed costs are weighing lighter.

However, purchase a bottle of $14.99 and you get $6.75 worth of wine (or 45% of the retail price) — following the same rationale.

In other words, a bottle of wine costing $14.99 is three times more expensive than the $4.99 one, but you're getting nine times as much wine for your money! From $14.99 most wines will retain the approximately 50% wine for money ratio.

And there is another compelling reason why I encourage you to buy wines from $15-25 or the equivalent elsewhere ($15-20 in Europe) for your tasting (and drinking!) wines. The lower the price, often the more manipulated the wine. Manipulation maybe just blending but could extend to acidification, the addition of sugar, correction of alcohol, use of chips or staves or a combination of these. These are all winemaking tricks to pair low cost with a style acceptable for mass market. However, by making these compromises, the wines will sacrifice typicity. And typicity is what we are looking for in wines when we want to learn about them.

2   More than a gadget!
Enhance your tasting experience

Coravin is an American invention, by Greg Lambrecht, which has added a new dimension to my wine tasting experience. Coravin's technology for still wines combines inserting an inert, noble gas (argon) into the bottle with a device, both to extract the wine and prevent oxidation. This can be done either with the classic Coravins needle devices or with the Pivot. With the Pivot, one opens the bottle and replaces the original closure with a specially designed stopper. The Pivot is then inserted through a special stopper to pour.

Lambrecht's invention has enriched my wine drinking and tasting experience in three ways. First of all, I no longer have to consider whether I am going to finish a bottle or not when I choose a wine; I just choose the wine I prefer to taste or drink — whether it is one sip or one glass, it doesn't matter anymore. As a result, on a typical day, I have 6 to 12 closed bottles 'open' without having to worry about shelf life. More important, Coravin has made my life as a professional wine taster easier. Previously, I only got one chance to taste a wine; once opened, it would oxidize within a matter of days. If I wanted to re-taste a wine, let's say, a week later, for instance with colleagues, I would have needed to order multiple samples. With Coravin, however, I sometimes taste the same bottle up to 5 or 6 times, sometimes over the course of several months!

3 Glassware is key
And Riedel is varietal specific

Each benchmark wine featured in chapters 7 and 8 comes with information about the price and shelf life, and advice about how to enjoy it even more, such as drinking temperature and the most suitable type of wine glass. Given the importance of grape varieties in this book, it's only logical that I chose Riedel glassware from Kufstein in Austria. After all, for decades, Georg Riedel has worked with winemakers, sommeliers and experts to discover that the key to the most suitable glassware was the DNA of the grape variety. They discovered that each variety needs a different size and shape of glass affecting how the wine is directed onto and delivered across your palate. It's all based on the rim diameter, curve of the lip, and how far you need to tip your head back to drink. This is why, I chose Riedel's varietal specific glasses, mainly from the Veritas collection, in a few cases from the Extreme collection.

In the process of selecting glasses, I discovered that I didn't need to match a different glass to each grape variety. In total, I selected about 10 different glass types to match the aromatic characters of the approximately 175 benchmark wines in this book.

The second reason I chose to feature Riedel in this book is my personal relationship with both the Riedel family and the company. Together with Georg Riedel, and later with his son Maximilian and a selection of Bolivian producers, we developed the ultimate glass for Singani — Bolivia's own grappa. It took us several interactive tasting sessions, starting in Kufstein (Austria), to find the ideal size, shape and stem. It was a great learning experience.

The third reason is that Riedel glassware is available all over the world; it's the number one brand for enthusiasts and professionals with a worldwide distribution network.

4 Practicalities
Create optimum tasting conditions

Optimal tasting conditions will enhance the experience. A quiet room where the ambient temperature is approximately 20 degrees is recommended.

To assess the color, the room should have bright (preferably natural) light, and the table a white background, like plain white paper.

To assess the smell, the room should have no strong odors and good ventilation. Avoid clothing that has the scent of perfume and/or tobacco smoke.

Make sure your table has enough space to place your glasses, bottles and spittoon.

Also, please drink enough water before, during, and after the tasting. If you don't, your taste receptors may dry out and become less sensitive. If you taste several wines, and especially if you want to compare them, try to pour approximately the same amount of each wine into your glass. Five centiliters are sufficient.

5 How to mature and serve your wines
Using EuroCave

Storing and serving wines at their right temperature is a key element of the enjoyment. And EuroCave is not only the creator of the wine cabinet, for me they are the global Gold Standard. That is why, in my home I store and serve my wines from EuroCave cabinets and rooms fitted with EuroCave cellar conditioners.

First of all, EuroCave cabinets guarantee a constant temperature, regardless of the outside temperature, thanks to unique insulation (and UV-proofed glass doors), heat and cold circuits and accurate sensors to effectively maintain the temperature, without effecting humidity levels. Furthermore, EuroCave cabinet frames and shelves absorb vibration. And last but not least, EuroCave cabinets have natural ventilation which gradually renews the air inside the cabinet with active charcoal filters to protect bottles from odors and mould.

Personally, I have also an INOA cellar conditioner which is not only the quietest conditioner in the market but also a beautiful design and guaranteeing to retain natural humity levels.

The temperature control in the cellar room allows a completely uniform temperature to be achieved, thanks to the principle of fanned cold air, it also allows control as close as possible to your bottles, via a wireless remote control. EuroCave's conditioners are also attractive, easy to maintain and allow incomparable freedom in terms of installation.

6   Stay Positive!
And do not give up

The number of different wines in the world is enormous. You're more likely to drink a Prosecco with the Pope than to blindly recognize a wine at the precision of grape, country, area and vineyard... (without cheating). Please regard each tasting as a way to get better at it, to get better in applying knowledge to method, and to build your own memory bank. Stay positive, even at times it feels you haven't learned anything at all. With experience, you will recognize more wines which will make blind wine tasting even more fun.

And once you've been bitten by the wine tasting bug, you may want to continue learning and take a wine appreciation course; an opportunity to put into practice what you have learned from this book. I recommend the courses offered by the Wine & Spirit Education Trust, or WSET for short. The WSET has grown into the largest global provider of wine, spirits and sake qualifications since its inception in 1969. The WSET offers 4 progressive levels of study through a network of course providers in more than 70 countries and translated into multiple languages.

After you've finished this book, most likely, WSET level 3 would apply to you.

Acknowledgments

First of all, I would like to thank my core team: Anna McKee and David Ramsay Steele (Carus books), Christa Jesse (Studio Christa Jesse), Karin Kerremans and Tess Savenije (DATBureau). They have worked with me wholeheartedly on *Anyone Can Taste Wine* and I owe them a lot.

I am grateful to Inga and Blouke Carus, who I knew from my former life in New Jersey and who believed in this book project. I also would like to thank my English colleague Tim Atkin MW and Jamie Goode, and my North American colleagues Dr. Liz Thach MW, Mark de Vere MW, Mary Ewing-Mulligan MW and Igor Ryjenkov MW. Also, thanks to Alison Cterckeko MW, Emma Jenkins MW, professor Kym Anderson, Executive Director of the Wine Economics Research Center and to George Gollin, Professor Emeritus from the School of Economics University of Adelaide for the up-to-date planting data. In addition, I would like to thank Carolina and Emma for their support, patience and distraction in between.

Anyone Can Taste Wine came about thanks to the commitment and support of many (in alphabetical order): Maria Andrade Lopes, Carmen Augschöll, Jaap Baan, Dan Balaban, Florent Baumard, Pierre de Benoist, Pablo Bergada, Nicolas Bonino, Angela Bonito, Denis Bottacin, Maartje van Broekhoven, Bob Bron, Marcela Burgos Abad, Martina Canterle, Elizabeth Caravati, Carla Castorini, Martin Champagne, Sebastiano de Corato, Merijn Corsten, Ilja Croijmans, Joan Cusiné, Nadia D'Annunzio, Roberto Damonte, Mathieu Dienst, Robert van Dijk, Adam Dijkstra, Paul Diterwich, Adrien Duboeuf-La Combe, Steven Duintjer, Ann Dumont, Maarten van den Dungen, Laura Ellwanger, Márcio Ferreira, Jordi Flos, Jasper Foppele, Mary Fritz, Karel Geers,
Thras Giantsidis, Matt Giedraitis, Lisanne Goossens, Annemijn van Gulick, Robert van Hastings, Ruud Heuvelmans, Roman Horvath MW, Peter van Houtert, Mira van Houwelingen, Alain Jacobs, Valentin Jestin, Petra John-Cooley, Christoph Kammuller, Duncan Keen, Petro Kools, Yvonne Kracher, Cristian Le Dantec, Mylène Lonjaret, Euan Mackay, Maria Manão, Eleonora Marzi, Nico McCough, Inma Menacho, Antonio Monteiro, Maxime Mostart, Penny Murray, Jolana Novotna, Osvaldo Nuzzi, Catalin Paduraru, Baldo Palermo, Kiriaki Panagiotou, Mireia Pauné Font, David Peabody, Gianmaria Peter, Marta Rafols, Oliver Rain, Marija Rajkovic Gasovic, Alexandre Relvas Jr, Laura Rhys, Maximillian Riedel, Elisa Rossetto, Annemarie Sauer, John Schell, Monika Schmid, Joep Speet MV, Cindy Stephan, Teona Talakhadze, Laura Tarmidi, Ana Tiefenbrunner, Patricia Toth, Jean Trimbach, Josef Umathum, Richard van Hemert, Erik Verboon, Mark de Vere MW, Javiera Vial Wunkhaus, Jonathan White, Annelies Wiersma, Heather Willson, Hinke van Woerden, and everybody else who contributed to the making of this book.

Thanks too, to the Wine Experts (Ben van Doesburgh, Willem Gaymans, Jorden Hagenbeek, Pieter Janssen, Edward van de Marel, Pim Mathot, Ernst Osinga, Hubert Prins, Joost Scholten, Gerhard van den Top, Rein Vehmeijer and Hans van de Wind) and the Red Wine Podium (Vincent Disselkoen, Willem van Gaasbeek, Daan Jonker, Bas Paddenburg, Bert Schram, Hans van Stam, Bernd Weeke and Ruud Winkels) who selflessly offered themselves as guinea pigs for developing what eventually became the CHARACTER Method. I also would like to thank Curtis Mann MW and Ivonne Nill MW.

And last, no matter how cynical it may sound, but *Anyone Can Taste Wine* is a book that came about due to the Coronavirus; without the virus, it is unlikely that I would have found the time and tranquility to write this book.

Index

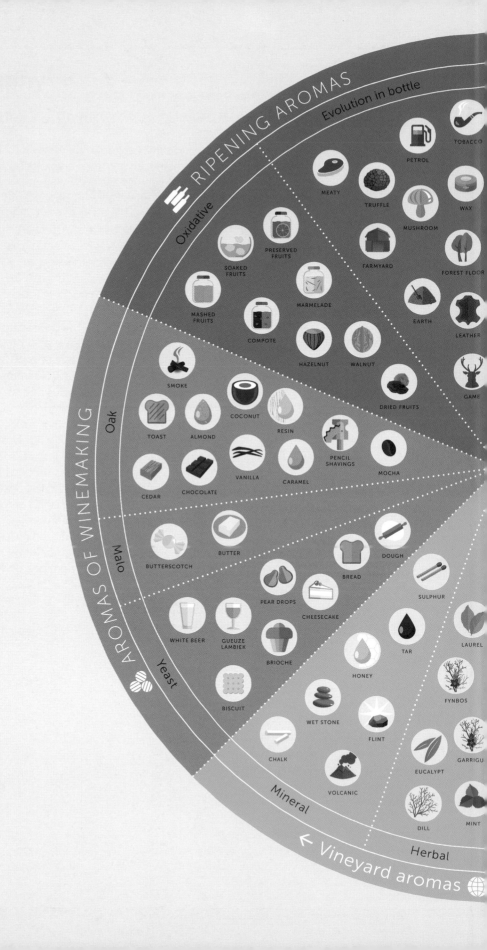

RIPENING AROMAS

Evolution in bottle

Oxidative

PETROL

TOBACCO

MEATY

TRUFFLE

WAX

MUSHROOM

PRESERVED FRUITS

SOAKED FRUITS

FARMYARD

FOREST FLOOR

MARMELADE

MASHED FRUITS

COMPOTE

EARTH

LEATHER

HAZELNUT

WALNUT

Oak

SMOKE

GAME

COCONUT

DRIED FRUITS

RESIN

TOAST

ALMOND

PENCIL SHAVINGS

MOCHA

CEDAR

CHOCOLATE

VANILLA

CARAMEL

AROMAS OF WINEMAKING

Malo

BUTTER

DOUGH

BUTTERSCOTCH

BREAD

SULPHUR

PEAR DROPS

CHEESECAKE

LAUREL

WHITE BEER

GUEUZE LAMBIEK

TAR

Yeast

BRIOCHE

HONEY

FYNBOS

BISCUIT

WET STONE

FLINT

GARRIGU

CHALK

EUCALYPT

VOLCANIC

Mineral

DILL

MINT

Herbal

← Vineyard aromas